A RESTORATIVE APPROACH TO FAMILY VIOLENCE

A Restorative Approach to Family Violence represents a substantive and timely contribution to the development of an emerging practice to a seemingly intractable problem. With a primary focus on New Zealand, an inspiration and a leader in the use of restorative processes for a variety of crimes, this book is beneficial to those who seek to understand how restorative justice, once forbidden in addressing family violence, has become a meaningful (and surprising) alternative to addressing these gender crimes. Questioning throughout, *A Restorative Approach* helps the reader understand the contours of the debate and the possibilities for creative solutions to intimate abuse that the criminal justice system has so often failed to address or repair.

Linda G. Mills, Center on Violence and Recovery, New York University, USA

A Restorative Approach to Family Violence

Changing Tack

Edited by

ANNE HAYDEN
Auckland University of Technology, New Zealand

LORAINE GELSTHORPE
University of Cambridge, UK

VENEZIA KINGI
Victoria University of Wellington, New Zealand

ALLISON MORRIS
Formerly University of Cambridge, UK
and Victoria University of Wellington, New Zealand

Routledge
Taylor & Francis Group
LONDON AND NEW YORK

First published 2014 by Ashgate Publishing

Published 2019 by Routledge
2 Park Square, Milton Park, Abingdon, Oxon OX14 4RN
52 Vanderbilt Avenue, New York, NY 10017

Routledge is an imprint of the Taylor & Francis Group, an informa business

First issued in paperback 2016

British Library Cataloguing in Publication Data
A catalogue record for this book is available from the British Library

The Library of Congress has cataloged the printed edition as follows:
A restorative approach to family violence : changing tack / by Anne Hayden, Loraine Gelsthorpe, Venezia Kingi and Allison Morris.
pages ; cm
Includes bibliographical references and index.
ISBN 978-1-4724-1230-0 (hardback) -- ISBN 978-1-4724-1232-4 (ebook) -- ISBN 978-1-4724-1231-7 (epub) 1. Family violence--Law and legislation--New Zealand. 2. Restorative justice--New Zealand. 3. Victims of family violence--Legal status, laws, etc.--New Zealand. 4. Marital violence--Law and legislation--New Zealand. I. Hayden, Anne, researcher II. Gelsthorpe, Loraine. III. Kingi, Venezia Marlene. IV. Morris, Allison, writer on domestic violence
KUQ4077.R47 2014
344.9303'28292--dc23

2013043989

ISBN 13: 978-1-4724-1230-0 (hbk)
ISBN 13: 978-1-138-24823-6 (pbk)

Contents

List of Figures

List of Tables

List of Abbreviations

BCS	British Crime Survey
CCP	Circles of Peace
CI	Confidence Interval
NGO	Non-Governmental Organization
NZ VAW	New Zealand Violence Against Women study
OR	Odds Ratio
P	Methamphetamine (New Zealand street term)
SAAS	Sexual Assault Archival Study

List of Contributors

Gale Burford has experience as a foster and group home parent, a social work practitioner and supervisor, a group and family therapist and a manager and senior administrator in services for children, young people and their families. After completing his MSW at the University of Washington in 1971, he worked for a decade with young people and their families in Montreal in a variety of positions until taking up an appointment teaching social work at Memorial University of Newfoundland in 1981. He completed a PhD at the University of Stirling in Scotland and provided training and consultation to local authorities in the UK. Gale is now a Professor of Social Work at the University of Vermont and Director of the Child Welfare Training Partnership between the University and the State of Vermont Department for Children and Families. He is also the principal investigator for a three-year evaluation of the child welfare and youth justice services. Gale has experience consulting, training and carrying out research in Canada, the USA, the UK, Australia and New Zealand. Gale's evaluation and research activities have focused on the use of teamwork in human services, drug courts, reparative probation panels, family team meetings in child protection and residential and day programmes for young people.

Kathleen Daly is Professor of Criminology and Criminal Justice, Griffith University (Brisbane). She writes on gender, race, crime and justice; and on restorative, Indigenous, innovative and international/transitional justice. First based in the United States, she travelled to Australia in 1995 as a Senior Fulbright Scholar to study restorative justice at the Australian National University. She has received five Australian Research Council grants to research restorative justice, Indigenous sentencing courts, the race and gender politics of new justice practices, innovative justice responses to sexual violence, and justice responses to Indigenous partner violence (with Elena Marchetti and Jackie Huggins). In addition to books and edited volumes, Kathleen has published 80 journal articles and book chapters. She is an elected Fellow of the Academy of the Social Sciences in Australia and a past President of the Australian and New Zealand Society of Criminology (2005–09).

Judith A. Davey is a Senior Associate of the Institute for the Governance and Policy Studies, Victoria University of Wellington and was Director of the New Zealand Institute for Research on Ageing from 2002 to early 2007. Prior to 1991, she was the Deputy Director of the New Zealand Planning Council and a consultant on social policy and social research. Judith is a graduate of London University and did her PhD at Durham University. Before coming to New Zealand, she was also a post-doctoral researcher at the University of Cambridge. Judith's personal focus for research is the ageing of the population and its policy implications. She has researched income, transport and housing issues for older people and has published several papers and reports on intergenerational issues. She has an extensive publication record, including academic papers, books and book chapters and commissioned reports and has provided advice to numerous policy-making bodies in the public, private and voluntary sectors.

Janet Fanslow is an Associate Professor in Mental Health Promotion at the School of Population Health, University of Auckland and Co-Director of the New Zealand Family Violence Clearinghouse. She has been engaged in violence prevention research since 1989. She is the principal investigator of the New Zealand Violence against Women Study, the largest epidemiological study on this topic yet undertaken in New Zealand. She is author of a large number of publications in the area of family violence, including reports commissioned by government departments. Janet's background is in psychology and public health. She worked with the Family and Intimate Violence Prevention Team of the US Centers for Disease Control and Prevention from 1997 to 1998, as part of a post-doctoral fellowship.

Loraine Gelsthorpe is a Professor of Criminology and Criminal Justice at the Institute of Criminology, University of Cambridge, UK. She has extensive publications across a broad range of topics, but most particularly: women, crime and criminal justice, the development and operation of community penalties, and youth justice. She teaches the Sociology of Punishment, Research Methods and the Ethical Dimensions of Research in Criminology. Recent research has included the criminalization of migrant women, female offenders and resettlement needs, and deaths under probation supervision. She has written about restorative justice and youth justice as well as restorative justice and family violence. Loraine is the current President of the British Society of Criminology. She also sits on a national Research Excellence Framework panel and advises on various governmental initiatives.

Naida Glavish has spent her adult life as an advocate for *Māori* people. In May 1984, as a humble telephone operator, Naida challenged the might of the then Post Office and won for *Māori* the right to use the *kupu*[1] (word) *'Kia Ora'* (hello) as a greeting on the New Zealand telephone. Naida's particular interest is health. Her role at Waitemata and Auckland District Health Board is General Manager and Chief Advisor *Tikanga* (customs and protocols), *Māori* Health Services. Additional areas of work and interest that serve *Māori* include: Advisor,

1 All *Māori* terms are italicised and explained when first used in a chapter. They are all listed in the Glossary in Appendix 1.

Police Commission, New Zealand Police; *Tikanga* Advisor, Forensic Pathology Auckland LabPlus; *Tikanga* Advisor, Organ Donor Department; and *Tuhononga* (standing in unity) of the *Iwi* (tribe)-led Crime Prevention Unit in Auckland Metro Police. She is also currently the Chair of *Te Rununga o Te Ngati Whatua* (the Council of Naida's tribe), a Justice of the Peace, an Officer of the New Zealand Order of Merit and the President of the *Māori* Party.

Anne Hayden's background includes both victim and restorative justice perspectives. She was a victim support volunteer for four years and had a Churchill Fellowship in 1996 to write on initiatives for victims of crime at local, national and statutory levels. In 1995, she became a restorative justice facilitator in the first contemporary restorative justice group in New Zealand (*Te Oritenga* (Equal Balance) Restorative Justice Group), becoming the coordinator around 1997. She was commissioned to write a manual on restorative justice for the Department of Courts, was a researcher for an evaluation of the youth justice system and then the New Zealand Court-Referred Restorative Justice Pilot with the Crime and Justice Research Centre, Victoria University of Wellington. Anne is no longer a practitioner, but in December 2010 completed her PhD which examined the use of restorative justice for intimate partner violence in the context of non-reporting. She has subsequently published chapters and journal articles on her research.

Julia Hennessy is the elected Chairperson of Restorative Justice Aotearoa, the national association for restorative practices in New Zealand. She is also the New Zealand representative on the board of Restorative Practices International. Julie is the General Manager for Family Works. She is a member of the Presbyterian Support Central leadership team and reports directly to the Chief Executive Officer. Julia has been a practising social worker and social work Senior Manager in the area of children and families for more than 20 years (both in the England and Wales and New Zealand). Julia has led projects in England and Wales which introduced family group conference practices and restorative justice practices into mainstream service delivery and was a member of the working group that contributed to guidelines for best practice in restorative justice in England and Wales. She was nominated for the national England and Wales Public Servant of the Year award for her work. She has spoken and trained worldwide on these practices and has contributed to resources published in these fields.

Mike Hinton is General Manager of Restorative Justice Aotearoa, after previously being Chairman of the same organization. He has been working as a restorative justice facilitator for 15 years. He was instrumental in the implementation of restorative justice services in one of the largest courts in New Zealand, the Manukau District Court, as well as servicing courts in Papakura, Pukekohe and the Auckland District Court. Mike recently featured in a poignant documentary about restorative justice practice in his community, produced by *Māori* Television, New Zealand. Before becoming involved in restorative justice, he spent 20 years in the military. Mike and Natalia Taurima work together, taking restorative justice referrals in South Auckland, West Auckland, Pukekohe, Papakura and Central Auckland.

Venezia Kingi is a research and evaluation consultant. She was a Senior Research Fellow at the Crime and Justice Research Centre at Victoria University of Wellington from its establishment in 2000 until its closure in 2011. Venezia has extensive experience of research in the criminal justice area and a comprehensive knowledge of issues relating to crime and justice and social issues in New Zealand. She has particular expertise in qualitative research and managing and conducting evaluations. Venezia specializes in interviewing difficult-to-reach populations about sensitive topics and has worked on projects about restorative justice, family violence, sexual violence, adult offenders' rehabilitation, prisoners' children, youth justice, jury decision-making, the public defence service and the families of homicide victims. She has also had first-hand experience assisting adult offenders in reintegrating into the community on release from prison when she worked as a Probation Officer for a short time in the late 1990s.

David Mather was appointed a District Court Judge in 1997, with a Family Court warrant. He sat primarily in the Family Court throughout New Zealand from 1997 to 2012. Recently he was appointed as a Panel Convenor member of the New Zealand Parole Board. Henceforth, he will sit on the Parole Board and also in the criminal division of the District Court. Before appointment as a Judge, David was in practice as a solicitor and later as a barrister for 25 years, following admission to the Bar in 1972. He has been actively involved with Family Court work throughout his years as a lawyer and judge. He worked as Legal Advisor for *Te Oritenga* Restorative Justice Group, the first contemporary restorative justice group in New Zealand.

Chris McGuire graduated with an LLB from Auckland Law School in 1973. His professional career commenced in private practice and was followed by periods in the New Zealand Army, the Crown Law Office and with a publicly listed company. Chris founded his own law firm in 1988. In 1997, he was appointed a District Court Judge at Rotorua with General and Jury Warrants. He has had a special interest in restorative justice from the time *Mana* Social Services commenced providing restorative justice services in Rotorua in 1998 and chaired the New Zealand District Court Judges' Restorative Justice Reference Group.

Ken McMaster has a 30-year history of working at the cutting edge of intervention work with men who are violent and who sexually abuse. He is known for his innovative practice ideas and the ability to translate theory into practice. He has held positions as a member and Chair of the Family Violence Advisory Committee / *Te Rangai Whiriwhiri Tukinotanga a-Whānau*. This committee was established to provide the Minister of Social Services and Employment with independent policy advice on matters related to government initiatives within the family violence arena. He was also a founding member of the National Network of Stopping Violence Services /*Te Kupenga Whakaoti Mahi Putanga* and is a past chair. Ken was involved in writing the Respondent Programme Regulation for the Domestic Violence Act 1995. In addition, he has worked as a part-time lecturer in Social Work at Canterbury University and is now involved full-time with Hall, McMaster and Associates Ltd as manager, writer of materials and principal trainer. Ken has published two books on family violence and has also co-edited three books.

Allison Morris was Professor of Criminology and Director of the Institute of Criminology at Victoria University, New Zealand until she retired in 2001. She graduated in law from the University of Edinburgh and studied criminology at the University of Cambridge and Columbia University, New York. She lectured in Criminal Law and Criminology at Edinburgh University and in Criminology at the Institute of Criminology, University of Cambridge. Allison has carried out research on women's prisons, youth justice systems, violence against women and restorative justice, and she has published widely in these fields. Her research into the early development of family group conferencing in New Zealand has been instrumental in greater focus on victims' needs and encouraging perpetrators to take more responsibility. She still takes an active interest in the development of restorative justice.

Paul Nixon has only recently moved to New Zealand. He is Chief Social Worker for Child, Youth and Family Services in New Zealand. He is a social worker from the UK who has worked for more than 20 years in child welfare and protection, always in a statutory setting. His previous job was as Head of Social Work for England's largest county, North Yorkshire. Paul is originally from Wales but has always been interested and inspired by practice and innovations from New Zealand, particularly restorative justice, *whānau*/kinship care and family group conferences. Paul has written a number of books on social work and numerous articles and chapters. He has provided training and consultancy on social work around the world.

Joan Pennell is a Professor of Social Work and Director of the Center for Family and Community Engagement at North Carolina State University (USA). She has conducted research on family group conferencing in child welfare, family violence, youth justice and schools. She is frequently consulted on implementing and evaluating family group conferencing in safe, culturally respectful, and effective ways and has presented papers on family engagement and family violence across the United States and Canada as well as in Australia, Guatemala, Netherlands, New Zealand and the UK. Joan is part of an international panel reviewing family group conferencing in New Zealand. She has co-authored two books and was the lead editor of a 2011 special issue of *Child Welfare* on family engagement in child welfare.

Maxine W. Rennie is a member of *Ngati Te Roro o Te Rangi Hapu – Te Arawa Iwi Aotearoa*/New Zealand and has had over 30 years' practice in the social service sector both at a community and national level. She established and managed three social service agencies in the Rotorua community, spending the last 10 years before her retirement in 2007 as Director for *Mana* Social Services Trust. This organization continues to offer a wide range of social services to the community free of charge. In 1999 Maxine developed and delivered restorative justice in Rotorua and assisted the establishment of the same programme in Tokoroa and Taupo including the training and supervision of staff. She received the Queen's Service Medal in 2006 for services to the community. She is currently working with both the local and national government.

Heeni Rongo is the pseudonym of a woman who has lived with violence for over 25 years.

Marie Ropeti is currently the Presbyterian Minister at Grey Lynn, Auckland, New Zealand. She is a New Zealand Samoan, with Bachelor's degrees in Arts and Theology (Otago University, New Zealand) and a Master of Arts degree obtained at the Pacific School of Religion, Berkley, California. She lectured in theology at Knox Theological College (1991–95). She gained experience in restorative justice when working as a facilitator for the *Te Oritenga* Restorative Justice Group, Auckland, before becoming the coordinator of PACT Restorative Justice Group also in Auckland (2000–2002). From 2000 through to 2006, Marie held the position of coordinator of Women Heart of the Pacific where she was responsible for providing and implementing programmes for disabled people.

Heather Strang is Deputy Director of the Jerry Lee Centre of Experimental Criminology in the Institute of Criminology, University of Cambridge and an Adjunct Associate Professor in the Regulatory Institutions Network at the Australian National University. She has directed many tests of criminological interventions, including a series of 12 experiments on the effects of restorative justice in Australia and the UK. She has published extensively in this area, and has edited two books on the application of restorative justice in family violence and other arenas. Heather is currently analysing a 10-year follow-up of victims and offenders who participated in the Australian restorative justice study. She is also engaged in two experiments with British police forces, one testing alternative strategies in addressing anti-social behaviour and the other a different approach to family violence.

Julie Stubbs is a Professor in the Faculty of Law at the University of New South Wales. She joined the Faculty in 2010, from her previous roles as Professor of Criminology and Director of the Institute of Criminology at the University of Sydney. Her research interests include intimate partner violence, intimate partner homicide, legal responses to violence against women, restorative justice, and women and criminal justice. Julie is an advisor to VicHealth on violence against women and a member of the Criminal Justice Reform Committee and the Advisory Committee of the Institute of Criminology.

Donna Swift comes from a background of working to end violence against women. A social anthropologist, she now focuses on the reasons young women use such behaviour against others. As the principal researcher of *The Girls' Project*, a groundbreaking study conducted over two years in the Tasman Police District, she explored teenage girls' use of violent and anti-social behaviour. Turning her findings into training workshops and presentations, Donna is now in demand as a speaker and travels extensively throughout New Zealand and overseas. She is also the Strategic Advisor on Young Women's Violence for the Stopping Violence Services Nelson, New Zealand and a Senior Social Science Lecturer at Nelson Marlborough Institute of Technology, New Zealand.

Natalia Taurima has worked extensively in the criminal justice field, including as a probation officer and cultural advisor working with *Māori* offenders and victims. She manages the *Te Whanau Awhina* programme based at *Hoani Waititi Marae* in West Auckland. It uses a restorative justice model to benefit offenders and victims. It enhances young *Māori* offenders' ability to redress the harm caused by their offending and provides opportunities for victims to participate in an environment that supports all participants. Natalia works alongside Mike Hinton as a facilitator in South Auckland and oversees the cases referred from the Manukau, Pukekohe and Papakura Courts.

Dannielle Wade is a Research Assistant in the Key Centre for Ethics, Law, Justice and Governance, Griffith University, where she works with Professor Kathleen Daly on her Innovative Justice research project. She has a BA joint degree in law and criminology from Griffith University. Danielle's interests include working as a volunteer for the Australian Innocence Project, which aims to assist in exonerating prisoners who are factually innocent, and theories of punishment, responsibility and reintegration.

Foreword

Rates of intimate partner violence remain shamefully high in New Zealand and elsewhere despite the fact that public awareness of the problem has risen markedly. There is growing recognition that the traditional adversarial approach in the criminal justice system has failed to deliver results and an associated interest in new initiatives, particularly in restorative justice. The publication of *A Restorative Approach to Family Violence: Changing Tack* is therefore timely. It is of practical interest for those whose work involves dealing with violent offending of a family nature, but it is also essential reading for all interested in the study of family violence generally and new measures for dealing with criminal offending.

The range of subjects and perspectives presented in the volume is wide. It includes empirical studies of the prevalence of family violence and perspectives on the use of restorative justice initiatives in the family violence context. It also includes accounts by those who have participated in restorative justice processes and have been victims of abusive relationships.

Restorative justice in New Zealand has been predominantly driven by practitioners. As such, it is to some degree under-theorized. *A Restorative Approach to Family Violence: Changing Tack* makes a valuable contribution to filling that gap in the literature. Particularly welcome is the editors' acknowledgement that the appropriateness of employing restorative justice processes where family violence has been involved is a fraught issue. The presentation of different views in this volume is commendable.

Family violence is a deep-rooted problem in our society and progress in reducing the levels of it has been slow. We do not yet know for certain how effective restorative justice initiatives have been. It will be many more years before we can see whether such initiatives have helped stem the tide of intergenerational family violence. What we do know is that the adversarial approach of criminal justice, which remains the default, has not worked to reduce levels of violence or to repair the damage it causes. The present volume represents a worthy contribution to the long-term project of working to ensure that family violence does not remain a national and international disgrace.

Right Honourable Chief Justice Dame Sian Elias
Wellington, New Zealand

Acknowledgements

Anne Hayden thanks her husband, David, for his enduring love and support. His insights and advice have been invaluable. She especially acknowledges and thanks her co-editors, Allison Morris, Loraine Gelsthorpe and Venezia Kingi for their forbearance, skills and knowledge, for being there and for the significant contribution each has made. They know that, in their different ways, they have enabled this book to happen. Loraine Gelsthorpe, Venezia Kingi and Allison Morris want to acknowledge Anne Hayden's work in the creation and development of this book. Without her calm dedication and perseverance, this book would not exist.

All editors want to thank the contributors to this book who have given it inspiration and a rare insight into the realities of family violence and the promise that is restorative justice. Their wide-ranging and, in many cases, international standing and experience in the academic, practice and policy fields have given considerable credibility to this collection. Our shared hope is that this volume will contribute to fruitful debate about the use of restorative processes in dealing with family violence.

Introduction

This book is about the possibility of using restorative justice to deal with family violence. However, there is no single or agreed definition of either of these concepts and so we first have to clarify briefly what we mean by them.

Restorative justice in New Zealand has a long history through its connection to the ways in which *Māori* traditionally resolved conflict, but it is its modern re-formulations which are of interest in this volume. New Zealand has gone further than most modern countries in its implementation of restorative justice for dealing with offences. Family group conferences for young people involved in offending, widely viewed as an example of restorative justice, were introduced by legislation in 1989 and since then various pilot schemes have been introduced for adults who have offended. More recently, various areas of New Zealand have tried to bring these practices to the field of family violence.

Restorative justice is a new way of thinking about justice. Conventional understandings are based on seeing crime as a violation of the criminal law and as a violation against the state, on blaming and punishing offenders and on decision-making by criminal justice professionals who act on the behalf of victims. Restorative justice, on the other hand, sees crime as a violation of relationships between victims and perpetrators and attempts to address these relationships as well as the harms done. It seeks to provide a voice to those most affected by the offences about not only how best to deal with them but also how to deal with the reasons underlying them and their consequences.

Because there is no single agreed definition of restorative justice or of how it is best practised, we prefer to identify it by its core values and to say that to be 'restorative', processes and outcomes need to reflect these. These core values include participation, respect, honesty, accountability, empowerment, hope, making amends, reintegration and inclusion. Thus, restorative justice processes enable victims, perpetrators and those closest to them to come together and, with the aid of a facilitator, to try to resolve how best to deal with the offence, its consequences and its implications for the future. Restorative justice processes also expect perpetrators to acknowledge responsibility for their offending and its consequences, to try to address the harm caused by their offending and to take steps to prevent its recurrence.

Restorative processes and practices, therefore, seek to empower perpetrators and victims by giving them a sense of inclusion in and satisfaction with these processes and practices. They seek to enable victims to feel better and safer as a result of participating in them; and they seek to hold perpetrators accountable in meaningful ways by encouraging them to apologize to their victims and to take steps to prevent a recurrence of their behaviour.

Researchers into family violence have included a range of different behaviours and have used diverse terminologies. Terms such as intimate partner violence, domestic violence, family violence and spousal violence have been used interchangeably. Some terms are used politically. For example, the word 'battering' was consistently used by the anti-domestic violence movement.

We have chosen to use the term 'intimate partner violence' to describe physical, sexual and psychological abuse, including but not limited to intimidation, harassment, damage to property, threats and causing or allowing a child to see or hear physical, sexual or psychological abuse between married or de facto couples, including same-sex relationships; and we have chosen to use the term 'family violence' where these same behaviours take place between children, parents, caregivers, extended family members including those related through marriage or cohabitation and anyone in a close personal relationship, but we do not include abuse between flatmates (as the Domestic Violence Act 1995 did in New Zealand).

Generally speaking and as alluded to in this volume, research has consistently shown that restorative justice processes can more fully involve victims than conventional criminal justice processes. Victims whose offenders are dealt with in restorative justice processes have more information, are more likely to meet with and confront their perpetrator, are more likely to have some understanding of reasons behind the offending, are more likely to receive some kind of repair for the harm done (for example, through an apology or reparation), are more likely to be satisfied with the agreements reached, are more likely to feel better about their experience and are less likely afterwards to feel angry or fearful than those victims whose perpetrators were dealt with by the courts.

Research has also shown, and again this is alluded to in this volume, that the participation and involvement of perpetrators is achievable through restorative justice processes. They get a better understanding of what they have done by hearing about its consequences either directly from their victims or others; they are held accountable for their offending in meaningful ways (for example, through an apology or reparation); they complete the tasks agreed to; they are satisfied with the agreements reached; and they may feel remorse for what they have done. Significantly, too, research suggests that restorative justice processes can impact on re-offending.

The challenge in this volume is to contribute to the debates about whether or not these benefits could be achieved also when restorative justice is used to deal with family violence, behaviour usually excluded from such processes. This is a contested area and we have invited a group of New Zealanders and others of national and international standing to share their expertise and thoughts on research and practice with regard to restorative justice processes.

The book is divided into six parts. Part I sets the scene and provides an account of the reality of family violence from the perspective of a woman who experienced it over a period of years and then of a judge who deals with it in court on a relatively frequent basis; Part II describes family violence as experienced by women, children, the elderly and teenage girls; Part III provides an in-depth case study of the practice of restorative justice with respect to family violence in one area of New Zealand; Part IV picks up on the theme of the importance of culture in the policy and practice of restorative justice; Part V describes some research findings on the use of restorative justice in family violence; and Part VI explores both the challenge to restorative justice by opponents to its use in family violence and the opportunities offered by it.

A Glossary of *Māori* and Samoan terms is provided in Appendix 1 and 2 respectively though each time a *Māori* or Samoan word is used in a chapter for the first time it is defined.

PART I
Setting the Scene

Family violence occurs in all communities and there is general dissatisfaction with the way in which criminal justice systems currently deal with it. The first two chapters in this book illustrate the complexity of family violence and some of the judicial dilemmas associated in dealing with it. In Chapter 1, a series of conversations between Heeni Rongo and Naida Glavish and between Heeni and Anne Hayden bring to life the reality of living with intimate partner violence. David Mather, in Chapter 2, describes common scenarios concerning family violence which judges in a range of courts are required to adjudicate on. He makes clear his frustrations with conventional judicial responses.

Chapter 1
Living with Intimate Partner Violence: Heeni's Story[1]

Heeni Rongo in collaboration with Naida Glavish and Anne Hayden

Introduction

Heeni has lived with intimate partner violence for over 25 years. Her partner, Charlie, is a gang member whose addiction to the drug P (methamphetamine) has taken her and their family on a roller coaster ride of emotional and physical violence, alternating with brief periods of congeniality when he is 'high'. As a gang member, Charlie has shown little interest in complying with the law; he has spent two years in prison for drug offences and is anti-police. This is in sharp contrast with Heeni's upbringing, where she was taught that the police were there to help. They have two children who are in their late teens. Their daughter is now the mother of a young child. Heeni's story highlights the reality of intimate partner violence and its effects on victims, their families and their support people.

Living with Violence

Although her partner's violence tends to be verbal, Heeni described his behaviour towards her in the early days of their relationship as very controlling:

> Can I say, it wasn't that bad? ... You'd get a slap. It was more the verbal abuse which [was] very sharp and meaningful ... and that action of standing over you ... If I was to make a call to the police and say he's abusing me ... down the track it's going to come back on me ... I would probably be bashed ... even put in the boot and taken somewhere. I know that's possible because he carries a knife with him and he has access to guns ... There's always been threats. 'I'll kill you, cut you up, stab you.' All of that. It's all there ... At the time you get told 'I'll poke you full of holes' ... In the back of your mind you know he's capable of it ... because knowing his history in his gang. It's like, 'Yeah,

1 This chapter is based on conversations between Heeni Rongo and her aromatherapy client Naida Glavish and between Heeni and Anne Hayden. These conversations were taped, transcribed and then edited by Anne. Heeni is a pseudonym, as with all personal names in subsequent chapters

> you're capable of doing it.' … It's 25 years that we've been together, on and off, because he's left at times and gone to prison, and he's buggered off and done his own thing somewhere. He could tell you … back then, he was harder. But today he's softer. Back then it'd be, 'I'd just smash her,' as he'd say. An' I'm like, 'No you didn't'. But maybe … you don't know. I don't know if I've blocked it out. I don't remember that bit.

Naida explained why she thought Heeni stayed with Charlie:

> I don't think you are hanging in there because of him. I really believe there are several reasons. First for the sake of peace for the kids; you see that the kids go to school, are alright, and to prevent disruption in their lives. Secondly, it's not easy to pack up and go, and thirdly, with his background, he would hunt you down. You know that, eh? … He knows people, and he could say, 'My missus has taken off. Can you fellas check it out?'

However, there are other reasons why Heeni stays with him. Although Charlie is not a good provider, he is a 'caring, wonderful father' who, despite his own addiction or possibly because of it, has told his children not to take drugs. On the other hand, he does not do the right thing by supporting the family and when he comes down from a high there are usually more threats, including taking the children away from Heeni. According to her, there is a frightening possibility that Charlie could get custody of their son.

Nevertheless, Heeni said it was her choice to stay with him:

> It might sound really weird … I hope he wouldn't do it. He's more verbal … very verbal … It's like, let him cool down and he'll be right after that. It's just one of his outbursts … the sad part is that the love you had was drugs. But that love is definitely thinning down a bit. That hope [thins down] as well … he's on the P now … This is a really horrible thing to say, but when he's on it, he's wonderful. He is. He's the man I first knew. But obviously he has to come down eventually, and that's when the horrid happens. That's when the gremlins come out and the family, the kids, they know and they walk around on eggshells when he's coming down.

Breaking the Silence

Before Heeni was asked by Naida about how she came to be bruised and limping, she had no one to talk to freely and frankly about what was happening. Although her parents lived nearby, a conversation of that kind with them was not possible:

> I could speak to Mum, but I didn't need to say anything, Mum would know. But she didn't need to know the details. She was always there to support me

and she didn't have a problem telling him where to go. She was very strong in that sense … [But there are] some thing[s] you don't want your mother to know.

As Heeni told Naida:

My mum would pick up on things, and she'd be like you, Naida, and she'd go, 'What's the matter?' She didn't have a problem speaking to him straight away. But I didn't tell her what was happening. No, not really … Just from the first couple of times when Charlie and I were going together and having our family, Mum would pick up any trouble between us and she'll talk to him directly. She'd confront him, sit down and talk to him about it. He would listen, but it was what would happen [to me] after that – the verbal abuse! If she did that too often, he would've just up sticks and taken us away. Out of my parents' way. And so a lot of the times I wouldn't want to tell her 'coz he'd just take us away from my family … And Dad would do nothing. But if he saw Charlie abusing me, he'd just say, 'That's enough boy.'

Naida: But you did talk to me, eh?

Heeni: That was the first time I talked to anyone outside of that … out of our circle. And it was scary 'coz he knew you came to the clinic at least once a week. He knew who you were; used to brag about you being a client of mine to his mates. And he knew you wouldn't take too much – that you'd just go and see him. You told me so, too. You'd go and see him … if you found out.

Heeni and Naida recalled the time when Naida first found out about the violence:

Heeni: You just looked at me and said, 'What's the matter?'

Naida: Yeah, yeah.

Heeni: (quietly) I think I tried to avoid it but …

Naida: You sure did. Tried to avoid any talk, 'No I'm alright, I'm alright'. So I'd let it go. Next time I'd come to you for a pampering, you'd be looking worse, and I'd ask, 'What's the matter with you?' So, in the end, next minute, you decided. You shut your clinic door, and then started …

Heeni: Bawling my eyes out. (She giggled nervously.)

Naida: And um, okay, while you were bawling your eyes out, I could see that there was a sense of relief that you could tell me, 'coz your concern was that you didn't want to bother me. Not that you didn't want to tell me, but you didn't want to bother me with all the other things that I do. And so we began talking

> about where things are at. And I wanted to go and see him then. But I could see the fear in your eyes, not for yourself, the fear in your eyes was for the children. From what you've told me I don't think he would ever do anything to the kids, but he would use the kids to threaten you by taking them away. Now that fear's going 'coz the kids are bigger. The kids are older.

Heeni spoke of how she feels Naida is like a mother to her; she trusts her and can feel safe with her. She also knows Naida can help. Naida explained: 'That trust is about the fact that I would keep your confidence provided you can show me you are safe. If you're not safe, I'll confront him.'

Feeling Stronger

Since telling Naida about the abuse and the reduced threat regarding losing her children, Heeni feels much stronger. She says she has changed. She is now reconciled to the fact that she cannot change Charlie; she can only offer him support by checking on his health, whether or not he has eaten and been sleeping properly. Although he hates the fact that others know about his behaviour, he cooperates with Naida's suggestion that Heeni talk about the P use with him. This has helped. Before Heeni did this, she used to get 'anti' and behave towards him in a confrontational way. After 25 years Heeni does not know how long that support will be there for him:

> It's all about the kids now. It's no longer about him. I've turned him using P into a positive. I just take in what he can offer when he's high … deep down inside he's a lovely man. He's just lost on drugs.

When first interviewed, Heeni commented that, if the violence were to happen again, she felt she could stand strong and probably make that move. It was through Naida's backing that, even though Heeni was very frightened, she found the strength on one occasion to pack the children up and leave home to spend a night in Naida's office. 'That was my first ever stand', she declared. She had come home to find Charlie heating a knife up on the stove so they could do some 'spotting' with P. There were other people there and Heeni did not want it happening in front of their children. Heeni also objected to P being in the house:

> Heeni: But he didn't want to be embarrassed in front of his mates, so he spun around on me. I'd never seen such anger or rage. I believed he was going to do something.

> Naida: I brought you and the children into my office and locked you in. I told you that there was no way that he could get into that office. You guys could get out but he couldn't get in.
>
> Heeni: Yeah, you made me feel safe. It was something I'd never done before. But I still felt him trying to come over to pick us up. If he wasn't texting me he'd text the kids. But that was the first ever time. And then there were quite a lot of abusive texts. His texts were threatening. Then they became, 'I'm sorry, come home.'
>
> Naida: The abusive ones were like 'You can't hide for long!' and 'Those are my kids!' Gee, sometimes I've been tempted to send the cops around to you, but I haven't because of the implications for you. And I'd need to talk to you first.

Heeni is slowly getting the courage to speak more with Charlie about what has happened to the relationship and she has told him that she doesn't like what he does:

> I've offered him the door, in a polite way but I have to pick my moment when I can talk like that. I said to him, 'Go and be the best gang member you ever wanted to be. The kids and I will be fine.' So we are at the stage where it is out in the open.

This is a big advance from when he used to say: 'Don't even talk about it!' or 'Mind your own business, woman!'

Being Prepared

Naida and Heeni set in place a safety plan. One way they considered Heeni could help prevent further intimate partner violence is for her to talk about it with Charlie. Although Heeni has not disclosed details to her parents, she knows she only has to visit them and she will be given immediate help and refuge. Naida and Heeni have agreed that Heeni will talk more openly with Naida about anything that was troubling her. This should take some of the pressure from her. Because of the terrifying threats Charlie has made to Heeni about the consequences of her reporting his violence to the police, in an emergency she is to telephone Naida, who will immediately call police she knows will be there 'so fast!' This way Charlie cannot blame her for narking and follow his menacing remarks with action. So they have contingencies set in place as far as Charlie's behaviour is concerned.

Consequences of Violence

One outcome of their living arrangements which provides a degree of safety for Heeni, but which is very concerning to her, is the presence of her daughter:

> If my daughter's there, and when Charlie and I do fight, and it gets heated, really, really heated, she'll intervene. Then he turns on her, you know, 'Mind your own business, ra, ra, ra'. And she's got both our genes of course, and she will stand up. And it gets a little frightening. It does. It's the same old, you know? Just get through the process and then, hello, it will be over again. It's like the weather, just ride it out and it will be alright.

Another unfortunate outcome is Heeni's daughter's use of aggression. Her ability to defend her mother has come at a price. Sadly, Heeni has seen her slapping her boyfriend a number of times. Heeni said to her: 'Don't you do that! It's ugly!' 'And it's her father again, all over.' So, in Heeni's immediate family, intergenerational violence is apparent, where her daughter, through witnessing her father's abuse of her mother, has adopted similar behaviour towards her boyfriend. The intimate partner violence has also influenced family dynamics in other ways. Heeni said:

> I couldn't help but be negative towards him. So I probably encouraged a backlash, caused us to fight more and the kids would see it … And it was the kids who said, 'Mum, why do you do that?' And I said, 'It pisses me off Dad's on that shit again!' And then I sat back and thought, 'Gee, this is not getting us anywhere! He's going to use the drugs, he can only help himself. He's got the support there but he's just greedy. He's got a good life, why should I change?'

Challenging Violence

Heeni's belief that she could stand up to Charlie the next time he was abusive proved to be correct. Heeni updated Naida on a recent altercation:

> Heeni: (her voice strong) Me standing up to him may have changed things, but the violence doesn't happen as much. There'll be times like the first time, still, but I stand up to him, and he doesn't know how to handle it. And … I haven't told you this before, Naida, but not so long ago it actually got more intense than ever.
>
> Naida: (looking up suddenly) Has it?
>
> Heeni: (more confidently) Yeah. I think it is because the support that you've given me, Naida, has given me that strength. 'Coz I do stand strong now. Like I have never ever before stood up to him, I now verbally give it back. And I

> remember your *kōrero* (speech) when you told me to be careful I don't end up hating him.
>
> Naida: Mmmmmmm.
>
> Heeni: Hating him, was that the word? And, when you get to that point, to know the signs. You know, recently when I was in the shed, he was on a downer and badmouthing me. I'd just had enough! I grabbed a screwdriver that was lying on the bench, and I gripped it like I really wanted to attack him with it. An' he was going, 'Betcha can't, you wouldn't dare.' And my daughter ended up getting involved, and then we all ended up getting involved ... I just said to myself, 'Why am I not going to speak to Naida about it?' Because I was alright. I was alright. I went through all that, and I still came through it. I know I have a plan. I can speak with you anytime. But I was alright. (Heeni's eyes were bright and her smile wide.)

Even more recently, when Charlie argued, 'bringing up anything and everything', Heeni had had enough. For the first time, she told him she hated him. Charlie responded in kind, saying he hated her and that he was going to kill her. Again, their daughter intervened:

> And then he went mad at her and told her to shut up. And then I just said 'I'm going to bed now'. 'Coz he'd kicked me out, I wasn't to have the car and it was the coldest night. It was just last week. It was freezing. And I said, 'No, I'm not going. I'm going to bed.' The next day he was still horrible. I was – just in one ear and out the other – and I just got ready for work.

The Burden of Supporting

While Naida's empowerment of Heeni is significant, and essential to Heeni's feeling of well-being, it has placed its own burden on Naida. As they sipped their tea, Naida commented thoughtfully:

> One of the things about you, Heeni, I've sometimes worried about ... I've wondered if my influence may have contributed to your getting a slap. Because, after we'd talked, my influence on you was to stand strong, you know, be strong and take no shit. Just deal to him. And so you would answer back. And that's when you'd end up getting a slap. And I wondered whether or not my influence may have contributed to unnecessary violence from him, simply because you wanted to be strong. You wanted to address those issues of domestic violence from within.

This is a significant consequence of being a support person for someone experiencing intimate partner violence. It can leave an emotional weight and sense of doubt on the shoulders of the supporter. This is where police can usefully become involved, sharing the load.

Unintended Consequences of Police Involvement

Not very long ago, Heeni said that, much to the surprise of Charlie, his abuse had been reported to the police. Neighbours, overhearing Charlie's loud verbal abuse towards Heeni, called the police. When they came, Heeni was asked to leave:

> Naida: You were asked to leave?
>
> Heeni: That was because it was his place.[2] It's just wrong. I said to him, 'You go.' But he wouldn't. It was one of those new police safety orders.
>
> Naida: Oh, where you've got to go while the police are there, otherwise they arrest you to make sure you go?
>
> Heeni: I had to go somewhere. And then the police spoke to me, and he goes 'Oh, Mam are you alright?' I said, 'Yep, I'm fine. You need to talk to him, it was his mouth, not mine', you know. And Charlie was like, 'Go on, Heeni, you tell him.' And I said 'No, it was your big mouth that brought them here, not mine.' The other thing was they had to watch me leave and escort me off the property.

Notwithstanding the apparent injustice of Heeni having to leave, this has not put her off seeking police assistance. She was thankful they had come. The only reason she will not call them herself is due to her conviction that Charlie will carry out his threats if she did.

2 The house is a state house (government owned rental property) on a lower rental in Charlie's name because he has been classified as a high-needs beneficiary with the New Zealand Ministry of Social Development (the government agency administering welfare benefits). Accordingly he is on a domestic purposes benefit, with the younger child named as in his care. Although officially Heeni does not live there, the family need this financial assistance to survive. According to Heeni this is Charlie's sole contribution to supporting the family, as the balance of his benefit is used to feed his addiction to P. Her work as an aromatherapist pays all their other expenses. Naida explained that this is how many families manage to meet their basic needs. The difficulty is that it has increased Charlie's power and reduced Heeni's.

The Restorative Justice Option

Heeni was asked what she thought about the possibility of using restorative justice for her and Charlie. She commented that she would be for it, but she did not know what he would think of the idea, mainly because he did not see his behaviour as being as bad as Heeni did. If it was contemplated, Heeni felt Charlie would need to be approached very carefully because he distrusted the police or anything to do with 'justice'. She commented, '… facilitators would need to be very careful about how they asked questions, maybe allowing each of us to have a say first, then put forward what you need to do from that'. Furthermore, facilitators would need to be able to handle 'anything thrown at them', figuratively speaking, as well as being fully informed about Charlie's background.

She considered that the presence of a *kaumatua* (male elder) or *kuia* (female elder) was vital and that, although 'a big ask', they could assist with monitoring the couple afterwards. In particular, they could see how the couple were, whether or not everything had gone to plan. She thought that one or more conferences might be necessary to perhaps offer some other options. 'Probably out of it all, [the conference] is saying that, even though he is the abuser, it is still safe for him to be able to speak.'

Ideally, as a result of a conference, Heeni expected that her partner would understand that what he had done was not right and that he would try to change and show that he could. 'If not, well, let me go!'

Chapter 2

Family Violence and the Courts

David Mather

Introduction

In this chapter I draw on my experience as a District Court Judge and Family Court Judge for the last 16 years. Family violence, including intimate partner violence, regrettably forms a substantial part of the daily diet of these courts. It presents at court in a variety of ways. Judicial experience and the following scenarios demonstrate how court processes are all too often neither timely nor necessarily appropriate responses. Restorative justice, on the other hand, offers another option. However, real caution is necessary when embarking on a restorative justice process because of the risks associated with it.

A significant percentage of cases that are dealt with in the Family Court involve family violence. This can arise in the context of a parenting dispute under the Care of Children Act 2004. It is the primary focus of proceedings under the Domestic Violence Act 1995. It can arise in other Family Court proceedings such as adoption applications, child support disputes, estate litigation and proceedings involving the elderly under the Protection of Personal and Property Rights Act 1988.

The police initiate prosecutions on a daily basis throughout New Zealand for a wide variety of offending involving family violence. The Waitakere District Court, where I am based, has for some years had a specialist Family Violence Court which sits at least one day each week. This has promoted greater consistency of approach to criminal prosecutions of this kind with important collaboration among a range of stakeholders including police prosecutors, lawyers, probation officers, victim services and programme providers.

Family violence features prominently as a factor in many of the cases which come to the attention of social services. Applications for declarations that children are in need of care and protection are often supported by evidence from social workers, families, schools and other people and agencies recounting the exposure of children to family violence and, on occasions, children being subjected to violence as well.

What follow are examples of situations which typically confront a judge in the District Court in its various jurisdictions. They show the widely differing issues and context in which family violence appears, the range of interventions and outcomes which are available to the court and the limitations of court processes in dealing effectively with family violence.

Intimate Partner Violence and the Family Court

Ms AB applies on a without notice basis for a protection order against her partner Mr CD. Her affidavit recounts recent relatively low-level physical violence, together with a history of physical and psychological abuse. She left the relationship (with her two children of a prior relationship) several weeks ago. She is currently living in a refuge.

The file comes before a judge in chambers. The judge then has to decide whether to make a temporary protection order or to direct that the application be served on Mr CD. If the order is made, and served on Mr CD, statistics show that there is a good chance he will take no steps to contest the order and it will become a final protection order after three months. If he does take steps to contest it, a hearing will be scheduled for some three months later. Prior to the hearing, the parties and their lawyers (if involved) may negotiate a settlement. This could involve the order becoming final or the application being withdrawn with or without undertakings (unenforceable, informal agreements by both parties not to use violence). There may be issues around the parenting of children to be resolved as well. The court will be asked to endorse the outcome, without disputed factual issues being tested, findings made and consequential court orders issued.

Another frequent scenario is Ms EF applying without notice for a protection order against Mr GH. She alleges recent and serious physical violence and a temporary protection order is made. Mr GH is served with the order and takes no steps to contest it. She also seeks and is granted an interim parenting order providing for her to have day-to-day care of their three children who have witnessed, and at times been subjected to, violence by their father.

Two months after the temporary protection order is made, Ms EF files an application to discharge the order. She has sacked her lawyer who assisted her when she obtained the order. Her handwritten affidavit records her view that what she said in her initial affidavit was exaggerated and/or untrue. She now has no concerns about violence from her partner and, in fact, is in the process of reconciling with him. They can sort out parenting arrangements for their three young children without the need for any court order and she wants the interim parenting order in her favour discharged as well.

The court is now faced with a litigant who has committed perjury, having sworn affidavits giving completely contradictory accounts of the same events. A judge is likely to direct that the application to discharge the temporary protection order and interim parenting order be allocated a short hearing, requiring Ms EF to come to court. She may or may not attend court and Mr GH likewise. Unless the court has input from a lawyer appointed to represent the children or a social worker's report which can be directed under the parenting proceedings, the court will have no independent, reliable information as to the dynamics in the household, the safety of the woman or the children. At the most serious end of the spectrum, Ms EF may be subject to intimidation, threats and coercion from Mr GH and at high risk of further violence, possibly life-threatening. At the other end of the spectrum, her initial application to the court, although filtered by a lawyer, may be an ill-considered reaction to some domestic argument, subsequently resolved and no longer meriting court or further official investigation. The Family Court will instinctively approach such cases with caution.

A third scenario might involve a professional couple Ms IJ and Mr KL. After a marriage of some 25 years, Ms IJ applies to the court for a protection order. She alleges relatively low-level physical violence early in the marriage but her main concern is sustained psychological abuse. She left the relationship three months previously and only now has regained her confidence to the extent that she can consult a lawyer and seek legal protection. She applies without notice for a protection order.

Family Court Judges are well aware that the effects of psychological and emotional abuse can be as insidious and damaging as physical abuse, if not more so (McKinnon 2008). However, such an application is likely to be directed to proceed on notice to Mr KL. He will typically defend the application with a complete and detailed rebuttal of Ms IJ's affidavit evidence.

At the defended hearing, both parties give reasoned and plausible, yet divergent, evidence of events through their marriage. Each has supporting evidence from family members. The presiding judge may have real difficulty in making clear findings of credibility with the result that a protection order can either be granted or refused with little confidence.

If a protection order is made, the respondent Mr KL must be directed to attend a stopping violence programme unless there are good reasons not to make such a direction (Domestic Violence Act 1995, s.32(i)). Typically, following a finding of intimate partner violence sufficient to justify the making of a protection order, the court will not excuse a respondent from attending such a programme simply because he does not consider it necessary, it is inconvenient, or he has done a similar programme in the past. A business or professional person like Mr KL may be affronted by the making of the protection order and resistant to attending a programme in the company of others with whom he might choose not to associate. The threat of prosecution for failing to comply with a direction to attend a programme, however, may be the only incentive for him doing so.

Further difficulties are confronted by the Family Court when dealing with applications to discharge protection orders. Some are relatively straightforward if they are filed many years after the order was made, when the parties have had little if any contact with each other and there is no evidence of ongoing risk of violence. Such applications can be filed by either the protected person or the respondent, and sometimes are filed by both. On the other hand, those applications brought by a protected person or by the respondent within a relatively short time of the order being made where assertions are made that the order is no longer needed are much more difficult. Concerns about the possibility of coercion or manipulation arise with unopposed applications of this kind.

It has been difficult, from the research evidence to date, to assert confidently that stopping violence programmes have been effective in reducing or eliminating violence. The Ministry of Justice (2011a) notes that there are mixed reviews of the effectiveness of these programmes to prevent re-offending and that international research is equivocal about their ability to address violence. Peter Boshier, recently retired Principal Family Court Judge, also cautioned that these programmes have not reached their full potential and are not as yet providing tangible results. He noted that while research has found that there were positive gains from the programmes in terms of a decrease in frequency of violent and abusive behaviour, these evaluations tend to overestimate the effectiveness of the programmes. He also noted the lack of completion of the programmes by respondents and the fact that many respondents had no good reason for this failure (Boshier and Wademan 2009).

I am aware from anecdotal evidence that some respondents (generally men) have acknowledged that, sometimes despite initial reservations, they have gained considerable benefit from these programmes. Similarly, it is hard to gauge the benefit to applicants (almost invariably women) who attend protected persons programmes under the Domestic Violence Act. Research by Maxwell, Anderson and Olsen (2001) found that large percentages of the women participating in these programmes reported that they believed the programme had actively contributed to them feeling safer and having the ability to keep their children safe. However, many were 'not completely confident that the person who had previously abused them would not re-enter their life and abuse them again and this factor was not under their control' (Maxwell et al. 2001: xiii). Furthermore, the women in the comparison group who did not attend the programmes also reported similar changes using safety strategies similar to those developed in programmes. This suggests that the programme may not be the only way to benefit victims of family violence, especially when other support networks are available.

Whenever possible, judges will reinforce the availability of such programmes and encourage women who have protection orders to obtain the benefit of them. The Ministry of Justice (2011a: 255), however, states that the uptake by protected persons is low; it was put at around one in four in an earlier report (Ministry of Justice 2007). Programmes are also available for children who are under protection orders, but again there is little research evidence to support their benefits for children and the level of uptake is disappointing. There was a review of three such individual programmes, including one *Māori* programme, published in 2002, using data collected between June 1999 and December 2000. This found that these specific programmes assisted the children to deal with the effects of intimate partner violence, including expressing their feelings on its impact, to understand family changes and to consider keeping safe strategies. Children and caregivers also self-reported being highly satisfied with the programme. This small sample, however, may not be representative (Cargo et al. 2002). The previous Principal Family Court Judge noted in February 2009 that a comprehensive evaluation of the effects of these protected persons programmes for children is overdue and that there is no reasonably attainable information about the children sent to such programmes or their completion rates (Boshier and Wademan 2009: 123).

Care and Protection Proceedings

The Family Court is frequently confronted with applications by social workers for custody of children exposed to or subjected to family violence. The violence can range from chronic low-level over-discipline to life-threatening violence to a child or parent by an abuser. Where appropriate, place of safety warrants are issued authorizing the immediate uplifting of children (Children, Young Persons and Their Families Act 1989 s.39) or interim custody orders with the same effect (s.78). The Family Court, when called upon, will act as urgently and protectively as the circumstances appear to justify. In the early stages when applications are filed by social workers without third party input, the court is heavily dependent upon the expertise and professionalism of the social workers involved.

Intimate partner violence has a hugely damaging and long-lasting impact on children who witness it in the home. According to the Ministry of Justice (2007):

> The damaging effects on children who have endured and/or observed violence include increased anxiety, fear, depression, aggression, emotional and behavioural problems and impaired social skills. There are also subtle symptoms associated with witnessing violence that can adversely impact on a child's future relationships, such as seeing violence as an effective means of getting what he or she wants (2007: 38).

Removal of children to a safer and more nurturing environment is clearly one option, often adopted by social services and endorsed by the court. However, against that must be balanced the loss of what might be considered as the nurturing features of that same home despite the family violence. Wider family or *whānau* options may not be available. The prospect of a succession of temporary and at times unsatisfactory placements is also relevant. The dilemma is even more acute when the court is asked to make orders allowing the removal of a child at or very soon after birth from a mother who cannot assure the child of a safe or protective home because of chronic partner violence. What level of anticipated intimate partner violence or neglect justifies the breaking of a mother-child relationship at birth? These cases certainly test the Family Court, particularly when reliable evidence and realistic options are lacking. Chapter 15 by Burford and Pennell in this volume explores a different route in a different jurisdiction.

Parenting Disputes

These comprise the single largest category of work in the Family Court. The Ministry of Justice has reported that applications filed under the Care of Children Act 2004 made up around 36 per cent of all substantive Family Court Applications in 2009/2010 (Ministry of Justice 2011a: 7, 48 and 56). The Ministry also advised that such cases occupied 50 per cent of all court fixtures requiring judge time as at September 2011 and are the most expensive cases to progress (Ministry of Justice 2011b: 2).

For many years, the Care of Children Act 2004 and its predecessor the Guardianship Act 1968 have mandated important constraints on the making of parenting orders where violence is established or even alleged. The court cannot make an order for day-to-day care or contact between a parent and their children in the face of allegations of physical or sexual abuse between the parties or to a child of the family, unless satisfied that such contact will be safe. The court is directed to determine, as soon as practicable, whether the allegations of violence are proved (Care of Children Act 2004 ss.58–62).

In practice, the allegations will be raised in affidavits and, when contested, will be the subject of affidavit evidence in reply. The court will, and routinely does, hear the parties (and any witnesses) give oral evidence and will make findings as to whether or not there has been violence, the extent and nature of the violence, and the effect on the parties and their children. These findings will inform any decisions as to day-to-day care and contact for the children and may result in supervised contact only by the violent parent.

Less easily resolved are cases where the parties negotiate a parenting outcome which does not involve them giving oral evidence and revisiting disputed events which may go back many years. Before the Family Court will sanction court orders on this basis, it must still be satisfied that the safety of the children is not being put at risk. The assistance of experienced lawyers, particularly those representing children, is extremely valuable in such situations. Judges are often reluctant to force parties who may have genuinely and effectively resolved their differences to revisit those issues in an adversarial court environment. Such a process is rarely conducive to genuine conciliation or reconciliation.

The court is mandated by the Care of Children Act 2004 to give effect to the principle that parents and guardians should have primary responsibility, and be encouraged to agree to their own arrangements, for the care of their children. A further principle is that care arrangements should be facilitated by ongoing consultation and cooperation between the parents (s.5(c)). On the other hand, the principle that a child's safety must be protected and children must be protected from all forms of violence is also of primary importance (s.5(e)). Needless to say, balancing these principles, which are not always or easily reconcilable, is a difficult challenge regularly confronted by the Family Court and its judges. The court can be faced with assessing, investigating and resolving family dynamics which involve intimate partner violence or other forms of family violence, without the willing engagement of even one parent.

Criminal proceedings Consider the following scenario. Mr MN is arrested one evening for a serious offence against his partner Ms OP. He has a long history of offending, including serious violence. He appears in court the following day charged with assault with intent to commit sexual violation and is remanded in custody without plea for two weeks. The police summary of facts alleges that Mr

MN held a steel bar to Ms OP's throat and threatened her over a period of several hours with serious sexual assault. The victim impact statement taken from Ms OP on the night of the assault records extremely serious physical violence over a sustained period. Ms OP clearly states she would feel unsafe if Mr MN is not in custody. He does not seek bail at this stage.

Two weeks later, Mr MN reappears in court. An updated victim impact statement has been provided, through a different victim adviser, in which Ms OP retracts her complaint of violence and expresses the strong view that she would not feel safe unless Mr MN is granted bail and in a position to protect her from others. Mr MN's counsel understandably places weight on Ms OP's most recent victim impact statement, noting that the court is obliged to take into account the views of victims (Victim Rights Act 2002 (ss.29–30)). The judge has serious reservations about the reliability of the second victim impact statement, suspecting (without evidence) that it is the result of threats from the defendant and/or his gang associates. On occasions, the court will be assisted by input, written or oral and direct or indirect, from a representative of a victim support agency alerting the court to the need for caution in relying on such victims' views. Preference is given to the initial victim impact statement and the defendant is further remanded in custody.

In another relatively common scenario, Mr RS is charged with assaulting his partner Ms TU with intent to injure. After an initial remand in custody, he is released on bail on strict conditions. He pleads not guilty and a hearing is scheduled for five months ahead.

On the day of the defended hearing, Ms TU fails to appear to give evidence. She has been served with a summons. The police are aware that she and Mr RS have been discussing reconciliation and may in fact have resumed living together. They have three dependent children. Ms TU has declined the offer of further support or input from victim services with whom she was initially in regular contact.

In this scenario, the judge has a number of options. One is to issue a warrant for the arrest of Ms TU, which may result in her being located and brought to court in time to give evidence on the scheduled hearing day. A second option is to adjourn the hearing to another date, which may be a further five months or more away, so the police can make further efforts to contact Ms TU and have her come to court. A further option, which predictably is frequently urged upon the court by defence counsel, is to dismiss the charge.

The police may or may not have attempted to maintain contact with Ms TU between the incident and the defended hearing date. Their views as to whether Ms TU's unwillingness to come to court reflects coercion or threats, a genuine wish to put the past behind her and not prejudice the future of the reconciled relationship, fear of the consequences if she were to give evidence or some other personal and quite possibly genuine reason may or may not assist in clarifying the matter. The court has to consider what ongoing supports are available to Ms TU and whether or not she is one of those victims who feel obliged to appear compliant with threats, promises or blandishments by a partner, but, at an underlying level, would prefer the court process to take its course and see her partner held accountable for his violence. The judge's task is to determine the appropriate course to adopt, taking a wide view of the best interests and safety concerns of Ms TU and, indeed, of the wider community.

The issue of accountability also arises when the court is asked to discharge a defendant without conviction (Sentencing Act 2002 ss.106–107). He may be a first offender, the level of violence may be quite low and the apparent consequences of conviction might be considerable. An early guilty plea is often followed by satisfactory completion of a stopping violence programme of up to 20 weeks. The victim/complainant may, with the assistance of competent victim advisers, report a change in her partner's behaviour and no ongoing concerns for safety. The court has the jurisdiction to discharge without conviction where the consequences of a conviction are out of all proportion to the seriousness of the offence. This involves a wide-ranging inquiry and a degree of speculation as to what might be the consequences of an event (conviction) which has not yet occurred. Public interest in such cases is often high, particularly where the defendant has a significant public profile. The judge has to decide on the extent to which s/he should take account of the sentencing principle that people should be held accountable for their actions and, at the same time, do justice to the individual perpetrator and take proper account of the views of his or her victim.

Conclusion

The authors of other chapters in this book address in detail the issues which arise when restorative justice processes are being considered in the family violence context and the benefits for individual participants and the wider community of restorative justice. The court is obliged to take into account any outcomes of restorative justice processes that have occurred or are likely to occur (Sentencing Act 2002 (s.8(i)). In addition, the same legislation provides that, in sentencing a perpetrator, the court must take into account any offer of amends, agreement to remedy any wrong, loss, or damage, the response of the perpetrator or his family and any remedial action taken or to be taken by the perpetrator (s.10).

Restorative justice in a family violence context has the distinctive feature that the parties have been, and often will continue to be, in a close personal relationship. For my part as a judge with experience dealing with intimate partner violence and other forms of family violence in both a family and criminal court context, and as a strong proponent of restorative justice as a powerful and effective process, I nevertheless urge caution in its application in the family violence area. Victims need time to heal and sensitive, effective ongoing support following an incident or incidents of family violence. Perpetrators need to be held accountable and prevented from exploiting the emotional, financial and other vulnerabilities of complainants, but also allowed an opportunity to genuinely address their behaviour and repair relationships. Skilled facilitation is essential. Real benefits can result from a well-managed restorative justice process and the learnings from experience and research worldwide will continue to inform the future of restorative justice in this area.

The above is unashamedly anecdotal. It is an attempt to convey a sense of the challenges and complexities which arise when family violence and intimate partner violence in particular are encountered in a court of law. Judges are obliged to deal with cases on the basis of the evidence and material provided to them. Due process must be observed. The rights of perpetrators as well as victims must be upheld in a system which respects the rule of law. For a variety of reasons, which include financial resources, the skill set and experience of lawyers and other professionals, pressure on court resources and delays in dealing with cases, we have a less than satisfactory court process. Outcomes are, as a consequence, often less than acceptable.

As a judge, I admit to frustration in many circumstances where I do not consider a family situation has been well served by the court process. I make that observation having regard to the interests of the perpetrators and victims of family violence, of the children impacted by it both directly and indirectly, and of the wider community. Legislation and legal structures and processes are essential and, if designed and implemented with individual and public safety as a priority, can make a significant contribution to confronting and effectively responding to family violence. Ultimately, of course, the reduction or elimination of family violence is a whole-of-community challenge. I wholeheartedly support the range of initiatives being undertaken and developed to ensure a better commitment by communities to eliminate family violence in all its pernicious forms and restorative justice has an important part to play here.

References

Boshier, P. and Wademan, J. 2009. Are Stopping Violence Programmes Worthwhile? *New Zealand Family Law Journal*, 6, 119.

Cargo, T., Cram, F., Dixon, R., Widdowson, D. and Adair, V. 2002. *Evaluation of Programmes for Children under the Domestic Violence Act 1995*, research report prepared for the Ministry of Justice. Wellington: Ministry of Justice.

McKinnon, L. 2008. *Hurting without Hitting: Non-Physical Contact Forms of Abuse*. Stakeholder paper 4. Sydney: University of New South Wales.

Maxwell, G., Anderson, T. and Olsen, T. 2001. *Women Living without Violence: An Evaluation of Programmes for Adult Protected Persons under the Domestic Violence Act 1995*. Research report prepared for the Ministry of Justice. Wellington: Ministry of Justice.

Ministry of Justice. 2007. *A Review of the Domestic Violence Act 1995 and Related Legislation: A Discussion Document*. Wellington: Ministry of Justice.

Ministry of Justice. 2011a. *Reviewing the Family Court: A Public Consultation Paper*. Wellington: Ministry of Justice.

Ministry of Justice. 2011b. *Family Court Review: Summary*. Wellington: Ministry of Justice.

Legislation

Care of Children Act 2004. Wellington: OHMS.
Children, Young Persons, and Their Families Act 1989. Wellington: OHMS.
Domestic Violence Act 1995. Wellington: OHMS.
Sentencing Act 2002. Wellington: OHMS.
Victims' Rights Act 2002. Wellington: OHMS

PART II
Violence in the Home

Before addressing the vexed question of whether or not it is appropriate to use restorative justice processes for family violence, it is important to consider it in more detail. Whereas Part I gives graphic information about the personal experiences of violence in the home from the points of view of a victim and a judge, Part II gives an overview of the extent and range of family violence. The multidimensional nature of intimate partner violence and its prevalence and impacts are set out in these chapters too. Janet Fanslow in Chapter 3 writes about the prevalence of intimate partner violence in New Zealand based on information derived from the New Zealand Violence Against Women study and how women have responded to their situations. Then, canvassing one end of the age spectrum, Paul Nixon discusses in Chapter 4 a number of cooperative initiatives to prevent and deal with child abuse. At the other end of the spectrum, Judith Davey explains in Chapter 5 the range of abuses that can and do befall the elderly. Donna Swift in Chapter 6 gives a rare view of girls' violence in the home and how this intergenerational violence can be one of the precipitating factors for these young women's violence.

Together these chapters demonstrate the pervasiveness and intergenerational nature of family violence and that no age group or family relationship is exempt. They also attest to our understanding that interventions to prevent and remedy family violence are still not effective despite the numerous initiatives at government level. People in families from infancy to old age continue to endure violence from within the family unit, the place where they should be and feel most safe and secure. These chapters illustrate why we must explore other ways of addressing such violence.

Chapter 3

Understanding the Prevalence of Violence against Women in New Zealand: Implications for Restorative Justice

Janet Fanslow

Introduction

This chapter presents information from the New Zealand Violence Against Women (NZ VAW) Study, the largest study ever undertaken in New Zealand to assess the prevalence and health consequences of violence against women.[1] The information is significant because it comes from face-to-face interviews with a sample of women who are representative of women in the country as a whole. As such, it provides an overview of the types of violence that women have experienced, irrespective of whether or not this experience was reported.

Information from the study is likely to be a more accurate estimate of the violence that has occurred in the community compared with estimates obtained from administrative data reported by government or non-government support agencies. This is the case for a variety of reasons, including the fact that no one government or non-government agency has a responsibility to ensure that consistent, reliable, complete data on family violence are collected and maintained. Also, agencies which do report family violence data are subject to both internal changes (for example, policy changes, systemic changes in identification and recording practices) and external changes (for example, changes in societal perceptions about the acceptability of violence can influence reporting) (Gulliver and Fanslow 2012).

In this chapter, I use data from the NZ VAW Study to outline the lifetime prevalence of multiple forms of violence against women, including child sexual abuse, physical and sexual violence by non-partners, and intimate partner violence. Since the focus of this book is on restorative justice approaches for family violence, I

1 I would like to acknowledge the women who participated in this study, members of the research team, the Advisory Group and Nicola Paton for comments on an earlier draft of this chapter. Funding for the study was provided by the Health Research Council of New Zealand (Grant 02/207). This study replicated the WHO Multi-Country Study on Violence Against Women (WHO/EIP/GPE/99.3).

also explore information about patterns of intimate partner violence in greater detail and outline what is known about women's help-seeking experiences related to it.

Methods

Study Population

A detailed description of the methods of this investigation has been reported previously (Fanslow and Robinson 2004). Briefly, the study population was women aged 18–64 years, who were usually resident in Auckland or North Waikato[2] and who resided in private homes. A population-based cluster sampling scheme with a fixed number of dwellings per cluster was employed. In households with more than one eligible respondent, one woman was randomly selected. If the woman was available to talk, consent was sought and an interview arranged; otherwise, contact details were obtained and further attempts were made to set up an interview. To maximize the chance of obtaining an interview, a minimum of three return visits were made to each household at different times and on different days.

The response for households was 88 per cent and for eligible women was 76 per cent, yielding an overall response rate of 67 per cent. Comparison of the demographic characteristics of the study sample with those of the general population of New Zealand indicated that the sample was comparable to the general population (Fanslow and Robinson 2004).

Questionnaire Development

The base questionnaire was developed by the Core Technical Team of the World Health Organization Multi-country Study on Violence Against Women (Garcia-Moreno et al. 2005). Minor modifications were made to increase the appropriateness to the New Zealand context and the revised questionnaire was pilot tested for acceptability. The questionnaire was produced in English and Chinese, as Mandarin/Cantonese speakers were the largest group who could not complete the questionnaire in English.

2 Auckland is the largest city in New Zealand (population 1.2 million) and, at that time, 27 per cent of the total New Zealand population of women aged 15–64 resided there; North Waikato is a rural region in which 3 per cent of the total population of women aged 15–64 resided at that time. These sites were selected in line with the protocol of the WHO Multi-Country Study, where the majority of countries conducted surveys in both the largest city and one rural region.

Definitions

Violence by non-partners Victimization by non-intimate partners was determined by respondents answering affirmatively to more than one of the following items:

- Before the age of 15, do you remember if anyone (in your family, at school, friend or neighbour, anyone else) ever touched you sexually or made you do something that you didn't want to do?
- Since the age of 15 years, has anyone (other than your current or past partner/husband) ever beaten or physically mistreated you in any way?
- Since the age of 15 years, has anyone (other than your current or past partner/husband) ever forced you to have sex or to perform a sexual act when you did not want to?

Violence by intimate partners *Intimate partners* were any male current or ex-partners that the woman had been married to, or had lived with, or current regular male sexual partners.[3] *Current partners* were those men with whom women were in a relationship with at the time of the survey. *Most Recent Partners* referred to the last man the woman had been in an intimate relationship with. Data related to current or most recent partner behaviour only are shown for controlling behaviours.

Type of violence refers to the categories of physical, sexual or psychological/ emotional violence. Each type of violence was operationalized by asking women if they had experienced specific *acts* by an intimate partner.

Physical violence was defined as having experienced one or more of the following acts: been slapped or had something thrown at them which could hurt them; been pushed, shoved or had their hair pulled (grouped as 'moderate violence' for later analyses); been hit with a fist or something else; been kicked, dragged or beaten up; been choked or burnt on purpose; or been threatened with, or had used against them a gun, knife or other weapon (defined as 'severe violence' for later analyses).

Sexual violence was defined as having experienced one or more of the following acts: been physically forced to have sexual intercourse when the woman did not want to; having had sexual intercourse because she was afraid of what her partner might do; or been forced to do something sexual that she found degrading or humiliating.

Psychological and emotional abuse was defined as having experienced one or more of the following acts: been insulted and made to feel bad about oneself; been humiliated or belittled in front of others; been intimidated or scared on purpose (for example, by a partner yelling or smashing things); or been threatened with harm (either directly or by a threat to hurt someone the respondent cared about).

---

3 Women were also asked about same-sex relationships, but numbers were too small to be generalizable to the population.

Controlling behaviour was assessed by asking women if it was 'generally true that their current or most recent partner engaged in any of the following acts: tries to keep her from seeing her friends; tries to restrict contact with her birth family; insists on knowing where she is at all times; ignores her or treats her indifferently; requires her to obtain his permission to seek healthcare for herself; is often suspicious that she is unfaithful; or gets angry if she speaks to other men'. The response categories were: yes, no, or don't know. 'Don't know' responses were later coded as missing data. The behaviour of previous partners was not canvassed in this question. Additional variables allowed us to determine if the woman's current or most recent partner had perpetrated physical or sexual violence against her, so this information was used to establish the extent to which women reported experiencing physical and/or sexual intimate partner violence *and* controlling behaviour by their current or most recent partner. Lifetime experience of intimate partner violence was determined by asking women if 'their current husband/partner or any other partner had ever' committed any of the acts. For any act experienced, women were asked when it had occurred (within the past 12 months or prior to the last 12 months) and the frequency with which they had experienced each act (once; a few times; or many times).Information was not obtained on the exposure period of the use of controlling behaviours (that is, we do not know if the acts occurred during the past 12 months or prior to the past 12 months).

Analyses

Descriptive statistics (percentages with confidence intervals (CI)) are presented to document the different acts of psychological/emotional abuse and controlling behaviours that women experienced and the frequency with which these acts were experienced. In all analyses, the complex sampling design has been controlled for. The survey procedures in SAS Version 9.2 were used for all analyses (SAS Institute 2008).

Safety and Ethics Considerations

All interviews were conducted in private (no other adults or children over the age of two years were present). Interviewers were trained to switch to questions about a neutral topic (food and nutrition) if the interview was interrupted and to terminate or re-schedule the interview if privacy could not be assured. All participants, regardless of whether or not they disclosed abuse, were provided with a list of support agencies. Ethical and safety recommendations for research on intimate partner violence developed by the World Health Organization were followed as part of the conduct of the present study (World Health Organization 2001). Ethics approval was granted by the Human Subjects Ethics Committee of the University of Auckland (Ref number: 2002/199).

Results

Sample

A total of 2,855 women completed the full questionnaire. Of these, 2,744 were ever partnered and 111 had never had partners. Of the 2,744 women who were ever partnered, 67 did not have current partners but did have (in the past) a male partner they did not cohabit with. Three cases had missing data related to their partner status. Thus, for analyses relating to intimate partner violence, data are reported from a total sample of 2,674 ever-partnered women.

Prevalence of Violence by Non-Partners

Child sexual abuse: around one in four women (26 per cent) reported that they had been sexually touched or made to so something sexual that they did not want to do, before the age of 15 years. Previous reports of these data indicated that the majority of perpetrators of child sexual abuse were male family members of the victims and that approximately half of the women had experienced these acts on more than two occasions (see Fanslow et al. 2007 for further details). Almost 1 in 6 women (16 per cent) reported having experienced at least one act of physical violence by a non-partner in their lifetime. One in 10 women reported having experienced at least one act of sexual violence by a non-partner in their lifetime.

Lifetime Prevalence and Women's Experience of Single or Multiple Types of Intimate Partner Violence

Of ever-partnered women who had answered questions about all three types of violence (2,646), 55 per cent (1,455) had experienced at least one type of intimate partner violence and 34 per cent (870) had experienced more than one type of intimate partner violence. Overall, psychological/emotional violence was reported most frequently (51 per cent), followed by physical violence (32 per cent) and sexual violence (17 per cent). Very few women reported experiencing physical violence (71, or 3 per cent) or sexual violence in isolation from other types of violence (15, or 1 per cent). Figure 3.1 shows this overlap in diagrammatic form.

Experience of Intimate Partner Violence is Repetitive

In addition to experiencing multiple types of intimate partner violence, women also reported that it was not restricted to isolated acts of violence. Of those who had experienced physical violence by an intimate partner (855), more than 80 per cent had experienced more than one act of physical violence (for example, they had been hit with a fist or something else *and* been choked or burnt on purpose) or had experienced more than one type of physical violence on more than one occasion. Of the 17 per cent who had experienced sexual violence by an intimate partner,

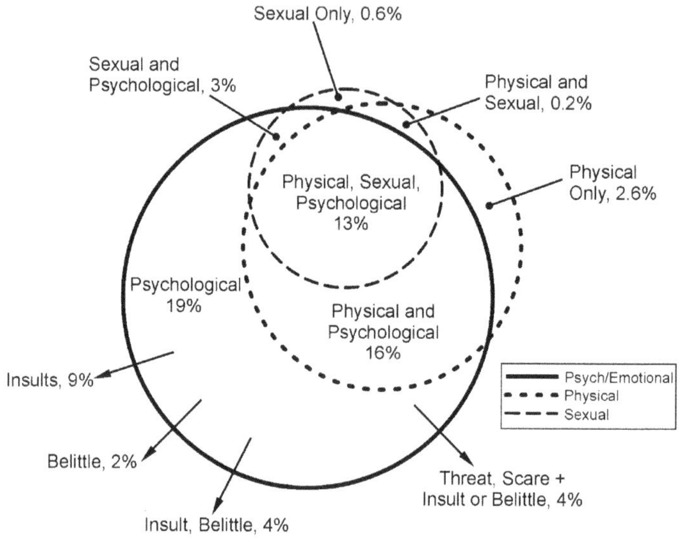

Figure 3.1 Overlap of types of intimate partner violence that occurred ever in a woman's life

over 90 per cent had experienced more than one type of sexual violence or had experienced sexual violence on more than one occasion.

Experience of Controlling Behaviours

Women's experience of controlling behaviours by their current or most recent partner was strongly associated with that partner's use of physical or sexual violence. Almost three out of four (73 per cent) 'most recent partners' who used physical and/or sexual violence also used controlling behaviours and almost half (49 per cent) of the violent current partners had used control. This contrasted with the use of controlling behaviours by 20 per cent of current or most recent partners who were not physically or sexually violent. Of those partners who used physical and/or sexual violence, 12 per cent (95 per cent) of current violent partners had used four or more acts of controlling behaviour, while 41 per cent of most recent violent partners had used four or more acts of controlling behaviour. Table 3.1 shows the number of different acts of controlling behaviour women experienced from their current or most recent partner.

Women's Help-Seeking for Intimate Partner Violence

Just under two-fifths (37 per cent) of women who had experienced intimate partner violence reported that they had told their parents about the violence; and 29 per cent had told a brother or sister about the violence. Friends were

Table 3.1 Number of different acts of controlling behaviour by use of physical and/or sexual intimate partner violence by the woman's current or most recent partner

	Number of acts of control by current or most recent partner	Frequency (n)	Row percent and 95% CI
Current partner perpetrates intimate partner violence	None	133	51.5% (44.9–58.2)
	One	41	16.8% (11.8–21.9)
	Two or three	47	19.9% (14.4–25.5)
	Four or more	24	11.7% (6.5–16.8)
Most recent partner perpetrated intimate partner violence	None	61	27.3% (21.6–33.1)
	One	22	10.0% (5.9–14.2)
	Two or three	46	21.9% (15.8–28.0)
	Four or more	82	**40.8% (33.7–47.8)**
Current or most recent partner not violent	None	1,729	**80.3% (78.2–82.1)**
	One	273	12.9% (11.3–14.5)
	Two or three	104	5.2% (4.1–6.3)
	Four or more	38	1.8% (1.2–2.4)

Note: Table 3.1 documents the number of different acts of controlling behaviour reported, not the frequency with which those acts occurred. Each of the acts reported could have occurred more than once (Fanslow and Robinson 2011).

also frequently told about the violence (48 per cent). Only a small per cent of women who experienced intimate partner violence reported that they spoke to aunts and uncles or to cousins (7 per cent). Women also told individuals in formal helping roles about the violence. For example, 16 per cent of the abused women disclosed to counsellors and other mental health professionals. Equal proportions (13 per cent) had spoken to the police and to doctors or other health workers. Only a few women discussed the violence with others such as other religious leaders or priests (3 per cent), women's organizations (2 per cent) and women's refuges (2 per cent). Almost one-quarter (23 per cent) indicated that they had not told anyone about their partners' violence.

Logistic regression analyses indicated that there were no differences in the percentage of women who told someone about the violence according to their ethnicity or the recentness of the violence. Among women who had experienced any physical or sexual violence, those who experienced severe physical violence were significantly more likely to have told someone about the violence (86 per cent) when compared with women who experienced moderate physical violence (65 per cent) or when compared with women who had experienced exclusively sexual violence (61 per cent).

Who tried to help? In the majority of cases, women reported that they had received a 'helpful' response from between one-half and two-thirds of those they had spoken with about the violence. Of the women who had talked about the violence with her partner's family or her children, less than a half reported that these individuals tried to help them.

Reasons help not sought from formal services Women who had not sought help from any formal services (456, or 49 per cent of the sample who experienced intimate partner violence) were asked for their reasons. The predominant reason for not seeking help was that women perceived the violence to be 'normal/or not serious' (63 per cent). The next most common reasons were that women were ashamed or embarrassed (14 per cent) and because they 'feared the consequences' (6 per cent). Ten per cent reported that they felt they should deal with it on their own. All other reasons (for example, fear of losing their children or the belief that telling someone would not help) were reported by less than 5 per cent of the women who had experienced intimate partner violence.

Reasons for seeking help from formal services Of those women who accessed one or more of the formal services (486), most reported seeking help because they could not endure more (49 per cent), followed by, in order of frequency, their children were suffering (17 per cent), they were encouraged to leave by friends (17 per cent), they were badly injured by their partner (15 per cent), they were fearful that their partner would kill them (11 per cent), their partner/ex-partner threatened or tried to kill them (11 per cent) and their children had been hit or threatened (8 per cent).

Discussion: Implications of these Findings for the Use of Restorative Justice

The sheer magnitude of the problem of violence against women in New Zealand and elsewhere[4] has important implications for the consideration of the appropriateness (or otherwise) of developing restorative justice approaches for family violence. The high number of cases involved could be used as an argument to support the development of alternative responses, as a 'one-size' type of response to violence through the criminal justice system is unlikely to be suitable for all. On the other hand, the information on prevalence and patterns of violence suggests other considerations which need to be taken into account if alternative responses are to be successful. Some of these implications are discussed below.

4 Of the countries which have participated in the World Health Organization Multi-Country Study, lifetime rates of physical or sexual assault by an intimate partner range from 15 per cent (in urban Japan) to 71 per cent (in Ethiopia province) (Garcia-Moreno et al. 2005).

Intimate partner violence accounts for the largest proportion of the violence against women in New Zealand, with one in three women reporting having experienced physical and/or sexual violence by an intimate partner within their lifetimes and half having experienced emotional abuse by an intimate partner in their lifetime. While the proportions are considerably smaller on an annual basis, this is less relevant when thinking about criminal justice based responses, which by their nature have been developed to respond to past events. Thus, one of the implications of expanding restorative justice to addressing intimate partner violence needs to be an awareness of just how big the problem is. Developing any option without providing sufficient resourcing to implement it effectively and consistently for all those who might want to take up the option will not enable good outcomes to be achieved or justice to be served.

The high levels of overlap of multiple types of violence (physical, sexual and psychological), the high proportion of women who experienced repeated episodes of violence and the co-occurrence of the perpetration of violence with the perpetrator's use of controlling behaviours is also noteworthy. Awareness of these findings would need to underpin any use of restorative justice for intimate partner violence. There will be considerable nuances in attempting to deliver restorative justice, for example, for those who have experienced ongoing patterns of violence compared with one-off incidents or for those who remain in a relationship with a formerly violent partner compared with those who no longer have a relationship with the perpetrator of the violence.

There are examples of restorative justice that have seemingly successfully navigated these complex waters (Pennell and Burford 2000). However, to do so safely requires significant investment in preparation pre-, during- and post-conference and follow-up. This is needed to ensure that victims will be safe and have the opportunity to be heard. It will require an ongoing commitment to monitor and evaluate adherence to the restitution and reparation plans that result from the conferences. It also requires that all participants involved (the facilitators, victims, perpetrators and the community (family) members) have a shared understanding of the power and control issues involved in cases of intimate partner violence, a commitment to address these and additional mechanisms such as criminal justice system protections to address ongoing safety issues if required. Busch (2002) has eloquently described the ways that restorative justice approaches can go wrong if these issues are not attended to.

Another important contribution to the success of all restorative justice processes concerns the involvement of community (Marshall 2003): usually the family and friends who are involved in supporting the victim and perpetrator and who help to ensure that agreed reparation plans are adhered to. Findings in this chapter also suggest important implications for this component of the process. In particular, the data available related to women's help-seeking in cases of intimate partner violence make it clear that not all responses from a woman's family and friends and still fewer responses from her partner's family were considered helpful. Coker (2002) describes some of the ways in which the views of friends and family members can either tacitly or explicitly endorse a man's use of violence. Clearly, if restorative justice is to live up to its promise there must be careful assessment of the capacity of those serving as the 'community' to understand the dynamics of power and control and the effects on victims of ongoing experiences of abuse. They also need to support the restorative justice aim of holding perpetrators to account.

It has been argued that the development of restorative justice approaches might increase women's reporting of intimate partner violence (Hayden 2010). However, results in the present chapter indicate that consideration of the available justice options is not the major motivator for women to seek help from formal agencies. Rather, the severity of the violence they experience, fear for their lives, threats to their children, and feeling like they could not endure any more are the primary reasons women report violence to formal helping agencies. Thus, if restorative justice approaches are to be considered, they need to be able to accommodate the most severe end of the spectrum of intimate partner violence and will need to be well linked in with alternative criminal justice sanctions. Restorative justice will not be successful if the violence is continuing.

Findings in this chapter also highlight the high prevalence of child sexual abuse, with one in four women reporting having been sexually touched before the age of 15 years, with previous work indicating that the majority of these cases were perpetrated by male family members (Fanslow et al. 2007). Previous opinion leaders within the field of restorative justice have noted the limitations of restorative justice for child sexual abuse where the victim is still a child (such as the lack of power held by the child and concerns that, if the community could not keep the child safe to begin with, they cannot be expected to support families or enforce reparation). The role of restorative justice in addressing cases of historical child sexual abuse has been less well canvassed (Proietti-Scifoni and Daly 2011) but may hold promise if important conditions can be met (Jülich 2006).

Conclusion

Restorative justice continues to be debated as an effective alternative mechanism for addressing intimate partner violence and other types of violence against women. There is a rationale for pursuing these discussions, as it is clear that current systems of justice do not always provide the best and safest outcomes for women and children (Tolmie et al. 2010). The pursuit is also justified by the positive examples of how, if thoughtfully and comprehensively implemented, restorative justice can assist families to make positive change (Pennell and Burford 2000). There are also suggestions that restorative justice has the potential to better meet the needs of Indigenous communities (Blagg 2002, Proietti-Scifoni and Daly 2011). However, these outcomes will only be possible if the preconditions for sustainable and effective justice models can be identified (Nancarrow 2010, Stubbs 2010).

Results from the present chapter highlight the need for the development of any restorative justice programmes to be created with mindfulness of the volume and the severity of the cases that might come forward. The results also highlight the importance of maintaining a clear focus on addressing issues of power and control. As others have noted in the field, 'the devil is in the detail' when seeking to implement safe and effective restorative justice processes (Koss 2010) and there is a high price for getting it wrong (Busch 2002).

The high prevalence of all types of violence against women also reminds us that there needs to be continued investment in prevention. Without addressing violence at the root source, there will be an ongoing stream of those who perpetrate violence and those who are victimized. Efforts to develop appropriate response systems need to go side by side with efforts that pursue societal transformation to end violence (Smith 2010).

References

Blagg, H. 2002. Restorative Justice and Aboriginal Family Violence: Opening a Space for Healing, in *Restorative Justice and Family Violence*, edited by H. Strang and J. Braithwaite. Cambridge: Cambridge University Press, 191–205.

Busch, R. 2002. Domestic Violence and Restorative Justice Initiatives: Who Pays if We Get it Wrong?, in *Restorative Justice and Family Violence*, edited by H. Strang and J. Braithwaite. Cambridge: Cambridge University Press, 223–48.

Coker, D. 2002. Anti-Subordination Processes in Domestic Violence, in *Restorative Justice and Family Violence*, edited by H. Strang and J. Braithwaite. Cambridge: Cambridge University Press, 128–52.

Fanslow, J.L. and Robinson, E.M. 2004. Violence against Women in New Zealand: Prevalence and Health Consequences. *New Zealand Medical Journal*, 117(1206), 1173–84.

Fanslow, J.L. and Robinson, E.M. 2011. Sticks, Stones, or Words: Counting the Prevalence of Intimate Partner Violence among New Zealand Women. *Journal of Aggression, Maltreatment and Trauma*, 20(7), 741–59. Available at: www.dx.doi.org/ 10.1080/10926771.2011.608221.

Fanslow, J.L., Robinson, E.M., Crengle, S. and Perese, L. 2007. Prevalence of Child Sexual Abuse Reported by a Cross-Sectional Sample of New Zealand Women. *Child Abuse and Neglect*, 31, 935–45.

Garcia-Moreno, C., Jansen, H.A.F.M., Ellsberg, M., Heise, L. and Watts, C. 2005. *WHO Multi-Country Study on Women's Health and Domestic Violence against Women: Initial Results on Prevalence, Health Outcomes and Women's Responses*. Geneva: World Health Organization.

Gulliver, P. and Fanslow, J. 2012. *Measurement of Family Violence at a Population Level: What Might be Needed to Develop Reliable and Valid Family Violence Indicators?* Auckland: New Zealand Family Violence Clearinghouse, The University of Auckland.

Hayden, A. 2010. Why Rock the Boat? Non-Reporting of Intimate Partner Violence. PhD thesis, Institute of Public Policy, Auckland University of Technology.

Jülich, S. 2006. Views of Justice among Survivors of Historical Child Sexual Abuse: Implications for Restorative Justice in New Zealand. *Theoretical Criminology*, 10, 125–38.

Koss, M. 2010. Restorative Justice for Acquaintance Rape and Misdeameanor Sex Crimes, in *Restorative Justice and Violence Against Women*, edited by J. Ptacek. Oxford: Oxford University Press, 218–38.

Marshall, T. 2003. Restorative Justice: An Overview, in *A Restorative Justice Reader: Texts, Sources, Context*, edited by G. Johnstone. Portland, OR: Willan Publishing, 28–45.

Nancarrow, H. 2010. Restorative Justice for Domestic and Family Violence: Hopes and Fears of Indigenous and Non-Indigenous Australian Women, in *Restorative Justice and Violence Against Women*, edited by J. Ptacek. Oxford: Oxford University Press, 123–49.

Pennell, J. and Burford G. 2000. Family Group Decision-Making: Protecting Children and Women. *Child Welfare*, 79(2), 131–58.

Proietti-Scifoni, G. and Daly, K. 2011. Gendered Violence and Restorative Justice: The Views of New Zealand Opinion Leaders. *Contemporary Justice Review*, 14(3), 269–90.

SAS Institute. 2008. SAS Version 9.2. Cary, NC: SAS Institute.

Stubbs, J. 2010. Restorative Justice, Gendered Violence and Indigenous Women, in *Restorative Justice and Violence Against Women*, edited by J. Ptacek. Oxford: Oxford University Press, 103–22.

Smith, A. 2010. Beyond Restorative Justice: Radical Organising against Violence, in *Restorative Justice and Violence against Women*, edited by J. Ptacek. Oxford: Oxford University Press, 255–78.

Tolmie, J., Elizabeth, V. and Gavey, N. 2010. Is 50:50 Shared Care a Desirable Norm Following Family Separation? Raising Questions about Current Family Law Practices in New Zealand. *New Zealand Universities Law Review*, 24(1), 136–66.

World Health Organization. 2001. *Putting Women First: Ethical and Safety Recommendations for Research on Domestic Violence Against Women.* Geneva, Switzerland: World Health Organization.

Chapter 4

Ma Matou Ma Tatou[1] – Working Together to Change Young Lives: Where to Next with Child Protection in New Zealand?

Paul Nixon

Introduction

New Zealand has a track record of innovation in child welfare practice. This owes much to ways of working and leadership from *Māori*, the Indigenous people, on how we best resolve matters for children and young people in need of care and protection. The full engagement of *whānau* (family), *hapū* (sub-tribe or clan) and *iwi* (tribe) and the wider engagement of community interests in decision-making have led to significant improvements in practice. *Māori* perspectives have had a profound effect on how practice is conceptualized; one of the strongest manifestations of this was *Puao-te-ata-tu* (Daybreak), a Ministerial Advisory Committee providing a *Māori* perspective on social work and chaired by John Rangihau (Ministerial Advisory Committee 1988). This report was instrumental in shaping the forward looking Children, Young Persons and Their Families Act 1989. The Act forged a new consensus on practice and thinking that endures today. New Zealanders, because of New Zealand's relatively small population, have a close proximity to their government. This has meant that New Zealand has often been able to be creative and nimble in response to social problems and their potential solutions. *Māori* perspectives challenged old institutional orthodoxies and created a new momentum with social work practice that placed family and its inherent and essential value on relationships, identity and culture at the heart of practice.

This chapter sets out some key developments in New Zealand that guide and shape the future of child protection services. It examines some current patterns and trends in child welfare and explores the strategic approach being taken to respond to these problems in which tackling family violence is an integral part. Like good social work practice, the road map to improvement involves a balancing of shared interests with a range of stakeholders – children and young people, families and communities, service providers and state agencies – in how they can collectively achieve change for children and young people. Underpinning any strategy, of course, there are key cultural concepts about how society thinks about its children

1 *Ma matou, ma tatou* – One for all and all for one, all of us.

and, particularly in the context of child protection work, about how we view children and young people as citizens in their own right rather than 'cases' or 'objects of concern' (Butler-Sloss 1988).

New Zealand is signatory to the UN Convention on the Rights of the Child (1989) and in the same year it legally mandated a Children's Commissioner to report to the government and monitor trends in the well-being of children in New Zealand. In 2009 anti-smacking laws were introduced. These changes have served to protect children better, but, at a more fundamental level, they make a statement about how we perceive children and young people as citizens and uphold their rights in the same way we do for adults.

In recent years, there has been a growing willingness across agencies and communities to notify Child, Youth and Family Services over concerns about children. There are now far more coordinated responses to child abuse and a renewed emphasis on families, communities and agencies working together than hitherto. In particular, a growing set of partnerships exists between health, education, police and child, youth and family services. There are also new interagency guides on keeping children safe (Department of Child, Youth and Family 2011).

The non-governmental organization (NGO) sector is well developed in New Zealand with NGO service providers working with *whānau*, *hapū* and *iwi* groups, making connections at a local level and providing a wide range of local and accessible services. Further, new technology is increasingly playing a vital part in the lives of children, families and agencies, with more and faster information being available than ever before. These growing sources of data tell us more about the lives of the children and families with whom social workers work.

Patterns and Trends in Child Welfare

Patterns in New Zealand in both child welfare and child abuse statistics show some striking trends over time. Comparisons of child abuse with other jurisdictions are notoriously difficult because there is no one accepted or agreed international definition of child abuse and different countries have different ways of defining, recording and responding to the problem of child abuse (Parton et al. 1997). This chapter reflects on what appears to be happening in New Zealand and the concomitant responses being put in place.

In 2003, a national review of child protection services, named the *Baseline Review*, was conducted and concluded that the Department of Child, Youth and Family Services should retain a sharp focus on its core business: care and protection and youth justice. In 2006, Child, Youth and Family then merged into the Ministry of Social Development. Systems were put in place to improve the notification, recording and response to child abuse. Since 2004, the notifications to Child, Youth and Family have risen incrementally year on year. Figure 4.1 sets this out. In 2004 approximately 40,000 care and protection notifications were received at the Child, Youth and Families National Contact Centre; by 2012 this number had risen to 152,000 notifications, close to a quadrupling of notified concerns about children.

The most dramatic rise in these figures was caused by the rapidly growing number of family violence referrals by the police which rose from 3,389 in 2004 to 78,915 in 2012. Violence in families affects the lives of many children and young people in New Zealand and it is a key priority area for government. In 2006, the Family Violence Interagency Response System was introduced. This was designed to create a collaborative, coordinated interagency response to family violence. It produced guidelines around the initial response, post event assessment, risk response planning, coordinated cross-sector support for victims' empowerment, children's safety, and offenders' management and accountability. The system has clearly identified and then notified increasingly high numbers to Child, Youth and Family Services as seen in Figure 4.1.

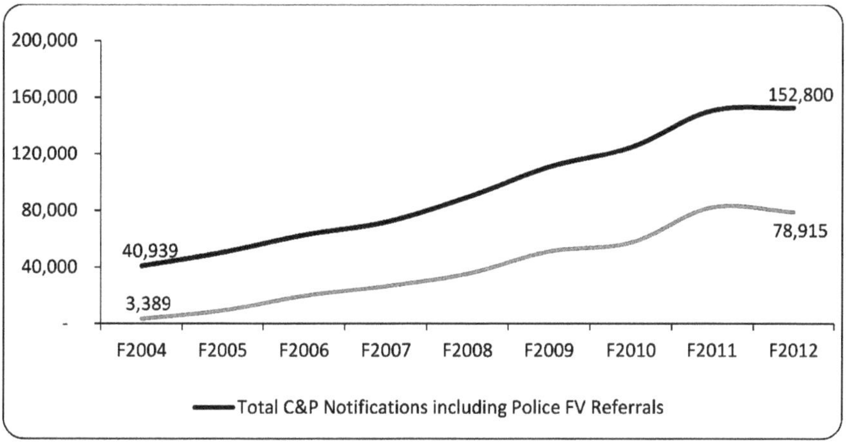

Figure 4.1 Number of care and protection notifications, 2005 to 2012

Tackling family violence is a fundamental priority because it is such a substantial part of children's safety and well-being. Violence in families affects the lives of many children and young people. Accordingly a coordinated response has been organized around:

- the establishment of the Chief Executive Interagency Taskforce to drive a coordinated interagency approach;
- the implementation in 2006 of the Family Violence Interagency Response System – a collaborative, coordinated interagency response involving police, child, youth and family services and women's refuge;
- the release of a well-resourced and high-profile public information campaign 'It's Not OK' – to raise public awareness and debate about family violence;

- the provision of a wide range of local NGO services for families experiencing violence;
- the creation of a Families Commission to provide regular reporting nationally on patterns and trends in relation to family violence and the nature of service responses to it.

A recent review of the Family Court by the Ministry of Justice (2011) focused on the question of how the service could ensure its efforts are targeted at the most vulnerable children and at the most serious cases, in particular in relation to family violence. This review recommended that there was a clear need to:

- improve family violence responses – to create more bespoke services and responses rather than a 'one size fits all' approach, given the complexity and the wide range of different types of family violence;
- ensure court professionals targeted those in greatest need – the most vulnerable families where the risk and needs were seen as higher;
- extend definitions of family violence to include 'economic abuse'.

Evaluating the underlying trends on child abuse raises some interesting policy challenges. Figure 4.2 sets out these data. Patterns in relation to child physical abuse and child sexual abuse and neglect appear to be somewhat stable, with a slight upward trend in all three areas. In some ways, the trends on child physical and sexual abuse are matched in other national jurisdictions (Barnett et al. 2011, Blagg 2002). Both physical and sexual abuse are characterized by more forensic assessment and diagnostic work, with the close working together of the police, the health service and the courts. It may also be that growing awareness amongst both the professional and public community about the nature of this abuse has provided for improved responses and has led to further and better awareness and management of the risk factors.

Neglect and emotional abuse are the two largest areas of child abuse. This trend is reflected in other countries too (Barnett et al. 2011) but the rise in emotional abuse appears to be largely caused by a constellation of risk factors operating together. The notable rise in substantiations of emotional abuse are characterized largely by the interplay of three key risk factors:

- family violence;
- parental alcohol and drug misuse;
- untreated parental mental health problems.

It is the interplay of these three factors which has a damaging effect on parenting and parents' relationships with their children. Together, these factors can create harmful environments, although singularly or even combined they do not in themselves guarantee emotional abuse will occur. Their coexistence, however, is clearly making life hard for children and their families.

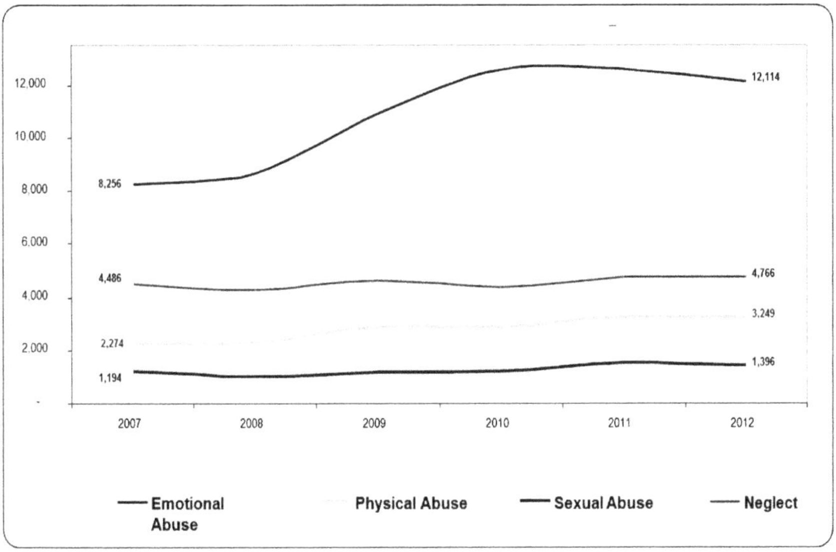

Figure 4.2 Substantiated abuse findings by type: 2006/2007 to 2011/2012

Note: We apologize for the imperfect distinction between abuse types in figure. However from top to bottom in the same order, they represent emotional abuse, neglect, physical abuse and sexual abuse.

New Zealand appears to have favoured using 'emotional abuse' and 'neglect' as the primary definitions for these behaviours by adults and their consequent risks to children. The policy challenge is that many of these parenting problems are underpinned by significant societal problems beyond the reach of social work resources alone. Tackling family violence often requires dealing with economic issues, poverty, housing, transport, structural issues around gender inequalities, sexism and attitudes to violence. Alcohol and drug misuse are significant public policy health issues, as is tackling mental ill health and creating good access to services. Police and court responses to violence in the home are often reactive and short-term and do not address the underlying causes.

It is important to make sure that a range of services is available especially drug, alcohol and mental health services. Further integration of policy and practice is needed across agencies to ensure the right response is appropriately matched to needs and risks. In particular, the interagency work on family violence now has to take account of:

- ensuring appropriate referral pathways for family violence so that families can be directed to the correct service response, help and support;
- better across-agency data and monitoring of the volume and complexity of family violence cases to support future strategic and operational responses;
- ensuring the consistent application of thresholds and decision-making;

- the development of multi-agency service responses – including both initial responses and high risk case management;
- the development of across-agency training focused on helpful interventions and services.

Quality Social Work Practice

In recent times, there has been a strong emphasis on government child protection agencies demonstrating their effectiveness and on introducing new levels of accountability for their performance. Given the complexity and uncertainty of the very nature of child protection work, many organizations have chosen to demonstrate their effectiveness through measures of organizational performance. This has largely been pursued through quantitative measures of organizational output – for example, the number of completed assessments within specified time frames. While this may provide a surface measure of organizational management or speed of service, it does not tell us about the outcomes or results experienced by the children and families involved.

A series of 'trade-offs' are inevitable depending on where the organization wishes to place its priorities – between measuring and reporting on either quantity or quality or measuring outputs and outcomes. Figure 4.3 sets out this dilemma. Furthermore, some of these indicators are far easier to measure than others.

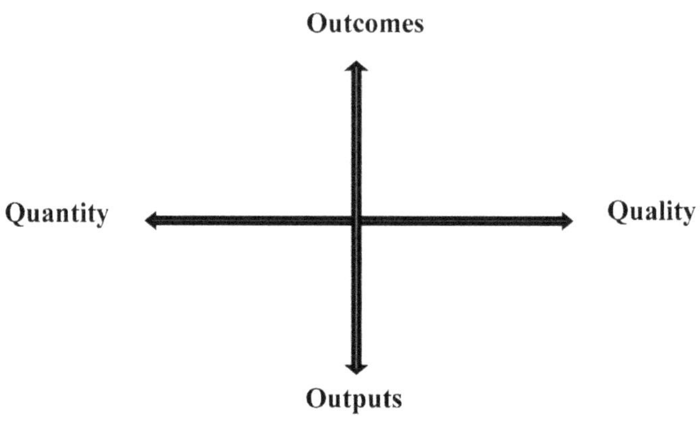

Figure 4.3 Balancing performance against organizational priorities

Child, Youth and Family's new strategy *Ma Matou Ma Tatou* places emphasis on quality social work practice but, to do so, it has to create the right environment for it to flourish. This means creating a suitable organizational culture. The organization signals what is important, in part by deciding on what it chooses to count, measure and report on.

Delivering high-quality social work in a statutory child protection setting is difficult. Agencies are overwhelmed with volumes of notifications; workloads are high; and the work is complex and uncertain. Good quality assessments – which are ecological and child-centred, which fully engage the immediate and wider family networks and which cross agency support – are highly skilled activities that demand quality social work practice (Smale and Tuson 1993). So, too, is the forging of close working partnerships with family and community groups for the effective running of family group conferences.

As indicated, implementing quality social work practice requires creating proper conditions. This means managing the volumes of caseloads, ensuring social workers have the skills and up-to-date knowledge and capability (Munro 2011). Supervision of a high standard, which is reflective and challenging is a prerequisite to good social work as is ensuring that the right information systems and learning opportunities are in place for staff. Research demonstrates that the quality of the relationship between the worker and the children and families they work with is the key to good outcomes (Department of Health 1995). Leadership within the organization – at all levels – is also crucial to creating the right organizational culture in which high-quality practice can thrive.

Creating the right space for quality practice is about leadership and challenging the prevailing assumptions of what public services should report on to demonstrate success. Historically, this has been output, organizationally centred, focused on quantity and tends to be fragmented (Adams 2003). Figure 4.4 demonstrates the shift in focus that needs to occur in order to start to understand improvements in terms of real outcomes for children.

Current quality assurance focus		**Future quality assurance focus**
Outputs	→	Outcomes
Organisational	→	Child Centred
Quantity	→	Quality
Fragmented	→	Systemic

Figure 4.4 Necessary focus shifts for improved outcomes

Family Group Conferences

Family group conferences are at the heart of child welfare and youth justice practice in New Zealand. Set in legislation, they provide a legal construct to manage the borderline between families and the state in matters about the care and protection of children. Family group conferences are also an early example of restorative justice, which aims to seek solutions, not allocate blame, and to involve *whānau*. The conferences are used in both care and protection and youth justice and they provide a mechanism to ease the tension between the right of families to self-govern and have freedom from interference from the state and the duty of the state to intervene in families to protect children if necessary.

In the context of family violence, the practice of family group conferences raises some specific challenges about how conferences involve perpetrators of violence in a decision-making process that leaves the family in control. Clearly good preparation, excellent information sharing, the involvement of the wider family and sometimes the exclusion of a perpetrator of violence from the conference can all be mechanisms to ensure the conference is successful (Nixon et al. 2005). Family group conferences have operated in New Zealand since 1989. The Child, Youth and Family Service is now looking to improve conferences further through improving *iwi* and community involvement in the running of conferences, by strengthening other agencies' contributions to providing information and services and to supporting conference plans.

Working Together with *Māori*

In particular, in working with *Māori* and *iwi*, an important programme of development is under way which includes:

- improved search for *whakapapa* (family networks and genealogy);
- increased use of *whānau hui* (family meeting) to help prepare for the conference;
- co-facilitated conferences with *iwi* representatives;
- co-constructed action-based research models to provide ongoing feedback about progress.

Twenty-six years ago, *Puao-te-ata-tu* was gifted to New Zealand providing a set of guiding principles to build a service that was responsive to *tamariki* (children) and *rangitahi* (youth) and their *whānau*. It still features strongly in the minds of practitioners today and has shaped the prevailing child welfare legislation significantly.

Work is underway to build stronger partnerships with *hapu* and *iwi* on how social work practice is better developed. In particular, this includes assessment and decision-making processes alongside the further development, identification and engagement of *whanau* and *iwi* caregivers. Furthermore, a process of consultation is underway looking at some of the best examples of both Indigenous and bicultural practice. This will help inform future practice development.

A key component of change is to incorporate the values, culture and beliefs of *Māori* and to promote *te reo* (language) in the everyday work of the Child, Youth and Family Service in order to provide a service that is truly responsive. A primary focus has been on children in care by promoting learning and identity through education and greater attention to their language and culture. As a child in a care residence commented: 'Learning about reo and tikanga lifts my spirits' (cited in Ministry of Social Development 2012: 11).

Voices of Children and Young People

Fully involving children and young people in decisions that affect their own lives is a prerequisite to good social work practice. Set within a wider rights framework for children, this is important politically as well because adults start to reconceptualize the importance of understanding children as people and citizens in their own right, rather than 'child protection cases'.

Changes in practice, policy and training are occurring to ensure children's participation and feelings shine through the assessment and planning processes. Specifically, this occurs through children's and young people's participation in assessment and decision-making in family group conferences. This means working differently and creating space and time for social workers and coordinators to spend more time with children and young people and to find new and innovative ways of engaging young people, particularly through the use of technology.

Creating a new approach to children's participation requires that social workers within the workforce have the knowledge and skills to listen to children and effectively engage them. Underpinning this are mechanisms to ensure the agency upholds and protect children's rights through a systematic real time complaints and feedback system. Involving children and young people in service development and improvement through the use of facilitated *hui* at both a regional and national level is being piloted currently to help to create services and practices that are designed to be more responsive to them. This accords them respect, one of the core values of restorative justice.

Connecting Communities

As previously discussed, a multi-agency approach is a significant aspect of improving children's welfare. No one agency can easily resolve the complex issues on their own (Department of Child, Youth and Family 2011). This shift in modality will require significant changes such as more integrated assessments and joint planning alongside families and communities. These will build on families' strengths while valuing the range of contributions and support they can offer around outcomes. Accordingly, they have a leadership challenge to bring people together around a common goal for the benefit of children.

Historically, concerns in communities about children's welfare have all been directed to Child, Youth and Family. If real change is to occur, reports of concern will need to have the right pathway immediately available which places the needs of children and their families at the appropriate level of response within the integrated system. This means closer work with families and communities to negotiate what needs and services are delivered and who is best placed in the continuum of need to receive them.

Improved information sharing, better access to shared data sets and a pooled knowledge on research and evaluation are all products of stronger cooperation. Work is occurring cross agency with a range of partners to establish a training 'hub' where social service providers and other agencies can collaborate. Furthermore, sharing this structure on an international level has the potential to benefit many communities. This way we can draw on different research and ideas about how to connect it to practice (Barratt and Hodson 2006).

Leadership and Workforce

Child welfare professionals have a leadership role in helping shape improvements in services for vulnerable children. Ensuring the appropriate behaviours and organizational culture is crucial to delivering plans and strategies for the future. Generally, it is better to change culture and behaviours than structures; experience has shown that culture shapes behaviour.

The leadership challenges are to develop more child-centred approaches where practice and services are focused on outcomes for children and their families and where families, agencies and communities are enabled to cooperate. The family group conference provides the ideal legal mechanism to deliver this, provided integrated strategies and plans are set in place.

To deliver greater integration of practice and working together, the workforce will need to be trained, skilled and supported to develop new behaviours and practice skills that can work readily across groups. Harnessing the skills of managers, senior practitioners and supervisors to coach, lead, challenge and support this type of practice will take time and resources.

Where Next?

At the time of writing, a *Children's Action Plan* is being launched by the government of New Zealand designed to improve outcomes for the most vulnerable children and to reduce patterns of child abuse. The aim is to strengthen accountabilities across all the agencies, taking a more integrated and holistic approach to children's needs – the child's *whānau*, *hapū*, *iwi* and community working alongside health, education, housing, social work, corrections and so on. A wide range of NGO providers at a local level will also join as key partners in providing services and support. A more coordinated and integrated approach will require a stronger interagency governance and resource deployment. To this end, a national Vulnerable Children's Board has been established to guide and oversee the targeting of the most vulnerable and for coordinating and integrating practice and services. In line with this, a series of intensive family support services in the shape of *Children's Teams* are being piloted to operate below the statutory child protection threshold, designed to pick up earlier concerns about children's well-being. These teams will be formed from local partnerships of community providers, *iwi* representatives and state agencies who will collectively provide support. Practice and services in New Zealand, like any jurisdiction, are constantly evolving and changing. There is still much to be gained by strengthening all the contributions of *whānau, hapū, iwi*, agencies and communities around the safety and well-being of children. This way, in accordance with *Puao-te-ata-tu*, we are hopeful it will be a new dawn.

References

Adams, R. 2003. *Social Work and Empowerment*. Basingstoke: Palgrave Macmillan.

Barnett, O.M., Miller-Perrin, C. and Perrin, R. 2011. *Family Violence across the Lifespan: An Introduction*. 3rd edition. Belmont, CA: Sage.

Barratt, M. and Hodson, R. 2006. *Firm Foundations: A Practical Guide to Organisational Support for the Use of Research Evidence*. Totnes: Research in Practice.

Blagg, H. 2002. Restorative Justice and Aboriginal Family Violence: Opening a Space for Healing, in *Restorative Justice and Family Violence*, edited by H. Strang and J. Braithwaite. Cambridge: Cambridge University Press, 191–205.

Butler-Sloss, E. 1988. *Report into the Inquiry of Child Abuse in Cleveland*. Cm 412. London: HMSO.

Department of Health. 1995. *Child Protection: Messages from Research*. London: HMSO.

Department of Child, Youth and Family. 2011. *An Interagency Guide: Working Together to Keep Children and Young People Safe: Me Mutu Ta Tatou Tukino Tamariki*. Wellington: Child Youth and Family.

Ministerial Advisory Committee. 1988. *The Report of the Ministerial Advisory Committee on a Māori Perspective for the Department of Social Welfare*. Wellington: Department of Social Welfare.

Ministry of Justice. 2011. *Family Court Review*. Wellington: Ministry of Justice.

Ministry of Social Development. 2012. *Ma Matou Ma Tatou – Changing Young Lives. Child, Youth and Family Strategic Plan 2012–15*. Wellington: Ministry of Social Development.

Munro, E. 2011 *The Munro Review of Child Protection: Final Report – A Child-Centred System*. London: Department for Education.

Nixon, P., Burford, G., Quinn, A. and Edelbaum, J. 2005. *A Survey of International Practices, Policy and Research on Family Group Conferencing and Related*

Practices. Englewood, CO: American Humane Association. Available at: http://www.fdgm.org.

Parton, N., Thorpe, D. and Wattam, C. 1997. *Child Protection Risk and the Moral Order*. Basingstoke: Macmillan.

Smale, G. and Tuson, G. 1993. *Empowerment, Assessment, Care Management and the Skilled Worker*. London: HMSO.

Chapter 5
Elder Abuse and Neglect

Judith A. Davey

Introduction

Despite evidence that elder abuse has occurred throughout history and across social groups and cultures, it has only recently been studied and named (Wilber and McNeilly 2001). This is in the context of increasing attention being given to all forms of family violence. In 2002, the work of the World Health Organization brought international attention to the issue of elder abuse and, increasingly, government agencies and professional groups have identified it as a social problem. There are several reasons for the lack of information and initiatives related to avoiding and addressing elder abuse: the relative newness of the field, conflicting causal theories and, as with other forms of abuse, the difficulty in obtaining data on its extent and characteristics.

Defining Elder Abuse

A particular problem is the lack of a single internationally accepted definition of elder abuse. The World Health Organization definition is: *A single or repeated act or lack of appropriate action, occurring within any relationship where there is an expectation of trust, which causes harm or distress to an older person* (www.who.int/ageing/projects/elder_abuse/en). Within this statement there are several elements which require clarification, highlighting the complex nature of the problem. Many organizations define 'older person' as 65 years or older. The phrase 'where there is an expectation of trust' means that 'stranger' crimes against older people, such as burglary, assault and fraud, are not generally included in the definition. Definitions may confine elder abuse and neglect to the interpersonal level. This approach leaves out institutional abuse, but it is important that this be covered in preventive and remedial action, given the vulnerability of older people in care services and facilities. In this context, deliberate acts by another person are classed as 'abuse' while omissions are classed as 'neglect'.

Definitions of elder abuse also require consideration of the cultural context. Interpretations of what constitutes abuse and the appropriate response can vary among ethnic groups and may involve beliefs about rights over property, what constitutes disrespect and dishonour to elders, and cultural needs (Glasgow and Fanslow 2006, Wainer et al. 2010). It is important to keep in mind the perceptions of older people themselves when determining whether elder abuse has occurred. These difficulties of definition, as well as problems of data collection and recording, inhibit meaningful comparisons of elder abuse and neglect, both locally and internationally.

Why Does Elder Abuse Happen?

Some of the theories about the nature and causes of elder abuse and neglect relate specifically to the situation of older people. Because of chronic health problems or disabilities they may be dependent on others, making them vulnerable. However, the abuser may also be financially and emotionally dependent on the older person. Where older people have significant disabilities, carers' stress can lead to abuse. Dementia or other medical conditions may produce behaviour which is abusive of carers. Social isolation from family and friends and from supportive services, experienced by many vulnerable older people, increases both the potential for abuse and the opportunities for concealing it.

There are analogies between elder abuse and neglect and other forms of family violence. Firstly, it is largely hidden, private and under-reported. It occurs within relationships characterized by abuse of power and control. Victims are often isolated, in a weakened, powerless and dependent position. In some families, violence is considered the normal reaction to stress; and it may continue from generation to generation. Sometimes there is a history of family conflict, alcohol and/or drug abuse, and psychological problems (Lachs and Pillemer 2004). As with child abuse and intimate partner violence, more than one type of elder abuse and neglect can occur at the same time (Wilber and McNeilly 2001). Gender differences are less clear-cut than in intimate partner abuse, with both men and women responsible for and experiencing elder abuse (Fallon 2006, O'Keeffe et al. 2007). Some elder abuse and neglect has its roots in long established spousal abuse.

In contrast to child abuse, older people are (generally) legally competent adults, able to make their own decisions about their lifestyle and living arrangements. They may choose to remain in a situation which is not physically, psychologically or financially safe for them. Such a decision made by a competent adult needs to be respected.

The 'ecological model' of violence links elder abuse and neglect with broader societal issues, instead of focusing solely on individual and family contexts, associating it with older people's relatively low status in society and lack of economic power (Peri et al. 2008, Wolf 2001). This suggests that explanations of why and how elder abuse and neglect occurs require an exploration of societal structures, ageist attitudes and human rights issues.

Why is Elder Abuse Important?

The experience of elder abuse and neglect may produce wide-ranging and long-term effects on older people's physical and mental health, finances, living arrangements, family relationships and social contacts (McAlpine 2008, Naughton et al. 2010, O'Keeffe et al. 2007). The greater fragility and vulnerability of many older people may mean that they never fully recover from the abuse physically or emotionally, as well as financially.

Older people may fear that telling someone else about the abuse will lead to the loss of close relationships, possible retaliation, or further loss of independence. They may be reluctant to believe that a trusted person is harming them. When the perpetrator is their son or daughter, they may feel shamed by the behaviour. They may not want the abuser to get into trouble, although they do want the abuse to stop. As with other abuse victims, they may fear that they will not be believed. Thus the impact of elder abuse and neglect may be worsened because shame, fear, and dependence on the abuser cause reluctance to seek help or because supportive services are not available. Elder abuse and neglect is likely to reduce an older person's ability to participate actively in their community and may, therefore, lead to social isolation.

Elder abuse and neglect may have significant health consequences. Age Concern New Zealand found that about half of the older people supported by their elder abuse and neglect services over the previous 10 years said that their health was significantly affected by the abuse they had experienced (Age Concern 2007). Two out of every five people experienced significant reduction in their independence, confidence and self-esteem and they reported feeling frightened, anxious or emotionally distressed. A qualitative study published in the UK found similar results, as well as an increased need for residential care and higher morbidity and mortality rates (Lachs and Pillemer 2004). Thus, as well as impacting on the well-being of older people, elder abuse and neglect brings increased costs to society in terms of social and health care, especially in a context of rapidly ageing population.

Types of Abuse and Neglect

Abuse, neglect and violence against older people take many forms – psychological, material/financial, physical, sexual and institutional. Abuse of older people's human rights is sometimes seen as an additional category (Cooper et al. 2008). Abuse and neglect occur in every social, economic and ethnic group, in every type of locality and in different settings (for example, in private homes and in residential care) (Heiser and Brownell 2009). Several types of elder abuse and neglect can occur at the same time.

Psychological abuse refers to behaviour that causes the victim anguish, stress or fear. It includes verbal abuse, intimidation, humiliation, harassment or excessive control of choices, taking away decision-making powers, threats of harm to property or pets, or threats of physical or sexual abuse:

> Edith is 77 and lives in her own home, with a separate unit where her adult grandson, Michael, stays. Michael sometimes helps his grandmother with shopping and other chores, although he does this begrudgingly, telling her 'You're useless. No-one needs you. Why don't you do the world a favour – don't wake up tomorrow.' Edith tells Michael that she does not want him there any longer. He starts yelling at her, telling her she is a 'selfish old cow' and threatening to break her windows. Edith is very distressed and frightened by Michael's attitude towards her.[1]

Material/financial abuse is the illegal or improper exploitation and/or use of older people's funds or other resources. Examples include theft of money or property and refusal to provide care or necessities, which can be paid for with the older person's assets, in order to retain inheritance money for the relatives:

> While Emily was in hospital, her daughter Karen removed a silver tea service and other valuable items to her own home. When Emily got home she thought she had been burgled and called the police, who found that Karen had removed the goods 'for safe-keeping. These are heirlooms, they don't just belong to Mum they belong to the whole family.'

Further discussion of financial elder abuse, its causes, prevention and mitigation can be found in Davey and McKendry (2011).

Physical abuse includes the infliction of pain or injury, physical coercion, inappropriate use of restraint or confinement that causes pain or bodily harm and chemical restraint, including abuse of medication.

Tilly's 80-year-old husband Ian has dementia and Tilly cares for him at home.

> To ensure he doesn't wander off while she goes shopping, Tilly ties him to a chair and locks him in the bedroom. When she comes home and finds he has urinated in the chair, she is so incensed that she beats him with her walking stick and threatens him.

Sexual abuse is non-consensual sexual contact of any kind with an older person; any coerced or exploitive sexual behaviour or threats imposed on an individual, including sexual acts imposed on a person unable to give consent.

Institutional abuse arises from the policies or practices of an institution that impinge on the rights and well-being of older people (as such it is comparable

1 These examples of elder abuse and neglect have been adapted from the Age Concern New Zealand website (www.ageconcern.org.nz/safety) and do not represent actual individuals.

to institutional racism). It may occur in a residential care facility, hospital, or other public or private sector institution, including financial and social service organizations. It may arise where there is insufficient or not sufficiently trained or supervised staff or where practice focuses more on organizational convenience or profit-making than clients' needs. Financial cutbacks may result in inadequate meals, hygiene or care.

People in institutional care may still be subject to abuse by their family and visitors, but abuse and neglect by staff also occurs. Examples include forced feeding, rough handling, inappropriate use of restraints, or cultural insensitivity. There are also cases of stealing from residents:

> Jane reports on disturbing practices in the rest home where she works. 'In one dementia unit, patients are constantly being flicked on the bottom by carers. They think it's funny. Some care assistants, who are meant to shower patients, do not do it. No one checks. Food is often left on the bedside table. After half an hour, someone else comes and takes it away. No one seems to notice that the older person needs help with feeding.'

Neglect results when someone fails to meet the physical, social or emotional needs of an older person. Passive/unintentional neglect may arise from carers' inadequate knowledge or inattention. Active/intentional neglect is the conscious and deliberate deprivation of care:

> Kathryn is worried about her friend, Jane, who lives with her daughter and son-in-law. Lately Jane appears to be depressed. When Kathryn asks her what is wrong she replies that her daughter is often too busy to make her lunch or take her shopping. Quite often her daughter and son-in-law go out for dinner, not leaving Jane anything to eat. She is embarrassed and hurt that her daughter is treating her like this but doesn't want to make a fuss.

Prevalence of Elder Abuse and Neglect

Because of issues surrounding definition and reporting, comprehensive and comparable statistics on the prevalence of elder abuse and neglect are difficult to find and, where available, may only represent 'the tip of the ice-berg'. Estimated prevalence rates from a range of countries, compiled by O'Keefe et al. (2007), ranged from 3 per cent to 6 per cent of older people experiencing elder abuse and neglect. In their systematic review, Cooper, Selwood and Livingston (2008) found that, in general population studies, prevalence rates ranged between 3 per cent and 28 per cent. In what they described as the 'best evidence', 6 per cent of older people reported significant abuse in the last month.

Cases may be reported to a range of authorities and services, including health services, the police and non-government organizations working with older people.

But many reported cases are not included in any formal data collection system. Older people may choose to seek support from family or friends rather than mainstream services, making estimates of its extent even more difficult to arrive at.

Most cases of elder abuse and neglect involve more than a single incident and often more than one type of abuse. The international literature suggests that neglect is the most common form of maltreatment, followed by financial, psychological and physical abuse (Cooper et al. 2008, Fallon 2006). Sexual abuse is not often reported for the older age group. Differences in ordering types of abuse by importance or prevalence, and in combination, reflect different measurement approaches (Clare et al. 2011, Lievore and Mayhew 2007, Naughton et al. 2010).

The prevalence of elder abuse and neglect in residential care or geriatric hospitals is difficult to estimate but it is thought to account for only a small percentage of cases (Daly et al. 2013). Cooper, Selwood and Livingston's (2008) review found that, although a high proportion of institutional staff reported having observed abuse occurring, much lower percentages admit to using psychological or physical abuse themselves. Estimates of the prevalence of abuse among older people with dementia range from 5 per cent to 12 per cent (Coyne 2001).

Who are the Victims of Elder Abuse and Neglect?

Even accounting for greater longevity, women are over-represented as victims of elder abuse and neglect relative to the older population (Lievore and Mayhew 2007, Naughton et al. 2010, O'Keeffe et al. 2007). In the UK, findings reported by O'Keeffe et al. indicated that women were more likely than men to have experienced neglect and interpersonal abuse (psychological, physical and sexual abuse). Older women living alone seem particularly vulnerable. The prevalence of financial abuse appears to be similar for both sexes.

Much of the international evidence suggests that the risk of elder abuse and neglect increases with age. Age Concern New Zealand's data suggest that a person aged 90 or more is nearly six times more likely to be a victim than someone aged 65–69 (Age Concern 2007). In the UK, the prevalence of neglect was highest among women aged 85 and over and the highest rate of financial abuse was found among men in this age group (O'Keeffe et al. 2007).

The increase with age may indicate that very old people have characteristics that put them at greater risk or there may be specific risk factors related to their living situations. Some studies have found that victims of elder abuse and neglect are more likely to be living with others in intergenerational households (Naughton et al. 2010), but in others they are more likely to be living alone (Age Concern 2007). The gender difference in vulnerability diminishes for the very old. This may be because risk factors become more similar or because very old men may develop particular risk factors of their own. Victims of neglect tend to be older than victims of abuse. Victims tend to be frail, vulnerable and dependent.

Those with cognitive and physical incapacities that are stressful for caregivers are at higher risk of abuse.

Who are the Perpetrators of Elder Abuse and Neglect?

Data from a range of sources confirm that the majority of perpetrators are family members, other household members, and paid carers – linking to definitions of elder abuse and neglect that involve expectations of trust or duties of care. Even where older people are in residential care, the majority of abusers are family members.

In the case of interpersonal abuse, research findings suggest that the majority of perpetrators are male, but women are just as likely as men to be perpetrators of financial elder abuse. Perpetrators tend to fall within the age groups likely to be the adult children of the victims (35–64 years). Older abusers are frequently the spouses or partners of the victims.

How Can Elder Abuse and Neglect Be Dealt With?

Primary Prevention – Public Awareness and Education

No single response will be sufficient to tackle the complex issue of elder abuse. A combination of approaches is required. Primary prevention initiatives focus on the general population and should therefore aim to influence ageist attitudes and behaviours. Government strategies and campaigns and public awareness initiatives can be helpful.

In 2006, the International Network for Prevention of Elder Abuse designated 15 June as World Elder Abuse Awareness Day and an increasing number of events are held across the globe on this day each year to raise awareness of elder abuse and neglect as a social and human rights issue that can be prevented. In their review of European initiatives (Sethi et al. 2011), the World Health Organization noted mixed findings on the effectiveness of awareness programmes but some promising evidence from school-based intergenerational programmes, informal caregiver support programmes and initiatives to encourage positive attitudes among those working with older people.

Secondary Prevention – Focusing on High Risk Groups

Older people considered to be at risk of abuse can be targeted through protective services, which often work through multidisciplinary teams and which provide interventions at the individual level, and also public-awareness-raising. Telephone helplines are used in several countries, usually offering free information and emotional support. Organizations advocating for older people provide information and guidance through leaflets, community outreach and websites for older people about their rights, strategies to keep safe, maintaining independence and control over personal affairs, future planning and where to get support, for example. The aim is to empower older people to help themselves.

Tertiary Prevention Initiatives – Providing Support, Reducing Harm and Preventing Further Abuse

Many countries have elder abuse and neglect services, often in the voluntary or health sectors, which investigate and assess referrals of suspected abuse and coordinate multidisciplinary responses according to the needs of victims and their carers. They undertake monitoring and follow-up and cases are referred to other sources of assistance. There are 24 specialist elder abuse and neglect-prevention services throughout New Zealand. They cooperate with other family violence intervention networks. Internationally, there are a few examples of emergency shelters designed specifically for elder abuse and neglect victims (Sethi et al. 2011).

Currently, older people make little use of the criminal law in dealing with abuse, although it is potentially criminal activity, as often they are particularly reluctant to press charges against family members. Advocacy organizations may have more ability to deal with abuse situations – for example, notifying rest-home managers about the inappropriate behaviour of staff members. But individual advocacy becomes difficult when the issues are more complex, where the concerned individual is uncomfortable with the legal and administrative processes required or is afraid to confront the abuser.

There are a range of alternatives to formal legal processes which avoid the adversarial processes of a court of law. Mediation is a possible option in elder abuse and neglect situations, but this works best where the relationship between the parties is equal. Restorative justice processes may be more appropriate than mediation as they require perpetrators to face up to the impact their behaviour has had on their victims. Restorative justice is also a more holistic approach, including the family/community context and giving consideration to the needs of the victim. A restorative justice conference can produce an agreement on reparation or restitution from the perpetrator to the victim and/or their families, as well as changes intended to alter the behaviour of the perpetrator. Advocates suggest that restorative justice processes, with careful selection, planning and skilled facilitators and with adequate protection and support for the victim, can provide a forum for addressing the needs of elder abuse and neglect victims in a safe environment, which conventional court processes may be unable to do. However, the close and ongoing nature of the relationship of a victim and perpetrator in elder abuse and the ongoing vulnerability of elder abuse victims may further complicate this issue. While restorative justice processes appear to be a promising way to deal with elder abuse, very little evidence is yet available on their use or outcomes. This calls for evaluation and action research.

Conclusion

A great deal of further work is required to develop means of preventing and responding to elder abuse and neglect in an ageing world. Sethi et al. (2011), on behalf of the World Health Organization (Regional Office for Europe), conclude that all programmes dealing with elder abuse and neglect should include an evaluative process which examines outcomes and cost-effectiveness. In order to produce valid comparisons, definitional issues need to be addressed, along with the development of a standardized system of data collection and outcome measures. As Daly, Merchant and Jogerst (2013: 361) note:

> Prevention of elder abuse will require a comprehensive approach involving a multifaceted intervention including multiple sectors of society.

References

Age Concern New Zealand. 2007. *Elder Abuse and Neglect Prevention. Challenges for the Future Including an Analysis of Referrals to Age Concern Elder Abuse and Neglect Prevention Services from 1 July 2004 to 30 June 2006*. Wellington: Age Concern New Zealand.

Clare, M., Blundell, B. and Clare, J. 2011. *Examination of the Extent of Elder Abuse in Western Australia: A Qualitative and Quantitative Investigation of Existing Agency Policy, Service Responses and Recorded Data*. Perth: Crime Research Centre, The University of Western Australia.

Cooper, C., Selwood, A. and Livingston, G. 2008. The Prevalence of Elder Abuse and Neglect: A Systematic Review. *Age and Ageing*, 37, 151–60.

Coyne, A. 2001. The Relationship between Dementia and Elder Abuse. *American Journal of Psychiatry*, 15(4), 634–6.

Daly, J., Merchant, M. and Jogerst, G. 2013. Elder Abuse Research: A Systematic Review. *Journal of Elder Abuse and Neglect*, 23(4), 348–65.

Davey, J. and McKendry, J. 2011. *Financial Abuse of Older People in New Zealand*. A Working Paper of the Institute of Policy Studies, Victoria University of Wellington. Available at: http://ips.ac.nz/publications/publications/show/324.

Fallon, P. 2006. *Elder Abuse and/or Neglect Literature Review*. Wellington: Centre for Social Research and Evaluation. Ministry of Social Development. Available at: http://www.msd.govt.nz/about-msd-and-our-work/publications-resources/research/scale-nature-family violence.

Glasgow, K. and Fanslow, J.L. 2006. *Family Violence Intervention Guidelines: Elder Abuse and Neglect*. Wellington: Ministry of Health.

Heiser, D. and Brownell, P. 2009. Elder Abuse and Neglect, in *The Corsini Encyclopedia of Psychology*, edited by I. Weiner and W. Craighead. New York: John Wiley and Sons.

Lachs, M.S. and Pillemer, K. 2004. Elder Abuse. *Lancet*, 364, 1263–72.

Lievore, D. and Mayhew, P. 2007. *The Scale and Nature of Family Violence in New Zealand: A Review and Evaluation of Knowledge*. Wellington: Crime and Justice Research Centre Victoria University of Wellington.

McAlpine, C. 2008. Elder Abuse and Neglect. *Age and Ageing*, 37(2), 132–3.

Naughton, C., Drennan, J., Treacy, M., Lafferty, A., Lyons, I., Phelan, A., Quin, S., O'Loughlin, A. and Delany, L. 2010. *Abuse and Neglect of Older People in Ireland: Report on the National Study of Elder Abuse and Neglect*. Dublin: National Centre for the Protection of Older People.

O'Keeffe, M., Hills, A., Doyle, M., McCreadie, C., Scholes, S., Constantine, R., Tinker, A., Manthorpe, J., Biggs, S. and Erens, B. 2007. *UK Study of Abuse and Neglect of Older People: Prevalence Survey Report*. London: National Centre for Social Research and Kings College.

Peri, K., Fanslow, J., Hand, J. and Parsons, J. 2008. *Elder Abuse and Neglect – Exploration of Risk and Protective Factors*. Wellington: New Zealand Families Commission.

Sethi, D., Wood, S., Mitis, F., Bellis, M., Penhale, B., Marmolejo, I., Lowenstein, A., Manthorpe, G. and Kärki, F. (eds). 2011. *European Report on Preventing Elder Maltreatment*. Denmark: World Health Organization, Regional Office for Europe. Available at: http://www.euro.who.int/__data/assets/pdf_file/0010/144676/e95110.pdf.

Wainer, J., Owada, K., Darzins, G. and Darzins, P. 2010. *Diversity and Financial Elder Abuse in Victoria*. Protecting Elders' Assets Study. Melbourne: Monash University.

Wilber, K.H. and McNeilly, D.P. 2001. Elder Abuse and Victimization, in *Handbook of the Psychology of Aging*, 5th edition, edited by J.E. Birren and K.W Schaie. San Diego, CA: Academic Press, 569–87.

Wolf, R.S. 2001. Understanding Elder Abuse and Neglect, in *Families in Later Life: Connections and Transitions*, edited by A.J. Walker, M. Manoogian-I'Dell, L.A. McGraw and D. White. Thousand Oaks, CA: Pine Forge.

Chapter 6
Violent Girls: A Casualty of Family Violence. 'She hits me first, then I hit her back. Can't let your mama hit you like that.'

Donna Swift

Introduction

> 'Girls in lunchtime punch-up'[1]
>
> 'Schoolgirls torture love rival'[2]
>
> 'Girl gang on playground rampage'[3]

Such captions permeate the written media. Subsequent text graphically details the physical violence of girl-on-girl fights. Many readers are both shocked by and condemn such stories. Behind the sensationalism lies the reality that family violence can often shape a girl's choice to use violence. The discussion of girls' violence in this chapter reiterates the importance of recognizing that these girls may have come from violent homes and can become future mothers. It uses data from *The Girls' Project* (Swift 2011) to illuminate the potential links between the impact and influence of family violence and the actions of teenage girls who choose to use violent and anti-social behaviour.[4] I begin with an overview of the literature on family violence and girls' violent and anti-social behaviour. I then summarize *The Girls' Project*, and use both quantitative and qualitative findings from the study to show the impact that family violence has had on the lives of girls who use violent behaviour. I focus on the girls' violent home environments and then explore the dynamics of family violence among members of the household. Finally, I examine how girls become part of the cycle of family violence.

1 www.stuff.co.nz/waikato-times/news/325482/Girls-in-lunchtime-punch-up (20.3.2008)

2 'www.stuff.co.nz/national 318519/Schoolgirls-torture-love-rival (6.3.2008)

3 www.dailytelegraph.com.au/news/nsw/girl-gang-on-playground-rampage/story-e6freuzi-1111116029025 (11.4.2008)

4 I am not suggesting this is the sole explanatory factor. Others include the influence of peer pressure, personality, addictions and parenting. Rather, it is the focus of this chapter.

What the Literature Says

Research has identified a range of detrimental consequences for children and adolescents associated with being raised in violent homes, experiencing parental conflict or suffering childhood maltreatment (Barnett et al. 2011, Becroft 2009, Denham et al. 2000, Hardy and Laszloffy 2005, Jenkins 2000, Kitzmann et al. 2003, Smith et al. 2010, Van Wormer 2010). Although not specific to girls, these authors offer an understanding that can be insightful for girls, as well as points for gender comparison. These consequences include substance abuse (Fagan 2005, Smith et al. 2010, Widom et al. 1999); anti-social conduct and delinquency (Fagan 2005, Smith and Thornberry 1995); post-traumatic stress disorder (Moretti et al. 2006); intimate partner violence (Black et al. 2010, Fagan 2005); peer violence (Noland et al. 2004, Park et al. 2010); sibling violence (Eriksen and Jensen 2006, 2009), and child-to parent violence (Ulman and Straus 2003, Walsh and Krienert 2009).

Social learning theories claim that individuals acquire behaviours or conditioned responses through observing others (Barnett et al. 2011, Button and Gealt 2010, Hoffman and Edwards 2004). The family is key to socialization and serves for the intergenerational and transgenerational transmission of violent and anti-social practices. It is here that children are exposed to the behaviours of their caregivers and witness adults' strategies for dealing with conflict and challenges. The use of corporal discipline or aggressive reactions modelled by parents further entrenches the practice of relying on violence as an appropriate solution or response (Bierman et al. 2004, Pepler et al. 2004, Zahn-Waxler and Polanichka 2004).

Studies of sibling violence acknowledge the family as a site where direct experience and repeated exposure to violence occurs. Consequently, the home becomes a training ground, providing opportunity for behavioural imitation of other family members, including being influenced by their rationale and motivation for violence (Button and Gealt 2010, Hoffman and Edwards 2004).

Moretti et al. (2006), studying aggressive and delinquent youth in correctional facilities, identified that young persons' exposure to their mothers' violence towards her partner increases their inclination for violent behaviour. For young women, this manifests itself in their own relationships with intimate partners and peers. They go on to suggest that because mothers are more central in familial relationships than fathers, their tactics for managing conflict are more influential. Ness (2004) offers an interesting angle on the mother-daughter dyad. In studying inner city minority women, Ness (2004: 37) describes mothers actively encouraging their daughters to fight in order to learn the skills to defend themselves and that 'she must stand her ground in the streets or face her mother's wrath'.

Writing specifically about girls, Underwood (2003) highlights the disparity in gender socialization. She contends that, from preschool age, girls are taught and expected to follow what is deemed as proper gendered behaviour. They are encouraged to quash expressions and overt displays of anger and, therefore, have minimal opportunity to learn how to manage their deep emotions. As a result, girls' violent and anti-social behaviour falls outside the gendered script and attracts the label of deviance with such transgressions then being pathologized (Chesney-Lind 1989, 1997, Hunt and Joe-Laidler 2001, O'Neil 2005).

Feminist research also progresses a deeper understanding of girls' offending. Scottish researchers Batchelor, Burman and Brown (2001) highlight the meaning and place of violence in the lives of teenage girls who described a social world where tough reputations brought rewards and displays of aggression were acceptable. These themes, along with opportunities to obtain a social identity and a sense of connection, were also prominent in Batchelor's (2009) study of girls' violence and gang affiliation. Adamshick (2010) found similar emphasis was placed on attachment and identity in her study of marginalized girls in the north-eastern United States.

With this deeper insight also came the increased awareness of the oppression and ill-treatment endured by many female offenders. Batchelor (2005), researching young women incarcerated for violent offending, suggests that aggressive and violent behaviour germinates from past victimization and the need for young women to adopt a defensive demeanour for self-preservation. Schaffner (2005, 2007) argues that the trauma and abuse experienced by girls in their private lives plays a key role in their more public acts of aggression and violence. She states that their victimization is not necessarily the result of girl-against-girl violence but results from societal abuse generated through sexism, racism and poverty. Victimization is well documented in studies of trauma in the lives of female offenders (Bloom et al. 2003, 2005, Covington 2011).

The varied place of violence in the lives of female offenders suggests that women's offending cannot necessarily be understood in the same way as men's violent crime because this assumes both genders are driven to their actions for the same reasons and in the same manner (Field 2003, Irwin and Chesney-Lind 2008). Feminist thought has presented a paradigm whereby deviant behaviour in the form of violence may contribute to strategies of survival for some girls (Adamshick 2010, Batchelor 2005, Brown and Tappan 2008, Chesney-Lind and Belknap 2004, Hine and Welford 2012, Hunt and Joe-Laidler 2001, Schaffner 2005, 2007).

The Girls' Project

The New Zealand-based *The Girls' Project* (Swift 2011), a two-year investigation of young women's use of violence and anti-social behaviour, began in August 2009. As well as providing data specific to New Zealand, the study strived to capture media and political attention to ultimately benefit services for girls. The need for such research surfaced after local non-government organizations and police could not secure funds to continue *Turning Point*, a 20-week intervention pilot programme that targeted girls who engaged in violent and anti-social behaviour (Swift 2005).

The Girls' Project utilized mixed methods of data collection. Quantitative findings, from 3,500 questionnaires completed by boys and girls aged between 14 and 16 in the Tasman Police District, recorded their experiences of and engagement in violent behaviour and allowed for gender comparisons. Forty focus group discussions with naturally forming groups of girls provided qualitative insight into the attitudes and experiences of both mainstream girls as well as those actively involved in anti-social behaviour. The author also conducted over 100 interviews with girls with a known history of violent and anti-social behaviour. While voluntary participants, these girls were introduced to the study through their connection with police, social workers, lawyers and school staff.

Key findings identified a range of themes, along with family violence, related to girls' violent and anti-social behaviour. The progressive stages of girls' anti-social behaviour were identified, as were the advantageous opportunities for prevention and intervention. The quantitative data found an overwhelming 98 per cent of the participants acknowledged involvement in peer-related violence, with little distinction between rural and urban locations. This suggested a normalizing of this type of behaviour amongst adolescents, while recognizing that this formed the foundation from which girls who went on to progress their use of violence established their reputation and loyalties. Details of *The Girls' Project* can be found at www.thegirlsproject.org.nz.

The Violent Home Environment

The phrase 'family violence' inadequately describes the turbulent home environments of some of these girls. Not only did they live with family violence between members of the household, but also with the ramifications of external, possibly more public, violent activities of family members. This included pub brawls ending up in the front yard or hostilities erupting in community settings. Family associations with rival gangs or reputed criminals meant that girls were besieged with grudges and, as potential targets, they learned to recognize and respond to their opposition. Ally (14) comments 'There's quite a few people that are pretty scared of me ... coz I come from a family that's in a gang.'

Such was the frequency and repetition of these events that girls took them in their stride. Ruby (12) could not recall ever learning to fight; it was just part of her. Rivals of her brother's gang would antagonize her and she would punch her way free, knowing her brother would retaliate on her behalf. Girls summarized the normality of violence in their lives with the phrases 'it happens' and 'it's what you do', reflecting the effectiveness of their socialization into a world filled with violence. Adamshick (2010), Batchelor (2009) and Batchelor, Burman and Brown (2001) and Hine and Welford (2012) all found much the same.

The aftermath of other people's violence brought chaos into the girls' home lives. When family members went to prison, girls not only missed their presence, but also had to explain their absence. Parental incarceration or the dual arrest of caregivers during a family violence incident sometimes meant that girls were placed in care, either with extended family or state-based services. Burdening unprepared or reluctant relatives with the responsibility for a teenager added further stress for all involved. This was the case for Britney (14) who had to use physical violence to fend off the physical blows of her grandparents. Such disruption could carry scores of unaddressed emotions and potentially set girls up as prime contenders for future offending (Thomas 2003, Van Wormer 2010, Zahn-Waxler and Polanichka 2004). Turmoil in the home also led girls to seek pseudo families, composed of street youth who had experienced similar circumstances or through gang involvement (Batchelor 2009, Hunt and Joe-Laidler 2001, Van Wormer 2010).

With home life in disarray, girls were exposed to changing household membership, reduced or inconsistent supervision by caregivers and disconnection from people and places, which had held some essence of security or stability. Often these girls then became vulnerable to sexual exploitation by visiting relatives or guests or by older friends who took advantage of their naivety and desperation. Sexual victimization was a common theme and quantitative findings identified that 11 per cent of the girls had been forced or tricked into unwanted sexual behaviour in the last year. Commonly these incidents were not a one-off event and they often involved perpetrators who had been considered family or as close as family. Jude (13) started drinking when she was eight after being raped by a family friend. She was raped again at 12 and again just recently. She now regularly drinks herself into a stupor to forget. For girls like Jude, the family home was not always a safe sanctuary.

Dynamics of Family Violence in the Home

Girls from *The Girls' Project* were entangled in a complex web of family dynamics within their home environments. Over a fifth (21 per cent) of the girls indicated that they had witnessed violence at home in the last year. This included altercations between parents, between a parent and a partner, or between an adult family member and a young person. Girls felt the tension build through a verbal row until it exploded into a physical exchange. They described being raised in a setting where 'might made it right'; they acknowledged the power physical violence had, which frequently came with the force of the fist. Gina (16) had been brought up in violence: 'I've seen my Mum get beaten up, I've seen my sister get beaten up so I thought, nah violence is all sweet … so I'd punch them, throw things at them and swear at them and literally abuse the shit out of them.' Brown (2005) and Artz (2004) contend that girls' exposure to man-to-woman violence entrenches the patriarchal privilege to control and dominate women, as well as modelling hierarchical behaviour patterns and expectations.

At times their mothers fought back, but more often, the girls commented, they watched them being physically beaten and emotionally broken. Some girls were infuriated that their mothers chose to remain with a violent partner or not to even attempt to fight back. Emily (12.5) describes her mother: 'She's just a dick. 'Coz she doesn't do anything about it … "I don't want to get your Dad in trouble." And I was like, "well you idiot he made you bleed" and she was like "I don't care".' Girls condemned passivity as weakness and vowed not to become this kind of woman. This attitude gave weight to girls wanting to be tough and able to defend themselves, brandishing an obvious objection to the stigma of women's fragility. They modelled what Hine and Welford (2012: 164) referred to as 'resilient femininity'.

Girls encountered physical violence directly from the adults of the household in many ways, including covertly through sexual violence, as mentioned earlier. However, more obvious violence occurred when they became ensnared in the hostilities between parents or between a parent and a partner, whether trying to placate the mood or deflect blows. This is Mere's (16) story: 'They were fighting, Dad was real drunk and I put my hand through a mirror to shut them up, and then I hit him in the eye … he pulled the scarf tight around my neck … He was done for assault.' Sometimes girls stepped into conflicts attempting to even the struggle or to defend the weaker or preferred person. Most often the girls spoke of experiencing direct physical violence through forms of corporal punishment, which included being slapped, spanked, thrown against walls, grabbed and held down, as well as having their pets harmed or possessions destroyed. At nine, Nikki's mother disciplined her with wooden spoons until they broke. Her mother then resorted to forcing spoonfuls of curry powder into her mouth, making sure it was damp so that it would stick. As she got older, Nikki threatened her mother with calling the police. Unable to control her daughter without physical discipline, Nikki spent the next four years shuffling every few months between her estranged parents, changing schools each time. Nikki recently defended herself against her mother, using violence. She faces assault charges and has trespass orders[5] against her. Today she lives with an abusive boyfriend and dreams of being a beautician, but first she has to finish school.

In households where adults model family management through acts of aggression and violence towards a child, children employ the same methods to deal with their parents (Ulman and Straus 2003). *The Girls' Project* identified that 18 per cent of girls experienced physical violence from their mothers or female guardians, compared to 15 per cent from fathers or male guardians; it also found that 8 per cent of girls hit their mothers or female guardians and 7 per cent hit their fathers or male guardians. However, in-depth interviews suggested that girls were more hesitant to physically challenge their biological fathers. Della (16) comments: 'The only person I'm scared of is my Dad. 'Coz he can bash, like really, really bash me, and I have to listen to him.' Girls responding to their mothers with physical violence more so than to their fathers fits with the findings of Walsh and Krienert (2009). However, consideration must be given to the fact that mothers are often the primary or only disciplinarian in many families and this may place mothers at greater risk of child-to-parent violence (Artz 2004, Ulman and Straus 2003).

It was evident from *The Girls' Project* that a parent's status or stature also swayed a girl's decision to use violence toward her parent. Mothers, deemed as weak because they had succumbed to men's violence or addictions, were less forthright in their demeanour or did not side with their daughter in an argument, garnered little respect. They were viewed on a par with rival peers and subjected to

5 A trespass order stops a person from coming onto another's property or place of residence.

the same aggressive behaviour as used on the street. Girls justified their violence towards their mothers with statements like 'she disrespected me so I disrespected her back' or 'she hit me first'. On the other hand, girls who spoke about their mothers with esteem stated they would never think of challenging their authority.

In contrast, the girls rarely challenged their birth fathers, especially if they had a reputation as a fighter. For several girls, this was reason to revere their fathers and to place them beyond reproach. Some girls were also scared of their fathers because they were aware of the beating these men could inflict, as Della's earlier comment indicates. The same regard did not usually transfer to other adult men who joined the household as stepfathers or boyfriends of their mother. Girls spoke of being physically and verbally aggressive to these men, sometimes out of jealousy over their mothers' attention or being upset by a replacement for their fathers. Other girls turned aggressive against the boyfriends for their own safety or to protect their siblings, especially if these men were abusive. Sue (16) describes such an incident:

> He came into the room and he's like 'Sue, get up and bloody look after (younger sibling)' … and he slapped me around the head … I picked it (a cup) up and just chucked it at him … That day was the most scariest day of my life, I just couldn't believe he hit me … He's not my Dad so why is he hitting me?

One girl told how she would retaliate against both her mother and her new partner by baiting him until his agitation spilled into a physical altercation with her mother.

The Girls' Project also recognized that aggression between girls and their siblings added another dimension of violence to home environments, albeit one that was often ignored or disregarded in the confusion over whether it was founded in sibling rivalry (Eriksen and Jensen 2009). Many girls from the study admitted that they frequently fought with their siblings over possessions, responsibility for chores or disclosure of secrets. Quantitative findings indicated that, of the girls with siblings, 34 per cent had hit their sisters and 39 per cent had hit their brothers, while 43 per cent reported being hit by sisters and 48 per cent being hit by brothers, all within the last year. This behaviour could reflect power struggles within the family or mirror adult patterns for dealing with discord (Button and Gealt 2010, Eriksen and Jensen 2009, Hoffman and Edwards 2004). However, some girls spoke of confrontations between similar aged sisters who were intent on settling conflicts. These often escalated in intensity to the level of a street fight against peer rivals and could result in serious physical or emotional harm. Yet girls viewed this type of fighting with their sisters as acceptable. As one girl explained in a focus group session: 'Got six sisters and fight with them all … It's different at home fighting, you don't want to kill them; just give them a hiding so they learn.' Girls rationalized that family ties tolerated the behaviour and one girl interjected that 'she will always be your sister, no matter what happens'. Ironically, girls never gave any thought that the same familial relationship did not always provide their sibling with a choice or a means to escape a potentially abusive situation (Hoffman and Edwards 2004).

Sibling violence provided a guise that allowed girls to step outside conventional women's behaviour (Eriksen and Jensen 2009) and an opportunity to hone skills for self-defence or to antagonize peers. Sibling violence also served as a training ground where older sisters passed on their fighting skills to younger family members, replicating how they had been taught. Through regular sessions, they toughened their novices by subjecting them to bouts of punching, encouraging them to stand tall and take it, while stressing the importance of holding back tears and not showing weakness. This is Kelli's (15) story:

> I smash my little sister so when she is older, if someone smashes her, she would say 'so what was that' (shrugs shoulders) because she is used to getting a hiding from me ... When Silvi was real young I started off real soft as I was punching her, she would say 'that did not hurt' so I would step it up a notch and punch her harder ... She can stand up for herself and if someone picks on her and gives her a hiding she does not come running to me all the time.

The qualitative aspect of *The Girls' Project* captured how entrenched family violence was in the private lives of girls who were known for their public engagement in violence. Not only did the home environment expose them to violence, but it was also the site where many experienced it and went on to use it against other family members as well as their peers. As Adamshick (2010) suggests, violent girls learn to fight from within the family situation.

Perpetuating the Cycle of Family Violence

The girls from *The Girls' Project* are at risk of joining the intergenerational cycle of family violence. Not only have many grown up in family environments where violence is acceptable, they have been socialized to consider violence as normal and an expected outcome or response. A consequence of this familiarity, as research attests, is that these girls are more apt to form relationships with like-minded partners, to be more accepting of their behaviour and to end up in violent intimate relationships (Noland et al. 2004, Zahn-Waxler and Polanichka 2004). Girls from the study provided examples of the controlling behaviours they were subjected to by boyfriends who would instruct them how to dress, check their phone messages, limit contact with friends and family and use physical violence to dominate them. Gina, now 16, has more assault charges than her age. She explains: 'I would get a hiding probably twice a day from my Mum's partners for standing up for my Mum ... I've been unconscious twice from Mum's partners.' At 15, Gina moved in with her boyfriend. She describes the relationship: 'He kicks me, he drags me on the ground, he punches the living fuck out of me, he strangled me, he's put me in hospital.' To her credit, Gina tried to stay at school, but the school did not provide an escape from violence. Gina's boyfriend hounded her through phone calls and texts. Then one day, ignoring the teacher's warning to put away her phone, Gina snapped at the teacher. 'I threw a chair at her and she ended up falling and I beat the living shit out of her head.'

Girls with a history of sexual or physical victimization are even more prone to intimate partner violence (Fagan 2005, Noland et al. 2004, Zahn-Waxler and Polanichka 2004). These same girls are often sexually active at a young age and are susceptible to the advances of older men, thus increasing the potential for teenage pregnancy (Leitenberg and Saltzman 2003, Ryan et al. 2008). *The Girls' Project* also noted that pregnancy did not deter some girls from engaging in physical violence. Therefore, children born into these familial situations would be more likely to be exposed to violence in the same way that their mothers were, to experience the chaos of being bounced between family and state caregivers and to become both a victim and perpetrator of violence in the home and in the community.

Where to From Here?

In conclusion, this chapter has shown that a girl's use of violence does not happen in isolation. She does not wake up one morning and decide to give another girl a hiding. The circumstances of her life have propelled her along a path where violence, because of its familiarity, has become a tool that she can readily grasp and use effectively.

The link between family violence and a girl's use of violence cannot be ignored. Therefore, it is pertinent that any intervention directed at a girl for her behaviour must address and unravel the socialization that she has gained through being raised in an environment of family violence. Yet, in doing so, it must also consider that violence has played a significant role in her life, at times keeping her safe and giving her a sense of personal power. Intervention must provide a suitable replacement. In turn, there is a need for any intervention into family violence to consider all members of the household.

References

Adamshick, P.Z. 2010. The Lived Experience of Girl-to-Girl Aggression in Marginalized Girls. *Qualitative Health Research*, 20(4), 541–55.

Artz, S. 2004. Violence in the Schoolyard: Schoolgirls' Use of Violence, in *Girls' Violence*, edited by C. Alder and A. Worrall. New York: State University of New York Press, 151–66.

Barnett, O., Miller-Perrin, C. and Perrin, R. 2011. *Family Violence across the Lifespan*. 3rd edition. Los Angeles, CA: Sage.

Batchelor, S. 2005. 'Prove me the Bam!': Victimization and Agency in the Lives of Young Women Who Commit Violent Offences. *The Journal of Community and Criminal Justice*, 52(4), 358–75.

Batchelor, S. 2009. Girls, Gangs and Violence: Assessing the Evidence. *Probation Journal*, 56(4), 399–414.

Batchelor, S., Burman, M. and Brown, J. 2001. Discussing Violence: Let's Hear it from the Girls. *Probation Journal*, 48(2), 125–34.

Becroft, A. 2009. *What Causes Youth Crime, and What Can We Do About It*. Paper to the NZ Bluelight Ventures Inc – Conference and AGM, Queenstown, New Zealand, 7 May 2009. Available at: http://www.justice.govt.nz/courts/youth/publications-and-media/speeches/what-causes-youth-crime-and-what-can-we-do-about-it

Bierman, K., Bruschi, C., Domitrovich, C., Yan Fang, G., Miller-Johnson, S. and the Conduct Problems Prevention Research Group. 2004. Early Disruptive Behaviours Associated with Emerging Antisocial Behaviour among Girls, in *Aggression, Antisocial Behavior, and Violence among Girls*, edited by M. Putallaz and K. Bierman. New York: Guilford Press, 137–61.

Black, D., Sussman, S. and Unger, J. 2010. A Further Look at the Intergenerational Transmission of Violence: Witnessing Inter-parental Violence in Emerging Adulthood. *Journal of Interpersonal Violence*, 25(6), 1022–42.

Bloom, B., Owen, B., and Covington, S. 2003. *Gender Responsive Strategies: Research, Practice, and Guiding Principles for Women Offenders*. Washington, DC: US Department of Justice, National Institute of Corrections.

Bloom, B., Owen, B. and Covington, S. 2005. *Gender Responsive Strategies for Women Offenders: A Summary of Research, Practice, and Guiding Principles for Women Offenders*. Washington, DC: US Department of Justice, National Institute of Corrections.

Brown, L.M. 2005. *Girlfighting: Betrayal and Rejection among Girls*. New York: New York University Press.

Brown, L.M. and Tappan, M.B. 2008. Fighting Like a Girl Fighting Like a Guy: Gender Identity, Ideology, and Girls at Early Adolescence. *New Directions for Child and Adolescent Development*, 120, 47–59.

Button, D. and Gealt, B. 2010. High Risk Behaviors among Victims of Sibling Violence. *Journal of Family Violence*, 25, 131–40.

Chesney-Lind, M. 1989. Girls' Crime and Woman's Place: Towards a Feminist Model of Female Delinquency. *Crime and Delinquency*, 35, 5–29.

Chesney-Lind, M. 1997. *The Female Offender: Girls, Women, and Crime*. Thousand Oaks, CA: Sage.

Chesney-Lind, M. and Belknap, J. 2004. Trends in Delinquent Girls' Aggression and Violent Behavior: A Review of the Evidence, in *Aggression, Antisocial Behavior, and Violence Among Girls*, edited by M. Putallaz and K.L. Bierman. New York: Guilford Press, 203–20.

Covington, S. 2011. Trauma Matters: Changing the World without Work. Paper to the 14th National Conference on Adults and Juvenile Female Offenders, Salt Lake City, Utah, 17 October, 2011.

Denham, S.A., Workman, E., Cole, P., Weissbrod, C., Kendziora, K. and Zahn-Waxler, C. 2000. Prediction of Externalizing Behavior Problems from Early to Middle Childhood: The Role of Parental Socialization and Emotional Expression. *Development and Psychopathology*, 12, 23–45.

Eriksen, S. and Jensen, V. 2006. All in the Family? Family Environment Factors in Sibling Violence. *Journal of Family Violence*, 21, 497–507.

Eriksen, S. and Jensen, V. 2009. A Push or a Punch: Distinguishing the Severity of Sibling Violence. *Journal of Interpersonal Violence*, 24, 183–208.

Fagan, A.A. 2005. The Relationship between Adolescent Physical Abuse and Criminal Offending: Support for an Enduring and Generalized Cycle of Violence. *Journal of Family Violence*, 20(5), 279–90.

Field, R. 2003. *Victim-Offender Conferencing: Issues of Power Imbalance for Women Juvenile Participants*. Paper to the Juvenile Justice: From Lessons of the Past to a Road for the Future Conference, Australian Institute of Criminology, Sydney, Australia, 1–2 December 2003.

Hardy, K. and Laszloffy, T. 2005. *Teens Who Hurt*. New York: Guilford Press.

Hine, J. and Welford, J. 2012. Girls' Violence: Criminality or Resilience?, in *Social Ecology of Resilience*, edited by M. Ungar. New York: Springer, 157–69.

Hoffman, K.L. and Edwards, J.N. 2004. An Integration Theoretical Model of Sibling Violence and Abuse. *Journal of Family Violence*, 19(3), 185–200.

Hunt, G. and Joe-Laidler, K. 2001. Situations of Violence in the Lives of Girl Gang Members. *Health Care for Women International*, 22, 363–84.

Irwin, K. and Chesney-Lind, M. 2008. Girls' Violence: Beyond Dangerous Masculinity. *Sociology Compass*, 2(3), 837–55.

Jenkins, J.M. 2000. Marital Conflict and Children's Emotions: The Development of an Anger Organization. *Journal of Marriage and the Family*, 62, 723–36.

Kitzmann, K.M., Gaylord, N.K., Holt, A.R. and Kenny, E.D. 2003. Child Witnesses to Domestic Violence: A Meta-Analytic Review. *Journal of Consulting and Clinical Psychology*, 71, 339–52.

Leitenberg, H. and Saltzman, H. 2003. College Women who had Sexual Intercourse when they were Under Age Minors (13–15): Age of Their Male Partners, Relation to Current Adjustment, and Statutory Rape Implications. *Sexual Abuse: A Journal of Research and Treatment*, 15(2), 130–47.

Moretti, M., Obsuth, I., Odgers, C. and Reebye, P. 2006. Exposure to Maternal vs. Paternal Partner Violence, PTSD, and Aggression in Adolescent Girls and Boys. *Aggressive Behavior*, 32, 385–95.

Ness, C.D. 2004. Why Girls Fight: Female Youth Violence in the Inner-city. *The Annals of the American Academy of Political and Social Science*, 595, 32–42.

Noland, V., Liller, K., McDermott, R., Coulter, M. and Seraphine, A. 2004. Is Adolescent Sibling Violence a Precursor to College Dating Violence? *American Journal of Health Behavior*, 28 (Supplement 1), S13-S23.

O'Neill, T. 2005. Girls in Trouble in the Child Welfare and Criminal Justice System, in *Problem Girls: Understanding and Working with the Troubled and the Troublesome* [ebook], edited by G. Lloyd. London: Routledge Falmer.

Park, S., Morash, M. and Stevens, T. 2010. Gender Differences in Predictors of Assaultive Behavior in Late Adolescence. *Youth Violence and Juvenile Justice*, 8, 314–31.

Pepler, D.J., Walsh, M.M. and Levene, K.S. 2004. Interventions for Aggressive Girls: Tailoring and Measuring the Fit, in *Girls and Aggression: Contributing Factors and Intervention Principles*, edited by M. Moretti, C. Odgers and M. Jackson. New York: Kluwer Academic/ Plenum Publishers, 131–45.

Ryan, S., Franzetta, K., Manlove, J. and Schelar, E. 2008. Older Sexual Partners during Adolescence: Links to Reproductive Health Outcomes in Young Adulthood. *Perspectives on Sexual and Reproductive Health*, 40(1), 17–26.

Schaffner, L. 2005. *So-Called Girl-on-Girl Violence is Actually Adult-on-Girl Violence*. Great Cities Institute Publication Number GCP-05-03 Working Paper. Available at: www.uic.edu/cuppa/gci/

Schaffner, L. 2007. Violence against Girls Provokes Girls' Violence: From Private Injury to Public Harm. *Violence against Women*, 13, 1229–48.

Smith, C and Thornberry, T. 1995. The Relationship between Childhood Maltreatment and Adolescent Involvement in Delinquency. *Criminology*, 33, 451–81.

Smith, C., Elwyn, L., Ireland, T. and Thornberry, T. 2010. Impact of Adolescent Exposure to Intimate Partner Violence on Substance Use in Early Adulthood. *Journal of Studies on Alcohol and Drugs*, 71(2), 219–30.

Swift, D. 2005. *Turning Point: A Violence Intervention Programme for Violent and Anti-Social Girls and Young Women*. Unpublished report. Nelson, New Zealand: Turning Point Governance Group.

Swift, D. 2011. *The Girls' Project. Girlfighting: An Investigation of Young Women's Violent and Anti-social Behaviour*. Nelson, New Zealand: Stopping Violence Services Nelson.

Thomas, S.P. 2003. Identifying and Intervening with Girls at Risk for Violence. *The Journal of School Nursing*, 19(3), 130–39.

Ulman, A. and Straus, M. 2003. Violence by Children against Mothers in Relation to Violence between Parents and Corporal Punishment by Parents. *Journal of Comparative Family Studies*, 34, 41–60.

Underwood, M. 2003. *Social Aggression among Girls*. New York: Guilford Press.

Van Wormer, K. 2010. *Working with Female Offenders: A Gender-Sensitive Approach*. Hoboken, NJ: John Wiley and Sons.

Walsh, J. and Krienert, J. 2009. A Decade of Child-Initiated Family Violence: Comparative Analysis of Child-Parent Violence and Parricide Examining Offender, Victim, and Event Characteristics in a National Sample of Reported Incidents, 1995–2005. *Journal of Interpersonal Violence*, 24, 1450–77.

Widom, C.S., Weiler, B.L. and Cottler, L.B. 1999. Childhood Victimization and Drug Use: A Comparison of Prospective and Retrospective Findings. *Journal of Consulting and Clinical Psychology*, 67, 867–80.

Zahn-Waxler, C. and Polanichka, N. 2004. All Things Interpersonal: Socialization and Female Aggression, in *Aggression, Antisocial Behavior, and Violence among Girls*, edited by M. Putallaz and K. Bierman. New York: Guilford Press, 48–68.

PART III
The Practice of Restorative Justice in Family Violence – A Case Study

Rotorua enjoys a reputation as a premier tourist destination, combining the best in *Māori* culture of the *Te Arawa* people, with the natural beauty of its lakes and the extraordinary geothermal features. Less well known is that the region has one of the worst crime rates in New Zealand. More serious crime is tried in the High Court in Rotorua each year than in Wellington or Christchurch even though those regions have a population catchment approaching twice the size of Rotorua. For this reason, we have chosen to focus on the practice of restorative justice in Rotorua with respect to family violence.

Māori make up 36 per cent of the population of Rotorua. In most smaller towns in the Rotorua region, *Māori* are a majority. As inferred above, *Māori* are over-represented in crime and imprisonment statistics; they are also over-represented in indicators of social deprivation generally. For example, unemployment for *Māori* across New Zealand, at 11 per cent,[1] is almost twice the average for the non-*Māori* population. In Rotorua, it is 13 per cent. Almost a quarter (24 per cent) of families in Rotorua are single parent families compared with the national average of 18 per cent.

Part III provides an in-depth view of one restorative justice programme offered by a *Māori* provider in Rororua which deals with family violence on a regular basis. Maxine Rennie in Chapter 7 gives a practitioner's perspective, Chris McGuire in Chapter 8 presents the experience of a local judge and Ken McMaster outlines the research findings on the programme in Chapter 9.

1 These statistics were accessed from Statistics New Zealand on 30 July 2013 (personal communication to Anne Hayden).

Chapter 7
Titiro Whakamuri – Looking Back: *Titiro Whakamua* – Looking Forward

Maxine W. Rennie

Background

Mana Social Services Trust was established in 1996 to deliver social services, counselling and programmes to the Rotorua community free of charge. The Trust was the first approved programme provider in New Zealand for *Māori* 'protected persons' under the requirements of the Domestic Violence Act 1995 and later provided programmes for *Māori* children who had experienced or witnessed intimate partner violence. The Trust staff at that time were mainly *Māori* but included some *Pākehā* (people of predominantly European descent). All were well trained and supervised to carry out their work and the *Māori* staff were actively involved in their *marae* (buildings associated with a *Māori* community) and *iwi* (tribal) affairs. Most of the *Māori* staff and four members of the Board of Trustees were *manawhenua* (of the *Te Arawa iwi*). In 1999 the Trust began a pre-sentence restorative justice programme which was conditional upon a guilty plea by a perpetrator. The restorative justice team consisted of two female facilitators (one *Māori* and one *Pākehā*) and a male court coordinator who attended court daily. The coordinator was available to meet with and assess perpetrators for their suitability to be referred to the restorative justice programme. The programme was Ministry of Justice funded. Initially court referrals to the Trust covered a wide range of charges including theft, burglary, disorderly behaviour causing damage, driving offences and male on male offences of assault, assault with a weapon, and threatening to kill. But intimate partner violence was excluded. There were no intimate partner violence referrals. At this time, levels of intimate partner violence in Rotorua were reported as being extremely high. Alcohol and drug use were also often found to be associated with incidents of intimate partner violence, with *Māori* figuring prominently in both categories.

Using Restorative Justice for Intimate Partner Violence Cases

The Trust's restorative justice team regularly discussed the high number of offences relating to intimate partner violence being dealt with in court and the resultant damage being done to the children in these homes through witnessing or experiencing such trauma. They believed that the restorative justice process offered the most appropriate intervention pathway to assist partners who were willing to take part in a conference by providing help and the necessary services to stop the violence.

The fact that the majority of offences involved *Māori* weighed heavily on the Trust whose guiding *kaupapa* (way of doing things) for service was to strengthen *whānau* (family) by utilizing holistic methods of restoring balance and healing to emotions and relationships, spirituality and the *tinana* (body). Strengthening child protective factors was another priority. Judges were also appalled at the unacceptably high number of offences involving intimate partner violence in their courts. Because they were fully supportive of the Trust's restorative justice programme and its staff, they eventually made the decision to refer intimate partner violence cases for restorative justice conferences.

Managing Power Imbalances

The process of managing power imbalances between a victim and a perpetrator begins from the first contact between the court coordinator and the perpetrator, usually in court. It is made very clear to the perpetrator that to be accepted on the programme a guilty plea is required and he has to be prepared to take responsibility for his offending. Only when the court coordinator is satisfied that the perpetrator is genuinely motivated to take responsibility for the assault, does he advise the judge that a referral to the restorative justice programme can be made. At times, the victim is also in court, so the court coordinator will have preliminary discussions with her. He will explain what a restorative justice conference is and ask questions about her willingness to attend a conference, the status of her relationship, her concerns about her safety, and who could attend with her. If the victim believes her relationship with the perpetrator is over, she is advised that the Trust can still provide services for herself and her children if she wants further help.

Once the court makes a referral, the onus is placed on the perpetrator to make contact with the Trust office. The court coordinator will provide the contact details, office location and time frame within which the interview is to be held. The perpetrator is advised that once he has had his interview and he is accepted for a conference, contact will be made with the victim. Bail conditions are discussed at this interview and compliance is urged. The perpetrator has to discuss his violent actions, as recorded on the police summary of facts, with a woman, for possibly the first time. Many perpetrators at this point attempt to minimize the seriousness of the assault, to shift the blame onto their partner or to dispute the police statements. They are reminded that they have already admitted their guilt to the charge in court. They are advised that if they now want to change their mind, they can return to court.

As the former senior facilitator, I cannot recall a perpetrator making that choice; most settled down and were able to discuss matters reasonably. This is an important time to hear his views on his relationship, what he thought led to his violent actions, his perception of the effects of violence on his children and what he is prepared to do to repair the damage.

Disclosures of childhood physical and sexual abuse, which for many had planted the seeds of hatred and violence and which had become evident as they grew older, often arose at these interviews. No perpetrator that I interviewed had ever received counselling to help them deal with their trauma. As well as listening, assessing, challenging beliefs and providing information, the first meeting focuses on building rapport and respect to ensure a safe conference. The rules of the conference are discussed with the perpetrator to make sure he clearly understands that any breach would see the matter returned to court. At the end of the interview, the perpetrator is advised that the conference will go ahead only if the victim agrees to attend. If the victim does not agree, he has to return to court where the judge will be advised of the victim's decision.

The interview process contributes to a shift in power that has up until then been held solely by the perpetrator. This allows a more cooperative approach to the conference by all participants. Furthermore, providing a clear understanding of the rules helps to maintain the power balance and to ensure the safety of everyone there.

Contact with the victim and subsequent interviews by the facilitator are handled very sensitively. This is the time to listen to her fears, validate her feelings of pain, humiliation and powerlessness, verify her concerns for the damage being done to any children, and to ascertain the status of her relationship. She is asked what she thinks led to her partner's violent assault and what would help him address his violent behaviour in future. Enquiries are also made about whether or not there are any *whānau* or other people who support her and her children and who would be willing to attend a conference with her. Information about conference safety procedures and about what community services are available to her, to her children and, of course, to the perpetrator are also provided. Victims are given a few days to decide whether or not they agree to attend a conference before they confirm with the facilitator that they will participate. The interview with the restorative justice facilitator mostly allows victims to reclaim some of their power to enable them to proceed. They usually say that they are thankful that someone is willing to listen and to help them sort things out.

From my observation, there were three types of victims. Firstly, there were those who chose not to attend a conference; these were mostly young women in casual relationships. They simply wanted to end the relationship. Secondly, there were those, mainly young couples, where the relationship was of short duration. These victims appeared less fearful. As a result, their conferences would often be feisty, with the victim exhibiting most of the power and the young perpetrator silenced in the face of her anger. The third type of victim was one in a relationship of longer duration. Couples with children who had long standing relationships were mainly there for help to get their lives back on track and to access the services they needed.

Participants' Safety

Careful planning of safety procedures for restorative justice conferences are adhered to particularly with perpetrators who face more serious charges. Participants need to know that a report will be written for the court and what it will contain: who will see it, who will make sure any agreements made are completed and what will happen if the perpetrator does not complete his programmes. Two facilitators usually attend the conference and the court coordinator often sits in to ensure everything goes smoothly.

Facilitators are careful to check with victims about any support person nominated by a perpetrator to ensure undesirable associates are excluded from conferences. Victims are encouraged to bring *whānau* support to a conference as this reconnects the safety network around both the victim and her children. By attending the interview between the victim and the facilitator, support persons are fully informed of all processes and procedures and any role they may have in a restorative justice conference.

Very few perpetrators ask to bring a support person with them to the conference despite being encouraged to do so. Victims, on the other hand, are generally pleased to have someone with them. The seating for the conference participants, particularly the victim and her support person, is usually discussed before the conference and they are taken into the conference room before the conference begins so that they can indicate where they would feel comfortable and safe, as well as where the perpetrator should sit.

Times of arrival are also important. Victims are asked whether or not they want to arrive first and also whether or not they want a facilitator to accompany them out of the building at the end of the conference, while the perpetrator is detained. If so, this time is used for the perpetrator and facilitator to complete any administrative matters, as well as to ensure that the perpetrator is calm when he leaves.

For many victims, the conference is the first time their partner has had to admit the harm he has caused, acknowledge responsibility for it and apologize for it – all in front of others. More times than not, the victim asks if the bail conditions could be lifted as the children miss their father or she needs her partner's help at home. In short, thorough pre-conference planning and preparation of the participants contribute to well-run conferences.

Agreements

Towards the end of each conference, participants consider what agreements are to be made. These will be forwarded to the court as part of the report of the conference. Perpetrators are asked what they are prepared to do to make amends for their violent actions and victims' agreement is sought before any final decisions are made. These agreements can include attendance at a 26 week violence prevention programme, counselling for unresolved childhood trauma, drug and alcohol counselling, cultural mentoring and relationship counselling. Service provision for victims and their children is also recorded and agreed at this time. *Whānau* violence cases often require drug and alcohol counselling for both partners and counselling for problem gambling can be offered as well.

Culture

The predominant culture of the Trust is *Māori*. Office décor, art, use of *te reo* (language) and *Māori* staff reflect the strong cultural base of the service so that *Māori* participants feel comfortable accessing any Trust service. As the senior restorative justice facilitator, my maturity, cultural knowledge and senior tribal status often assisted with the correction of any power imbalances between victims and perpetrators.

Karakia (prayer) is offered as a starting point for all conferences and *kaumātua* (male elders) and *kuia* (female elders) are encouraged to attend as part of their *whānau* to bring balance and their wisdom to proceedings. Sometimes a perpetrator offers to do the *karakia* and, if the victim is agreeable, this is allowed.

One example of how the restorative justice conference more than met the needs of *Māori* occurred when an older *Māori* couple were accompanied by five of their adult children to their conference. Each sibling had a say in denouncing the violence and in voicing their objections to the continued abuse toward their mother by their father over the years. They regretted that they had not previously intervened; however, they had attended the conference to support their mother, while letting their father know that no further violence would be tolerated. The powerful *whānau* dynamics of 'shaming' their father and standing up for their mother were incredible to witness. Only after their father accepted how wrong he had been, how much he had hurt all of them and he had apologized, did the tears of forgiveness flow. This was a safe, facilitated conference that gave a whole *whānau* the space and forum to speak openly and honestly to one another. The restorative justice conference provided an environment where this *whānau* demonstrated admirable courage.

Debriefing Facilitators

Debriefing restorative justice facilitators is carried out immediately after a conference ends. This allows a complete review of how the conference has gone, any issues or high points that occurred, specific learnings from the participants' discussions and, overall, how well facilitators had managed the conference. Immediate debriefing captures the essence of the conference for facilitators and is viewed as an extremely important part of the whole procedure of bringing closure to a process that has raised emotions and anxieties for all conference participants, including the facilitators.

Monitoring Sentencing Decisions

The court coordinator monitors all court sentencing decisions. The majority of conference outcomes are taken into account at sentencing by judges. Even in the most serious cases where the outcome might still be imprisonment, a positive restorative justice conference outcome can result in a significant reduction in the prison term. In most cases judges postpone sentencing for the agreed tasks from the conference to be completed and then wait for the court coordinator's report to confirm this. External community providers are contacted regularly to check perpetrators' attendance at the programmes and the court coordinator will take the necessary steps to deal with non-compliance unless there are legitimate reasons for absences. These steps are as follows: (a) notification to the perpetrator that, due to non-compliance, the matter is being returned to court for sentencing; (b) the victim is notified of this decision; and (c) an application is made to the court for sentencing to take place.

The Trust provides individual counselling and programmes for children. This becomes part of the internal monitoring procedures. These entail the Trust monitoring supervision reports from counsellors and programme facilitators that advise how well the perpetrator is keeping appointments in addition to providing a general statement of his progress. If *whānau* support persons have offered to provide monitoring at home, they are contacted by the court coordinator for updates that all is going well. Final reports are provided to court by the court coordinator before any sentencing decisions, if these have been temporarily adjourned to allow for completion of services by the perpetrators.

Conclusion

As the longest serving member of the *Māori* Advisory Board to the police in Rotorua I can categorically state that today in Rotorua the number of *whānau* violence call-outs requiring police intervention continues to rise. Currently police respond to seven call-outs daily. The monthly figures of 200 call-outs equates to 2,400 a year. These involve mostly *Māori* in situations where children are often present witnessing the trauma.

The yearly figures of children exposed to *whānau* violence are totally unacceptable. We must look at alternatives that can be used to intervene in and stop such damage continuing. Restorative justice conferencing could be made more available in communities for those who wish to avail themselves of a safe, professionally facilitated process. This way conflicts, personal or *whānau* issues and employment grievances could be resolved. The Restorative Justice programme in Rotorua continues to be funded by the Ministry of Justice and is today viewed by *Māori* as a normal part of court procedures. Alternative funding should be considered to allow wider community access to restorative justice with outcomes that are primarily of benefit to individuals, couples, family and *whānau* who are willing to meet to peacefully resolve issues around family violence.

Chapter 8
Changing Lives through Restorative Justice: A Judicial Perspective

Chris McGuire

Introduction

Rotorua District Court was the first court in New Zealand to have restorative justice routinely considered as a realistic response to crime, alongside all other sentencing options. Five judges, three male and two female, serve the region. All have a strong problem-solving ethos. And, although all have a strong belief in restorative justice, it has not been suggested that in this region we are 'soft' on crime. Rotorua District Court was also the first court to achieve 'critical mass', that is when all cases where restorative justice seemed a good option are referred to an appropriate service provider – approximately 250 cases per year.

The Process

The influence of restorative justice has been enduring. On criminal list days, the restorative justice coordinator is in court seated alongside other essential stakeholders – the probation officers and the mental health nurse. As often as not, the possibility of a restorative justice referral will be initiated by defence counsel or the police prosecutor and discussed with the restorative justice coordinator prior to the court hearing. If there is agreement between these stakeholders (and there almost invariably is), the judge's order that there be a restorative justice referral is a formality. Typically, such a perpetrator will have only a few, and sometimes no, previous convictions. In other cases, often more serious cases by repeat perpetrators, the judge, in open court, might initiate discussion on the possibility of a restorative justice referral. Defence counsel, the police prosecutor and the restorative justice coordinator would all speak their minds and the decision would then be made. Candour is encouraged. Indeed, the years of experience and wisdom of those stakeholders is much valued by the judge. I recall on one such occasion the coordinator speaking last and saying: 'We tried hard twice last year to get Mr Anthony to engage with us. He wouldn't. We're sick of him.' So, for Mr Anthony, the more formal and traditional criminal justice followed.

This approach, which has strong connections with the local *iwi* (tribe), was shortly thereafter replicated at this region's satellite courts at Tokoroa and Taupo, each about an hour's travel from Rotorua. Thus in our region three different *Māori* providers connected with three different *iwi* deliver restorative justice.

Maxine Rennie's initiative with *Mana* Social Services Trust (described in Chapter 7) and those at Tokoroa and Taupo appear to all intents to be something of an anathema to some in the halls of power in Wellington where central planning and control prosper. But what was undeniable was the success of our community-based models which had a measure of credibility with all the stakeholders, including the courts, police, lawyers, the probation service and, most importantly, perpetrators and victims that other providers since then have aspired to.

For *Māori* perpetrators with *Māori* victims there is likely to be some *whakapapa* (lineage) or tribal links both between them and those facilitating restorative justice. In Rotorua, the ancestral carving in the meeting room brings a subtle formality and often a calming effect to the occasion. The eyes of *Te Arawa's Tupuna* (ancestral) chiefs look down from the portraits on the walls. Tuning out because the speaker is wearing a police uniform or a judge's gown is no longer an option. It is time to be honest and to confront the behaviours that have brought the perpetrator to court.

Pākehā (European) perpetrators and victims are dealt with in the same way with equally positive results. Through a purely *pākehā* lens, the restorative justice facilitators are demonstrably grass roots members of the local community with a passion to make the community better and safer.

Restorative Justice Processes and Intimate Partner Violence

Restorative justice is routinely considered in Rotorua District Court for cases of intimate partner violence. These types of offences have consistently made up approximately a third of all referrals to restorative justice conferences. The debate that has raged elsewhere as to the appropriateness of restorative justice in cases of intimate partner violence has passed us by.

Intimate partner violence is as commonplace here as elsewhere, perhaps more so. Drugs and alcohol play their inevitable part as do other triggers like financial stress, unemployment, jealousy, infidelity, poor impulse control, poor coping skills, chaotic and violent upbringing, and a general inability by male perpetrators to identify for themselves a coherent, positive and fulfilling male role in post-modern society. A default position for a small but disturbing minority is to 'capture' a solo female with a child or children, who is receiving welfare support from the state which includes accommodation support and benefit payments. That sets the perpetrator up with an income (hers), a sexual partner and a place to stay or, more accurately, a place to come and go from as he pleases. Often enough he is simply acting out what he has observed of the male figures that passed in and out of his life as a child.

In the case of some *Māori* male perpetrators who are severed from pro-social cultural influences, what also may be at play is a warped and bogus understanding of the role of the *tāne* (man) within *Māori* culture, informed by some of the factors mentioned above, as well as 'gangster' culture and the worst offerings of the electronic media. So instead of *tāne* being the protector of *wāhine* (woman), as the source of new life, he is instead the indiscriminate, violent abuser having convinced himself that this is his cultural right as a *tāne*.

Restorative Justice in Practice: Some Case Histories

Ducati and Tania

Ducati was a 39-year-old *Māori* male. While on bail for dangerous driving and refusing to take a blood test, Ducati was arrested for assault on his partner, Tania, and for breach of a protection order prohibiting violence against her. The assault followed a domestic argument over the roadworthiness of the family's two old motor vehicles. Tania asked Ducati to leave. He grabbed her by her clothing and forcibly threw her out the front door. Ripped clothing aside, she suffered no physical injury. When spoken to by the police, he admitted the assault, telling them he had had a bad year and was not coping. His record showed three previous convictions for assaults, two of them for assaults on females but they were 12 and 13 years earlier. He also had convictions for dishonesty and moderate drug offending. However, in the five years prior to the current offending, Ducati had been effectively offence free.

A week after the latest assault, Tania wrote to the court outlining the stress the family had been under. She said that she and Ducati were seeking grief and relationship counselling to deal with their present issues. The probation report on Ducati identified the following as contributing factors to his offending – a sense of entitlement to be in charge; a harmful pattern of drug use (cannabis and methamphetamine); a willingness to resort to violence; and relationship difficulties. The probation officer regarded him as being at medium risk of re-offending. A death in the family during the previous year had added considerable stress to their relationship. The assault charge had resulted in their separation after 15 years together. However, Tania remained supportive of her ex-partner.

The couple each declined the option of individual pre-conference meetings and proceeded to a full conference at which they sat together. Unusually, their teenage daughter also attended. Ducati expressed what Tania believed to be sincere and genuine regret and remorse and apologized for his behaviour. He became tearful.

Interaction at the conference was positive and mother and daughter said they had no fears for their safety and well-being. Forgiveness was offered. Their daughter spoke of losing one family member and not wanting to lose her father to jail. The conference report recommended to the judge that grief counselling be pursued; that Ducati write a letter of apology to his family further expressing his remorse and regret for the extra grief and burden he had placed on them; and it added the victim's request that the court show leniency to Ducati at sentencing. The court sentenced him to 12 months supervision with conditions to undertake the recommended counselling to address the other factors identified as contributing to his offending.

Blaze and Liz

Blaze, a 21-year-old *pākehā* man, was charged with assault on his partner of two years, Liz. They resided at his parents' house. He was in employment and had no previous convictions. The two argued in bed one evening. He dragged her along the bed and punched her in the chest three times. She fell to the floor and he kicked her twice in the chest, all the while shouting and swearing at her. She sustained bruising and sore ribs. His explanation to the police was that he was under a lot of stress and just 'lost it'.

He was remanded for a probation report and referred to *Mana* Social Services for a restorative justice conference. The probation report revealed relationship issues, a propensity for violence, a poor attitude and a sense of entitlement to be the boss as contributing factors. Lack of insight and remorse and failure to take full responsibility were also identified.

At Liz's restorative justice pre-conference meeting (without Blaze), she identified a major stressor as being friction with Blaze's parents with whom they were residing at the time of the assault. They had since then moved into a flat of their own and this had relieved a lot of the stress. Bail conditions that had initially been set prohibiting contact had been amended to allow cohabitation, with the condition now being that Blaze not offer violence to Liz. At his pre-conference interview, Blaze acknowledged the negative role his family had played, believed that finding a place of their own had assisted in eliminating some of the stressors and said he wanted to apologize to Liz at the full restorative justice conference.

The restorative justice conference commenced with Blaze apologizing to Liz. She accepted his apology as sincere and his remorse as genuine. She said she forgave him and offered her support for him. She said she had no concerns for her safety and well-being and she believed that living on their own had assisted in improving their relationship. After discussion, a reparative plan was formulated and agreed, namely that Blaze undertake anger and relationship counselling and this was to be put forward for consideration by the judge at the next court appearance. Liz was also going to ask that the court consider a discharge without conviction.

At the next court appearance, the judge agreed with the reparative plan and adjourned the matter further for the counselling to take place. Blaze duly did the counselling and his positive participation was reported to the court. He was discharged without conviction.

Chevvy and Charlotte

Chevvy, a *Māori* male aged 35, was charged with assault on his estranged partner, Charlotte. He had been in a domestic relationship with her for 15 years. They have two children together but had separated some seven months prior to the assault.

In the middle of one afternoon, Chevvy went to the house where Charlotte resided. She saw him coming and she went out to meet him on the driveway. Chevvy accused her of spreading rumours about him and pushed her up against the side of the dwelling. Holding her with his right hand, he then pushed her into a nearby bush. She kicked out at him in an attempt to escape. Charlotte managed to get up and he backed away. She made her way up the side of the property and attempted to phone the police. He chased her, tackled her to the ground and took her cell phone. Chevvy verbally abused her and walked out onto the street. Charlotte voiced her displeasure at his actions. His response was to throw her cell phone on the ground and to move towards her with clenched fists. Seeing this and fearing for her safety once again, Charlotte ran to the neighbouring property and took refuge inside the neighbours' house. Chevvy attempted to follow her into the dwelling but was prevented by the occupant. Chevvy verbally abused Charlotte and then left. She suffered a sore finger from the assault but did not require medical treatment.

Chevvy had previous convictions for moderate drug offending (cannabis) as well as for drink driving on three occasions. His last conviction was three years earlier, for obstructing the police. Police records showed that there had been 10 family violence 'call outs'; that is to say, occasions when the police had called following complaints from someone in the household or from third parties, but these had not resulted in charges being laid.

Pre-conference interviews were held with both Chevvy and Charlotte. Charlotte said that their relationship had been 'just the best' and spoke of a good man who had changed during the year prior to the offending. She spoke of Chevvy's frequent physical abuse during this period. Stressors mentioned included his being now unemployed; her past addiction to gambling; suspicions of his infidelity; and two miscarriages. She was concerned at the effect the conflict was having on their two children and she saw her main priority as ensuring their well-being. She said she did not want him to go to jail but that she wanted some honesty.

At his pre-conference interview, Chevvy said he went to Charlotte's house that day to confront her about 'false accusations'. He acknowledged the essence of what occurred. He spoke of Charlotte's friends feeding her false accusations. He too described an earlier 'awesome' relationship with the victim and his remorse at the effect of the conflict on their children. He became tearful when speaking of the children.

He spoke of his wish to do what he could to rebuild the relationship. Counselling options were discussed. The matter did not proceed to a full conference, Charlotte ultimately saying she was 'not ready' to meet with Chevvy. The perpetrator of his own accord commenced relationship counselling and he received a sentence of 60 hours of community work.

Tempest and Pat

Tempest, a 34-year-old *Māori* male, was charged with assault with intent to injure on his partner of 19 years, Pat. It occurred at 3.30 a.m. after they had both spent the evening with associates consuming alcohol. Tempest became jealous after seeing Pat in conversation with a male associate of hers. He went up to Pat and punched her several times to the face, head and arms, causing her to drop to the ground.

He then kicked her twice in the head using his right foot; he was wearing running shoes at the time. Three of their five children who were present intervened. The police were called but Tempest decamped before they arrived. Pat was admitted to hospital overnight. Her injuries were bruises to her arms and neck. As well as bruising, she experienced abrasions and swelling around her right eye socket. Tempest admitted the assault saying that Pat was cheating on him. Tempest had offended as a youth some eighteen years earlier. However, since that time, there was just one conviction for drink-driving.

Although their relationship commenced 19 years earlier, they had been living separately since the birth of their first child two years into the relationship. Following his release on bail, Tempest, of his own volition, commenced alcohol counselling. Three weeks after the assault, on the day he pleaded guilty and was referred to a restorative justice conference, Pat tendered a letter through the court's victims' adviser supporting such a referral and seeking relaxation of his bail conditions to allow contact between the two to resume.

At her restorative justice pre-conference meeting, Pat said she believed the incident to be alcohol related; that Tempest had jealousy and anger issues; that she did not want him to go to prison; but that she wanted him to have counselling to deal with his issues. She said she had no concerns for her safety.

At his restorative justice pre-conference meeting, Tempest expressed remorse for the harm caused and said he had apologized to Pat and their children. He expressed interest in anger management counselling in addition to the alcohol counselling that he had already commenced.

The full conference identified a number of matters. Insecurities in Tempest arising from their separate living arrangements led him to become jealous and angry when he consumed alcohol. He said 'I just want us to be a family.' Pat said she wanted them to be together 'full-time' but was hesitant on account of Tempest's anger. Both acknowledged the negative effect of this on their children. The reparative plan required completion of both sets of counselling (anger management and alcohol). It also included the request from Pat that no term of imprisonment be imposed.

On his return to court, the judge ordered a probation report, on account of the seriousness of the offending and to explore the possibility of a home detention sentence. At sentencing, the judge acknowledged the progress made through the restorative justice process and Tempest's honest participation in the two sets of counselling. In view of these factors, the term of imprisonment that would otherwise have been imposed was reduced by a third, from one year to eight months and was converted to a home detention sentence of four months[1] with strict conditions, including that Tempest undertake further rehabilitative work as directed by his probation officer and that this continue until completed, for up to six months after the completion of the home detention sentence.

1 This meant Tempest spent four months in prison followed by four months at home wearing an electronic ankle bracelet, confining him to their residence or other place approved by his probation officer.

Razi and Roz

Razi was a 32-year-old *Māori* male charged with assaulting his partner and their teenage son. He had got angry at the noise his son's dog was making. His partner, Roz, unsuccessfully tried to calm things. Razi threw a coffee cup smashing a window, pushed over a bookcase breaking it and punched his partner on the back of her head. Their son ran to help Roz and was punched on the jaw by his father who threw Roz on the floor and again punched her on the back of her head. She managed to walk outside and sat in the driver seat of their car. Razi followed and punched her twice to the face causing her nose to bleed. Mother and son then managed to drive away. She sought medical treatment as she had suffered cuts to the bridge of her nose, bruising around her eyes and scratches. Razi had consumed a considerable amount of alcohol prior to the offending and had one previous conviction for assaulting a female some 10 years earlier. A probation report was ordered, as was a referral to a restorative justice conference.

The probation officer prepared the probation report following an interview with Razi and a telephone chat with Roz. By coincidence, these things took place before the restorative justice meeting occurred. To the probation officer, Razi presented as showing no shame, empathy or remorse for the victims. He was 'very dismissive' of what his children might be feeling and of any long-term effect it could have on them. He presented as very self-absorbed and with a 'sense of entitlement'. He had chosen to ignore lessons learned from past alcohol related offending. He was assessed as being of high risk of harm to others. Prison was recommended.

The report from the restorative justice meeting, which occurred two weeks later, presented a completely different picture. That meeting was attended by Razi and his partner as well as their other son, a young teenager. Their son who was the victim did not attend but wrote of a great relationship with his father except for occasions like this. Throughout the restorative justice process, Razi was described as acknowledging his offending and being very remorseful. He said he 'lost the plot' and that his 'anger and bullying was b ... s ... and uncalled for'. He said 'I hurt you all because I was angry.' He apologized to his children and his partner. As spokesperson for the children, the son present at the meeting spoke of their love for him and acknowledged the great things he had done with them as a father, but he said they did not like it when he 'does things to Mum'. It was their wish that he re-engage with counselling for alcohol and violence.

Faced with the two reports, as well as a number of 'glowing' work-related testimonials, the court sentenced Razi to nine months supervision with special conditions that he undertake alcohol and anger management counselling.

Discussion

This snapshot of five cases is reasonably representative. A majority of referrals involve first time perpetrators or at least those not yet entrenched in violent behaviour though the latter are not excluded. In reality, it is rare for a victim of repeated violence to be willing to participate in a restorative justice conference because they are too frightened, because they are completely under the thrall of the perpetrator or, more rarely, because they never want contact with the perpetrator again.

As with Chevvy and Charlotte's case, it is not uncommon that the referral does not result in a full conference. Indeed, as is the victim's unquestioned right, she may choose not to participate at all. In my view, the referral still has value. If the perpetrator is genuine, the referral assumes that he acknowledges publicly, probably for the first time, that he has a problem with violence and that he needs to take the first steps on the road to rehabilitation. The snapshot also reflects the reality of relationship arrangements that our society regards as unremarkable, but which no doubt would have appalled our grandparents. And, as always, where there are children, they are the collateral damage.

The case of Razi and Roz is instructive. There, over a period of two weeks between the interview with his probation officer and the restorative justice meetings, the perpetrator managed to move from a position of being unrepentant, boorish and staunch to one of acknowledging the wrong he had done and expressing sincere remorse. Both interventions played their part in my view. Some people just take a bit longer to figure things out. Active involvement by his children in the restorative justice process also played a significant part, as it did with Ducati and Tania.

Conclusion

Is restorative justice worthwhile in cases of intimate partner violence? Emphatically yes. And it is proven to be so by independent empirical research carried out here in 2006 (Tisdall et al. (2007) and discussed in Chapter 9). But as with all interventions aimed at changing human behaviour, in many cases deeply entrenched human behaviour, results may vary or take time.

The restorative justice coordinator at Taupo recently told me of a perpetrator, the subject of a successful referral for intimate partner violence some three years ago, contacting her twice since to re-engage in further anger management counselling because he felt he needed to. He has not re-offended in the last three years, but he has been honest and realistic enough to understand he has more work to do to consolidate his violence-free behaviour.

Finally, I well recall an exchange with a defendant, Harley, in his late 30s who might justifiably be described as a career criminal. He had spent much of his adult life in prison for crimes including aggravated robbery. As well as having been under the malevolent influence of a gang, he had issues of addiction. However, Harley was the unintended beneficiary of a restorative justice conference after a street robbery where the co-perpetrator was a young man with no previous serious convictions. It was the young co-perpetrator that the restorative justice referral was primarily aimed at. However, Harley conscientiously took part and, as a result, the term of imprisonment he was later sentenced to was reduced. Time passed and as he continued to be absent from court lists I dared to think that his referral to a restorative justice conference had brought about a turning point in his life, away from crime.

Then, there he was one day, standing in the dock, charged with criminal damage, having got drunk and smashed the glass panel in the door to his girlfriend's house. I voiced my dismay to him saying to him 'Well, nothing's changed has it?' Bypassing counsel his response to me was: 'Well, I think it has. This is far less serious than what I used to do.' He was right, of course.

Reference

Tisdall, M., Farmer, S., Robinson, M., Wells, A. and McMaster, K. 2007. *Review of the Use of Restorative Justice in Family Violence Cases in the Rotorua District*. Wellington: Ministry of Justice.

Chapter 9
Restoring the Balance: Restorative Justice and Intimate Partner Violence

Ken McMaster

Introduction

Extending restorative practices to intimate partner violence is not straightforward. Many doubts have been raised, principally because such violence differs from other kinds of crime by being a 'gendered harm' which is based on dominance and subordination. Intimate partner violence is usually characterized by long-standing power imbalances, secrecy, economic dependencies, the vulnerability of children and pressures from relatives (Coker 2002, Curtis-Fawley and Daly 2005). Key questions to be addressed are when (if at all) is it appropriate to use restorative justice processes for intimate partner violence, with what safeguards, and in what relation to the criminal justice system?

Rather than not viewing restorative justice as an option in cases of intimate partner violence I argue that with the right conditions (careful assessment, skilled facilitators and structured support) then restorative justice is a possibility. I also argue that the use of formal sanctions may not always be in the best interests of the family for healing the hurts caused and moving on. Further to this argument is the need for a thoughtful understanding of the wishes of those victimized by the abuse and allowing them to reclaim their voice in any decision-making regarding their safety. This chapter also refers to a largely qualitative study conducted into restorative justice in intimate partner violence (Tisdall et al. 2007).

What Makes Intimate Partner Violence Different from Other Types of Offending?

The use of restorative justice processes in intimate partner violence and sexual violence must be carefully considered given the unique dynamics involved. This is because the power imbalances inherent in this type of behaviour (contrast Anne Hayden's comments in Chapter 18 of this volume) pose significant risk to the physical and emotional safety of those victimized. By the time intimate partner violence comes into the public gaze, the behaviour is often cyclical and reflects deeply entrenched gendered attitudes and beliefs – a one-off intervention may therefore not be effective or safe (Morris 1997). It is now well recognized that where a restorative justice process takes place, providers need to ensure that facilitators possess the specialized skills and experience required to facilitate these cases and that additional safety and support measures are in place. Compared with many other crimes of violence, the legal and social dimensions of intimate partner violence present several complications for effective legal control and intervention. It differs significantly from other forms of public violence and crime in several important ways:

- There are often strong emotional ties between victims and perpetrators including having children in common. The parties often love one another. The bond may be traumatic, complicating victims' resolve to enter into processes of restoration as well as creating internal conflict regarding separation.
- Financial dependency may be a factor with the victims being financially dependent on the perpetrators or, alternatively, they may face a severely diminished standard of living if separated. Arguably, she (the overwhelming evidence suggests that women are the most likely victims of intimate partner violence) faces an economic life at or below the official threshold of poverty upon leaving the relationship, as do any children.
- Intimate partner violence, unlike violence occurring outside the family context, can be a recurring event between individuals in daily contact. Violence that occurs behind closed doors in the privacy of the home is bereft of the usual forms of guardianship and surveillance that are available in public spaces. Unlike robberies, in which victims and perpetrators are often unacquainted, or other assaults involving acquaintances, victims and perpetrators often occupy the same space, share and compete for the same resources and have emotional ties. In other words, they have to go to bed together as well as get up the next day and face each other. In this context, threats are readily conveyed and quite believable. On the other hand, it is extremely difficult to mount and maintain a deterrent threat within a context of ongoing and unsupervised contact between the victim and the abusive person. The notion of surveillance in relation to private behaviour is very different from what we might experience in the public sphere.
- Rates remain high relative to other violent crimes (see Chapter 3 by Janet Fanslow for a detailed analysis of intimate partner violence in New Zealand). Intimate partner violence rates are highest among subgroups that also have a history of stranger (or public) violence. It, therefore, has a sense of 'normality' in the public arena and shifting attitudes and beliefs have a relatively short history (McMaster and Swain 1993).

Restorative justice makes as its strongest claim that it holds perpetrators directly accountable to the people they have victimized in a way that the criminal justice system on its own does not. It is argued that it does this by providing the opportunity for victims to confront perpetrators in person, face-to-face, in a safe setting. They are thus enabled to speak openly and fully in front of the perpetrators and other relevant people about what their experience of victimization was like and how they were affected by the offences. Following this, apologies may be made and reparation and other consequences set in place, with an emphasis on restoring perpetrators to their families and communities whenever possible. In addition, restorative justice seeks to involve communities, particularly engaging the strengths of Indigenous communities, in order to influence the behaviour and rehabilitation of perpetrators.

Assisting victims to reclaim their voice has been a call for a very long time in the field of intimate partner violence. By its very nature, it renders silent the stories of those victimized. Violence robs them of their *mana* (dignity) and so good practice aims to enhance the victim's agency.

Restorative Justice and Intimate Partner Violence within the Court Process

As Maxine Rennie described in Chapter 7, *Mana* Social Services is a *Tikanga Māori* (culturally oriented) service based on and geared to meet the demands of this population. In addition to restorative justice it also offers: social workers in schools, counselling, family conflict resolution and parenting assistance. *Mana* Social Services is also involved in restorative justice across a broad range of other offending behaviour. Around a third of the cases referred to it are for offences related to intimate partner violence. *Mana* Social Services uses a *kaupapa Māori* (cultural) approach in its work. Being the only provider of restorative justice in Rotorua, a region commonly characterized as having a high incidence of intimate partner violence often fuelled by poor economic conditions, alcohol and drug abuse, and cycles of intergenerational violence, the cases presenting are often of a serious nature.

The Mana Restorative Justice Programme

Mana Social Services runs a pre-sentencing restorative justice programme which is conditional upon a guilty plea by the perpetrator of intimate partner violence. The steps in the restorative process as described below are outlined in Figure 9.1.

The Research

The methodology chosen for the evaluation was qualitative with the researchers gathering data primarily through focus groups and semi-structured in-depth interviews with key informants (stakeholders, programme providers, affiliated agencies and programme users), victims and perpetrators. Other information was gained through the examination of District Court files, *Mana* Social Services files

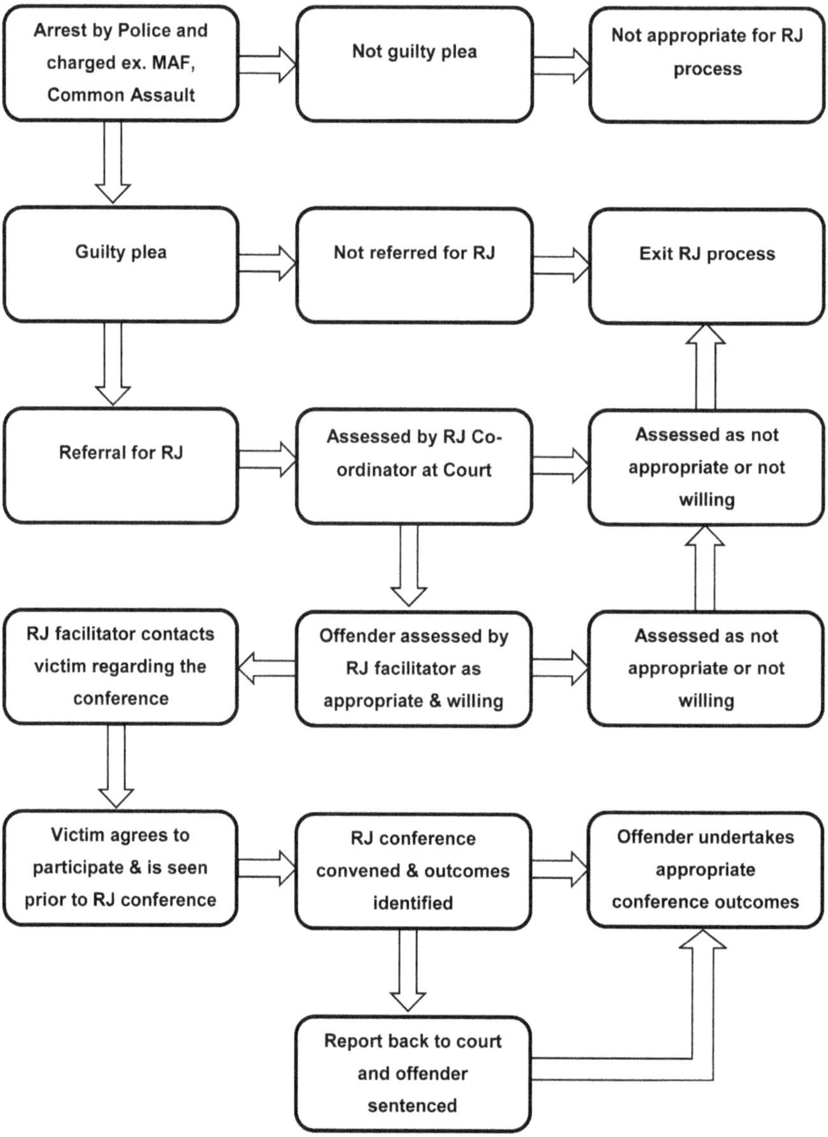

Figure 9.1 *Mana* Social Service Restorative Justice process

Note: Mana Social Services has a team who work specifically in restorative justice; the restorative justice coordinator attends court and is available to meet with and assess men who have been arrested for their suitability for the programme.

and a review of the literature. Quantitative follow-up information was obtained from 48 police call-out files.

Approximately eight open-ended questions were prepared for discussion in the focus groups, exploring the following themes: perception of intimate partner violence in Rotorua, the influence of *Mana* Social Services, the role of restorative justice in addressing intimate partner violence, agencies' relationships with *Mana* Social Services and models and training for restorative justice facilitation. Semi-structured interview schedules containing around 20 questions were developed for the victims and perpetrators, which focused on the restorative justice process, including before, during and after the conference, preparation, safety, accountability and changes.

All who had consented were interviewed over a period of two separate weeks. Most agency interviews were conducted by one member of the research team while the other simultaneously transcribed the responses. Out of the 20 cases chosen as primary participants selected by *Mana* Social Services, six perpetrators and eight victims, including five couples, were interviewed. The majority of the interviews with victims and perpetrators were audio-taped and transcribed. Each interview took around 45 minutes.

Referral

The referral for restorative justice is usually made by the presiding judge, lawyers or, in some cases, the police. The pre-sentencing programme required defendants to plead guilty to the charges before a referral could be made. This is standard restorative justice good practice in that it avoids disputes about the summary of facts which would tend to re-victimize the victim. Once a referral is made the coordinator meets with the defendant.

Interestingly, the data from the three police representatives interviewed showed that it was stated on several occasions that that they did not know if a perpetrator had previously participated in a restorative justice conference and they considered that this might have influenced their decisions about prosecution. None of the eight victims mentioned receiving contact from the court's victim adviser. Victims found out about the restorative justice conference as follows: four from *Mana* Social Services, one from a police officer, and three from the court.

The Pre-Conference Meeting

The perpetrator is responsible at all stages of this process for its successful completion. He must take the initiative and contact *Mana* Social Services and arrange to attend a pre-conference meeting. The meeting is held with one of the restorative justice facilitators and the perpetrator may bring along a support person if he wishes. Younger perpetrators, for example, are encouraged to bring an older *whānau*/family member such as a mother, father, aunt or uncle. In the pre-conference meeting, the facilitator establishes the perpetrator's suitability for a restorative justice conference and emphasizes his need to accept the facts of the case and his responsibility for his actions. The facilitator also emphasizes that the victim's view will be upheld and the conference will only take place if the victim is willing to participate. Some perpetrators reported not knowing what to expect, although most understood it was a means of 'getting some answers about what was going on' or 'to try and sort out what happened' (Tisdall et al. 2007: 71). This lack of knowledge may have been due as much to difficulties in recalling what went on as it did to the level of explanation offered to them. When considering the purpose of the restorative justice conference, some considered 'we went there for me ... not for her' (ibid.: 71). One perpetrator remembered being asked to 'write some things down on a piece of paper about what I had done and to bring it to the conference' (ibid.: 71).

Contacting the Victim

The facilitator will contact the victim, who at this stage may have already talked to the victim adviser.[1] The facilitator will explain the restorative justice process, address safety issues and also empower the victim to choose for herself whether or not she participates. If the victim chooses not to do so, the conference will not go ahead. If the victim agrees, however, the facilitator will give her the option of bringing a support person to the conference, which the facilitator will then arrange.

Our research showed that although victims were also unsure about what to expect, most remembered being asked whether or not they would like to bring a support person. Many declined this option. Among the motivators for victims to agree to a conference were the following: 'I've got a family so I needed something to work' (Tisdall et al. 2007: 75) and 'just to help us really' (ibid.: 75). No respondent felt pressured to attend.

The Conference

Generally, the facilitator will arrange for the perpetrator and victim to arrive separately at staggered times to ensure the safety of the victim. The facilitator will address any special cultural needs or beginning rituals and outline the process of the conference. After reading the police summary of facts, the facilitator will then ask for the victim's story and the effects of the violence on her and her family. The perpetrator is not asked to comment on this or given the opportunity to dispute the victim's story. An apology may be made at this point. The facilitator will then ask the victim what she thinks needs to happen to make amends for the violence and from this an agreement is reached with regards to what actions the perpetrator should do to redress the harm done. These actions or conditions vary and may be any combination of attending a stopping violence programme, counselling, attendance at an alcohol or drug treatment programme, community work, and/

1 Victim advisers are court appointed lay people whose role is to support, advise and occasionally speak for the victim.

or a payment to a charity. During the course of the conference, the facilitator may explore issues either individually or relationally associated with the violence and, on the basis of this, make his/her own contribution to the conditions. The victim's safety and the perpetrator's accountability are emphasized at this stage.

All respondents indicated that both the victim and the perpetrator had an opportunity to talk: 'we want to speak out what was in our mind and what was in our heart' (Tisdall et al. 2007: 71). There was some frustration and anger acknowledged toward the facilitator who 'might've been more for women and not for men ... there's not much help for men' (ibid.: 71). However, there was also an acceptance that 'I was in denial ... I was acting like a boy so she had every right to treat me like one' (ibid.: 71). Some perpetrators found it difficult or declined to describe their thoughts and feelings about the impact of their violence upon their partner and (where relevant) children. Feedback from victims was very positive. 'The facilitator listened, even when both parties were talking' (ibid.: 77) and 'when the perpetrator got defensive, the facilitator shut him down in a way that did not offend' (ibid.: 76).

Report to the Court

The facilitator writes a report for the court outlining the outcome of the conference and the agreements reached. The judge will then often adjourn the sentencing until satisfied the agreements have all been fulfilled; usually this entails reports back from the agencies concerned. The completion of the agreements is left up to the perpetrator to initiate and accomplish. *Mana* Social Services play no role in the process of initiating contact with respective agencies, but as part of the court process will report back to the court on whether or not this was undertaken. It is believed that having the perpetrator initiate action demonstrates responsibility. If the perpetrator fails to complete the agreements then this is also reported back to the court and sentencing takes place.

Two judges were respondents in the research. In terms of the influence of the restorative justice report on sentencing, one commented on the following as relevant: 'the attitudes that were displayed, that the defendant has expressed remorse and apologized, and if the complainant has accepted. Any agreements that have come out of it and what's going to happen from here' (Tisdall et al. 2007: 58). One of the judges acknowledged that 'It's hard to think there's a checklist about whether the victim is going to be safe or not safe' (ibid.: 59). However, the judges also considered that 'restorative justice can also provide ... empowerment in resolving the case; it is not just left in the hands of the judge. We owe it to them and ourselves to try and give it our best shot' (ibid.: 59).

Perpetrators' Level of Responsibility Taking

It is most important that the perpetrator is taking meaningful responsibility for his actions, is showing remorse and is open to hearing about the impact of his actions on his victim. It is critical that he agrees beforehand – and is held to it during the conference – not to use the conferencing as an opportunity to challenge the victim's account of her victimization. In other words, the nature of the offending will not be open for discussion in the restorative justice process. A fundamental requirement, therefore, is acceptance of responsibility for the offences *as described by the victim* (which might best be done via a written or verbal communication received early in the process before meeting the victim). This measure is to counter perpetrators' tendency to minimize their violence, blame their victims, and under-report the seriousness of their violence, the number of violent acts carried out, the extent of any sexual violence, their partners' injuries and their controlling behaviour generally. If the perpetrator strongly wishes to argue that there are distortions of fact in the victim's account, this effectively should preclude the case from a restorative justice conference, leaving it up to the court to adjudicate. His airing of any disagreements in the restorative justice session, even if they are justified, would subvert the process and render it ineffective to redress the power imbalance and fear felt by the victim.

All eight victims reported that the perpetrator had said sorry during the conference and that they considered that he meant it. One victim commented: 'he doesn't say sorry to anybody … so what happened that night he really was in the wrong and he apologised' (Tisdall et al. 2007: 78). Another victim described the conference as a turning point. 'It was like being taken out of your life and watching your own life unfold … it was like the penny dropped and he realised what he had done and how bad it really was' (ibid.: 79).

Outcomes

Follow-up quantitative research based on call-outs in police reports from 1 July 2005 to 31 December 2006 showed that *Mana* Social Services had a positive impact on perpetrators. Of the 48 perpetrators in this part of the study, 42 (87 per cent) completed their tasks, leaving six (13 per cent) who did not (Tisdall et al. 2007: 105).[2] Those who completed the agreements made at the conference prior to being sentenced had a much reduced level of re-offending compared to their re-offending rate before undergoing the process (down to 5 per cent from 63 per cent). Of the 13 post disposal police call-outs, 11 perpetrators were not charged. On the other hand, all five who did not complete their restorative justice agreements had further charges against them after their disposal date (ibid.: 109).

The Fit with Best Practice Principles for Restorative Justice

The process is clearly in line with what would be considered best practice principles in restorative justice. For example, the perpetrator must acknowledge responsibility for the offence before a case can be referred to, or accepted for, a

2 One case was unresolved.

restorative justice process. Agreed outcomes provide an appropriate and realistic response to the violent behaviour with outcomes reflecting what participants think can be done to put right the offending – this will depend on a range of factors, including the needs of the victim and perpetrator and the circumstances of the offending. In addition, agreed outcomes should be fair, realistic, achievable, credible and able to be completed within an appropriate time frame. They must also be monitored and action should be taken when an agreed plan breaks down. There is an inherent tension between a hands-off approach to action and being overly instrumental in ensuring agreements are carried out. Given that in many situations of intimate partner violence reconciliation between the parties is not uncommon, follow-up after the conference to assess both its positive and negative impact is essential.

The emotional and physical safety of participants is an overriding concern. This includes ensuring that restorative justice processes are safe for participants at all times, that potential risks are carefully managed, and that processes are discontinued at any time if the facilitator(s) consider it inappropriate or unsafe to continue.

Feedback from victims was positive – they felt safe due to the neutral setting, the facilitator being someone in authority, the way the conference was facilitated and because their partner was sober. For example, one said: 'Yeah I felt safe, because at home it's both our territory whereas in a room, 'coz it's neutral territory I could say what I felt' (Tisdall et al. 2007: 79). Another commented: 'I've never felt not safe with him, it's just the alcohol combined with him being angry' (ibid.: 79).

Discussion

Considerable agreement is emerging as to the conditions that must be met for restorative justice to be used in cases of intimate partner violence (Strang and Braithwaite 2002, Ministry of Justice 2004, Stubbs 2002, 2007). However, the point should be clearly stated that acknowledging wrongdoing does not necessarily equate to remorse and responsibility for abusive behaviour. The motivation of avoidance of the consequences rather than making long-lasting changes in one's behaviour is a key concern which emerges from much of the debate and thinking.

Pennell and Burford (2002) are emphatic that family group conferencing can stop family violence, but only if it is resourced adequately so that all family members are safeguarded. Their model uses conferencing explicitly to mobilize resources. Resources also need to be invested from the outset in careful planning, consultation and selection of participants and subsequently in support and monitoring. Barbara Hudson (1998) argues that the aim of restorative justice of creating a forum for community disapproval needs to be backed up by extensive resources including programmes for perpetrators, recourse to injunctions, curfews and strong sanctions. Concerns have been expressed in the literature about who will take responsibility for ensuring that disclosures made in sessions do not result in retribution for the victim at some later time, who will give ongoing support to the victim and who will provide monitoring of the perpetrator (Stubbs 2002).

There is consensus that thorough screening and prior casework (usually over several sessions) should be done before proceeding to a restorative justice conference. Screening of perpetrators must focus on victims' safety, not just on the wish or willingness of both parties to participate, and on offence seriousness (although this is, of course, relevant to the level of risk to victims in face-to-face conferencing). Screening needs to ensure that the victim's participation is well-informed and genuinely voluntary: that the victim has the desire, strength and feeling of safety to talk in depth about the perpetrator's abusive behaviours; that she feels safe outside the sessions; and that she feels able to terminate the sessions at any point. Adequate assessment of perpetrators requires the use of appropriate risk assessment tools. Men who have a tendency to higher dependency needs in relationships are more likely to engage in the process with the express purpose of reconciliation. This same group are also most likely to breach protection and safety orders resulting in further harm and in some cases homicide/suicide (McMaster 2006).

In good practice, facilitators of restorative justice sessions should not adopt a neutral stance (equipoise), but rather one that is clearly focused on redressing the inequality between the victim and the perpetrator which was implicit in the offending. A bottom line for Strang and Braithwaite (2002) is anti-subordination; this requires that the system absolutely guarantees the woman a right to a contest in court with well-funded legal aid. It also guarantees her right to a restorative justice process in which she will not confront her partner alone, but with the advocacy of as many lay and professional supporters as she chooses, including publicly funded intimate partner violence advocates. An alternative view is to allow the woman at the centre of the process to choose not to engage in a public event around what has taken place and to opt instead for a restorative justice conference.

Barbara Hudson states the advantages of restorative justice for intimate partner violence cases as follows:

> The conference or meeting offers the victim the opportunity to choose how to present herself; to abstract herself from the relationship; to select her own supporters and representatives. The abuser cannot ignore her, as he could in a conventional court while she is giving her evidence; her story will be told not refracted through legal language; it will be told in her words, the words with which she always communicates with him so he cannot claim not to have understood any more than he can claim not to have heard. Her story will be about *her*, she will not be confined to dwelling on those elements that relate to him, elements relevant to establishing his guilt and his culpability. He cannot claim, then, not to have been told about *her* feelings, *her* understanding of events, *her* wishes and demands for the future (Hudson 2003: 183, emphasis in the original).

What is not negotiable, in my view, is the need, as Bannenberg and Rossner (2003) indicate, for facilitators to take a stand against violence and draw attention to how abusive behaviour silences the voice of those victimized. In addition, they suggest that facilitators must develop methods to balance the power of the parties such as limiting speaking time and using pre-formulated victims' comments and demands. Other reports suggest the importance of maintaining a gender balance, preferably in favour of women in order to offset the influence of men in the conferencing. Writing in the German context, Bannenberg and Rossner (2003) suggest having two specialist mediators able to conduct preliminary discussions with the victim and the perpetrator. They discuss managing multiple sessions over a longer time frame than is usually offered in restorative justice conferencing or mediation. Curtis-Fawley and Daly's (2005) study of the views of victim advocates in South Australia and Queensland is very positive about using restorative justice. However, concern is expressed about possible re-victimization when the imbalances of power become difficult to manage in informal processes where the facilitators lack appropriate skills. In reality, facilitators need multiple skills, including the ability to work with victims' representatives, use pre-recorded victims' statements and be able to stop a conference at the first sign of intimidation.

Strang and Braithwaite (2002) note strong support in the literature for victim/perpetrator conferencing to be held separately in the first instance, with the parties being brought together subsequently only if cycles of denial and intimidation have clearly been broken. When joint meetings begin, the victim needs to be able to opt out at any time, requiring facilitators to check with the victim throughout the process about her willingness to continue.

There is agreement among authors (Bannenberg and Rossner 2003, Hudson, 1998, Stubbs 2002, 2007) that, if apologies are expected or encouraged, there should not be an expectation of forgiveness or even for 'acceptance' of the apology which is only a further demand by the perpetrator on the victim. Instead the focus should remain on the victims' safety and the perpetrators' responsibility. Some authors are highly sceptical about this aspect of restorative justice processes, arguing that apologies may give victims false hopes. Pagelow (1981), for example, found that 73 per cent of a women's refuge sample returned to their partner because he had apologized and they hoped he would change. Men who use violence against their partners are often adept at using apologies as a strategy to buy back favour and exercise further control over their partners and others or to foreclose discussion: 'I've said I'm sorry, so let's move on.' Such apologies and expressed contrition are frequently a phase in a pattern of repeated abuse and violence (Stubbs 2002). Apologies may, therefore, oil the wheels of a renewed cycle of abuse, intimidation and violence rather than bring these to a stop.

If apologies are to be a part of a restorative process they must receive careful attention. An adequate apology must contain a clear acceptance of responsibility, recognition and acknowledgement of the effects of the violence on the victim and a statement of the perpetrator's plans to undertake the necessary steps (in terms of programmes, support and removal of their presence) to initiate and maintain a change of behaviour. An apology should be witnessed by a wider range of those involved than the victim only in order for it to be effective as a public condemnation. Thus the perpetrator's own family and supporters should be included.

Conclusion

The use of restorative justice for intimate partner violence remains controversial because the nature of intimate violence is such that there is always a risk that victims may be subtly re-victimized in any contact with the perpetrator. However well managed, there is a potential for a perpetuation of the imbalance of power that was present in the violence itself. Nevertheless, in all the places where it has been tried, in North American and Canadian settings (Pennell and Burford 2002, Strang and Braithwaite 2002) and in Australia (Sherman et al. 1998), many victims have reported satisfaction that they were free to make the choice of entering into a restorative process and were enabled to follow through with it. They were pleased that the process galvanized community participation on their behalf and because it enabled them to tell their story to an audience of their own and the perpetrator's supporters, as well as to receive a publicly witnessed apology from the perpetrator.

Whereas courtrooms limit the stories that can be told by the victim to those that are legally relevant, restorative justice, its advocates claim, re-empowers victims by institutionalizing active listening to victims' fuller stories about the harms experienced. This increases the community's empathy for the pain of victims and creates a space for dialogue where consequences will flow from this listening. Restorative justice also provides a way for family and community members who have been in denial of the problem to recognize their broader community responsibility. This way, they can take action through a collective process of problem-solving rather than stand by feeling helpless and inadequate while the justice system acts on their behalf. Kay Pranis, Restorative Justice Planner with the Minnesota Department of Corrections, sums up the main strength of restorative justice in simple terms: 'Listening respectfully to someone's story gives that person dignity and worth' (Pranis 2002: 30).

It is noteworthy that one of the outcomes of the evaluation undertaken in Tisdall et al. (2007) was that women reported that, when in court, they heard clearly from the judge where the responsibility for the abuse lay. A more disturbing finding about the perpetrators was that they remembered little. This may be indicative of the anxiety that occurs when being sentenced in public. It was only after sitting with the restorative justice facilitator that they were able to fully realize the implications of what was said.

There still remains much to clarify and evaluate about applying restorative processes to intimate partner violence. It is too soon to say that the critics' objections have all been met or can easily be met. However, restorative justice processes arguably have some less tangible gains, such as increasing the motivation and willingness of perpetrators to follow through with undertaking a stopping violence programme and increasing the likelihood of families staying together; or, when there is a separation, increasing the motivation and willingness of both parents to cooperate in child care and parenting roles. That it also makes a difference to the outcomes of repeat offending is not yet fully clear, but the indications so far are positive (see, for example, Nelson Restorative Justice Service Report 2011). The growing consensus is that the way forward lies in the working together of criminal and restorative justice, so that the seriousness of intimate partner violence receives a state-sanctioned response while also enlisting the active involvement of the community to provide a reintegration of the perpetrator. As one perpetrator explained: 'You look at why you do things and how come you've done it. These things don't get touched upon normally' (Tisdall et al. 2007: 73).

References

Bannenberg, B. and Rossner, D. 2003. New Developments in Restorative Justice to Handle Family Violence, in *Restorative Justice in Context: International Practice and Directions*, edited by E.G.M. Weitkamp and H. Keiner. Cullompton: Willan Publishing, 109–33.

Coker, D. 2002. Transformative Justice: Anti-Subordination Processes in Cases of Domestic Violence, in *Restorative Justice and Family Violence*, edited by H. Strang and J. Braithwaite. Cambridge: Cambridge University Press, 128–52.

Curtis-Fawley, S. and Daly, K. 2005. Gendered Violence and Restorative Justice: The Views of Victim Advocates. *Violence against Women: An International and Interdisciplinary Journal*, 11, 603–38.

Hudson, B. 1998. Restorative Justice: The Challenge of Sexual and Racial Violence. *Journal of Law and Society*, 25(2), 237–56.

Hudson, B. 2003. Victims and Perpetrators, in *Restorative Justice and Criminal Justice: Competing or Reconcilable Paradigms?* edited by A. von Hirsch, J. Roberts and A. Bottoms. Oxford: Hart Publishing.

Nelson Restorative Justice Service. 2011. *A Comparative Quantative Analysis of Restorative Justice with a Family Violence Context in the Nelson/Tasman Area* 2011. Available at: http://www.restorativejusticeaotearoa.org.nz/files/File/Papers,%20Research/%20RJ%20DV%20Statistics%20Analysis.pdf.

McMaster, K.J. 2006. Predicting and Managing Risk in Men who are Domestically Violent, in *Will They Do It Again: Assessing and Managing Risk*, edited by K. McMaster and L. Bakker. Lyttelton, New Zealand: HMA Books.

McMaster, K.J. and Swain, P. 1993. *A Private Affair: Stopping Men's Violence to Women*. Wellington: GP Books.

Ministry of Justice. 2004. *Restorative Justice: Best Practice in New Zealand*. Wellington: New Zealand Government.

Morris, A. 1997. *Women's Safety Survey*. Wellington: Victimisation Survey Committee.

Pagelow, M. 1981. *Woman Battering: Victims and Their Experiences*. Newbury Park, CA: Sage.

Pennell, J. and Burford, G. 2002. Feminist Praxis: Making Family Group Conferencing Work, in *Restorative Justice and Family Violence*, edited by J. Braithwaite and H. Strang. Cambridge: Cambridge University Press.

Pranis, K. 2002. Restorative Values and Confronting Family Violence, in *Restorative Justice and Family Violence*, edited by J. Braithwaite and H. Strang. Cambridge: Cambridge University Press.

Sherman, L. Strang, H., Barnes, G., Braithwaite, J. and Inkpen, N. 1998. *Experiments in Restorative Justice Policing: A Progress Report to the National Police Research Unit on the Canberra Shaming Experiment (RISE)*. Canberra: Australian Federal Police, Australian National University.

Strang, H. and Braithwaite, J. (eds). 2002. *Restorative Justice and Family Violence*. Cambridge: Cambridge University Press.

Stubbs, J. 2002. Domestic Violence and Women's Safety, in *Restorative Justice and Family Violence*, edited by H. Strang and J. Braithwaite. Cambridge: Cambridge University Press.

Stubbs, J. 2007. Beyond Apology? Domestic Violence and Critical Questions for Restorative Justice. *Criminology and Criminal Justice*, 7(2), 149–80.

Tisdall, M., Farmer, S., Robinson, M., Wells, A. and McMaster, K. 2007. *Review of the Use of Restorative Justice in Family Violence Cases in the Rotorua District*. Wellington: Ministry of Justice.

PART IV
Recognizing Culture in Restorative Responses to Family Violence

The case study in Part III indicated the importance of culture and in this part we elaborate on this. Restorative justice processes operate differently within and across different countries. However, there is no single *'right way'* to deliver restorative justice. The essence of restorative justice is not the adoption of one form rather than another; it is the adoption of any form which reflects restorative values and which aims to achieve restorative processes, outcomes and objectives.

Part IV comprises three chapters about restorative justice policy and practice. Loraine Gelsthorpe explores in Chapter 10 the possibility of using restorative justice for intimate partner violence, basing her comments on the jurisdiction of England and Wales. In Chapter 11, Julia Hennessy, Mike Hinton and Natalia Taurima write about practice in New Zealand, presenting three case studies. A different cultural perspective is provided in Chapter 12 by Marie Ropeti who gives an overview of *ifoga* as practised in Samoa and, on occasions somewhat differently, in New Zealand. This approach has clear links with the core values of restorative justice. Together these chapters address the 'nuts and bolts' of restorative justice process and the development of expertise through information sharing and wider experiences.

Chapter 10

The Promise and Possibilities of Restorative Justice as a Way of Addressing Intimate Partner Violence in England and Wales[1]

Loraine Gelsthorpe

Introduction

This chapter explores the possibility of using of restorative justice to address men's violence against women, particularly intimate partner violence, in the specific cultural context of England and Wales. It is certainly an auspicious moment to consider this. A newly revised draft of the 'Victims' Code' (Ministry of Justice 2013), launched in April 2013, promises, amongst other things, extra support for victims of the most serious crimes, specialist help for young victims

1 There are three legal jurisdictions in the UK, involving four separate policy initiatives in the sphere of intimate partner violence. The focus of this chapter is largely on policy initiatives and developments in England, although some of the research data relate to England *and* Wales. Scottish policy is outlined in the Scottish Government and the Convention of Scottish Local Authorities' (2009) report *Safer Lives: Changed Lives. A Shared Approach to Tackling Violence against Women in Scotland.* It focuses on prevention; protection of victims; provision of services and participation of all agencies to ensure policy-making and practice development around violence against women is informed by those who use intimate partner violence services. In Northern Ireland, the current strategy is set out in *Tackling Violence at Home A – Strategy for Addressing Domestic Violence in Northern Ireland* (Department of Health, Social Services and Public Safety Northern Ireland 2005) and is supported by Action Plans up to 2013. In 2008 the Northern Ireland Government published *Tackling Sexual Violence and Abuse – A Regional Strategy* (Department of Health, Social Services and Public Safety Northern Ireland 2008). These two strategies ran in tandem for a while but in March 2012 a joint Domestic and Sexual Violence and Abuse Action Plan was published taking forward actions on a collaborative basis. In 2005, the Welsh Assembly Government published its first national strategy *Tackling Domestic Abuse: The All Wales National Strategy* (Welsh Assembly Government 2005). It supports also bi-yearly action plans. This was superseded in 2010 with the publication of *The Right to be Safe* which is a six-year integrated strategy for tackling all forms of violence against women and has an increased focus ensuring that the whole violence against women agenda is tackled effectively (Welsh Assembly Government 2010). The Welsh, Scottish and Northern Ireland authorities have all looked at restorative justice possibilities, although there are no concrete plans within policy developments as yet.

and, most importantly, sets out the services that should be provided to victims of crime in England and Wales, including restorative justice. The Code describes what victims can expect and what they are entitled to:

> The Government's seeming commitment to increasing the use of restorative justice also emerges in attempts to ensure quality and consistent restorative justice services (Ministry of Justice 2012). In partnership with the Restorative Justice Council,[2] new minimum standards are expected to be launched in 2013. The standards will include the Council's Restorative Services Quality Mark Restorative (Restorative Justice Council 2013). This adds to the Association of Chief Police Officers' report (2011) *Restorative Justice Guidance and Minimum Standards.*

But turning to the substance of this chapter and by way of preparing the way for a consideration of restorative justice, I first briefly summarize policy developments in relation to intimate partner violence in England and Wales and outline some of the issues relating to the effectiveness of the law and the criminal justice system in dealing with violence towards women. Policy developments in England and Wales are characteristically slow and incremental. Secondly, I point to what we know about what women want in response to violence against them from their partners. In the third section, I explore the promise and prospects for restorative justice in relation to men who commit violence against their partners.

Intimate Partner Violence and Policy Developments in England and Wales

A key question, of course, concerns how effective the law and criminal justice system is in dealing with violence towards women. One of the difficulties in trying to address this question is that we do not really know the 'true' level of violence against their female partners. We know that the number of arrests is a poor indication and that changes in arrests may result from changes in reporting and recording practices rather than increases or decreases in offending. Victim surveys have helped us to gain a clearer picture of the extent of violence but, even here, increases in prevalence rates over time can be attributed to an increased willingness to report incidents of violence or to improvements in research methodology.

Assessment of the level of intimate partner violence in England and Wales is beset with difficulty and one sometimes reads wildly different figures reported in the media. The problem arises from referring to different findings in the British Crime Survey (BCS). The most recent figures for intimate partner violence can be found in *Crime in England and Wales 2010/2011* (Home Office 2011a). The BCS asks around 50,000 men and women aged 16–59 about crimes they have experienced in the last year. Using the experiences of the respondents for each type of crime, the

2 The Restorative Justice Council is the independent third sector body for the practice of restorative justice in the UK. Available at: www.restorativejustice.org.uk.

BCS then estimates its prevalence.[3] It estimated that there were 392,000 incidents of intimate partner violence across England and Wales in 2010 to 2011. However, this report also highlights the shortcomings in the survey (Home Office 2011a). The statistics quoted were gathered by face-to-face interviews, which is a method recognized to be unreliable when used to measure intimate partner violence, due to a significant degree of unwillingness among respondents to disclose such details personally to an interviewer. To address the problem, the survey also captures data on intimate partner violence via a self-completion module, which allows the respondent to write experiences directly onto the interviewer's laptop. Indeed, the results for this self-completion module do show overall rates five times higher – 2 million in total.

There have been major changes in the national policy regarding intimate partner violence in England and Wales over the past 30 years in response to advocacy and campaigning by the women's movement and non-governmental organizations providing services to abused women (Harwin 2006). Police services, in particular, have been involved in configuring criminal justice responses to the problem of intimate partner violence, but health and social care services have also been key players in reshaping policy. Moreover, many government and non-government institutions have commissioned research on intimate partner violence and have formulated policy recommendations. In the 1990s, two events had particular influence on the development of policy on intimate partner violence in the UK: first, the increasing interest in aligning UK policies with the strategic objectives agreed in the Beijing *Platform for Action* to promote the human rights of women (United Nations Women 1995); and, secondly, New Labour (as a political party) coming into government in 1997 with a manifesto commitment to take forward policy development to combat this type of offending. During the period between 1997 and 2010, the main focus of policy and legislation on intimate partner violence was on implementing measures based on prevention, protection and justice and the provision of support for victims of family violence, to be implemented by partnerships of service providers at local and national levels. Interestingly, in formulating policy, the Labour Government defined intimate partner violence in a gender-neutral way.

The 2005 Home Office[4] publication of *Domestic Violence: A National Report* marked a shift in central government policy, recognizing the importance of partnership with voluntary organizations working in the field of intimate partner violence (Home Office 2005a). The Report made seventeen commitments to support and develop public services to respond proactively to domestic abuse and included support for new measures including Specialist Domestic Violence

3 The British Crime Survey (BCS) is now called the Crime Survey England and Wales (CSEW).

4 In England, the Home Office is seen as the lead government department for the coordination of intimate partner violence policies and initiatives, providing guidance to other governmental departments and cooperating with non-governmental organizations to develop and implement policy (Matczak et al. 2011). The Home Office undertakes research, provides information and releases statistics on the prevalence of intimate partner violence.

Courts and Independent Domestic Violence Advisers. The concomitant *National Domestic Violence Delivery Plan* (Home Office 2005b) set out objectives focusing on the reduction of the prevalence of intimate partner violence and related homicides; increasing the rate intimate partner violence is reported to the police and referred to the courts; and the provision of support and protection to victims. Performance indicators were listed to measure progress in these areas, with yearly reviews time-tabled, and annual progress reports were published in the period 2006–09. Although this could be seen as the first major step in national planning in which the government took a clear lead, criticisms were made of this approach: for example, there were failures to implement the policy and there was a disproportionate focus on criminal justice responses at the expense of early and effective prevention (House of Commons 2008).

Subsequent to this, there was a government Consultation Paper *Together We Can End Violence against Women and Girls* (Home Office 2009) which focused more explicitly on actual violence against women and girls, noting their fear of this and its impact on everyday lives. It made fresh proposals regarding prevention, supporting victims and bringing perpetrators to justice (ibid.).

Following a change in the administration in 2010 to a Coalition Government (Conservatives and Liberal Democrats), the new government introduced another consultation exercise. They criticized the previous administration for adopting a 'top-down' approach to intimate partner violence and called for more localized responses to the problem – with an emphasis on prevention, the provision of support to victims, partnership working with third sector agencies, and risk reduction. This marks a return to the approach taken before 2005. It focuses firmly on gender based violence (recognizing that men and boys can be victims too) and includes 'honour based violence' and female genital mutilation as well as considering the impact of intimate partner violence on children (Home Office 2011b). It was backed by a £28 million fund to support the provision of specialist services for victims and prevention work.

What Do Women Want in Response to Violence from Their Partners?

Notwithstanding legal and policy developments in terms of the state recognizing victims more, there is strong evidence to suggest that victims want a less formal process where their views count (see, for example, Strang 2002). It is very clear that victims wish to participate more in their cases – where proceedings have been instituted – and that they want to be treated more respectfully and fairly (Tyler and Lind 1992). But this does not amount to an unalloyed *belief in* or *reliance on* the law and the criminal justice system. Drawing on the evidence base in England and Wales in the main (and selectively for reasons of space), research consistently shows that only a few of the women who experience violence at the hands of their male partners rely on the law, police or courts to deal with it, at least in the first instance (see, for instance, Mirrlees-Black 1999 and Walklate 2004). Some women 'accept' the violence and see it as part of 'ordinary life' (Bush and Hood-Williams 1995).

Almost all have to overcome a reluctance to take action; their preference seems to be to turn first to friends or family, and then to medical general practitioners, lawyers and other 'helping' agencies as much to the police. Although police policy on violence in relationships in most Western jurisdictions specifies that perpetrators should be arrested except in exceptional circumstances, research findings suggest that the police have not always followed this policy (see, for example, Hester and Westmarland 2005, Hoyle 1998, Kelly 1999). In Hoyle's (1998) sample of 33 victims, for example, only a third wanted their partner arrested and many of these women did not want the police to proceed further; they wanted immediate protection but not necessarily prosecution. In Hoyle's (1998) view, some victims judged interventions as successful even though they did not result in a prosecution; and whether or not their partner was arrested was unrelated to women's level of satisfaction with the police. There have been attempts to empower female victims in relation to police and criminal justice processing, of course, but there are complex issues relating to women being compellable witnesses in some jurisdictions (see, for example, Crown Prosecution Service 2010). One key issue concerns considering where the public interest lies, especially where the safety of children and young people is at stake.

It is also important to identify the challenges faced by female victims of intimate partner violence who experience undesirable arrest outcomes (Hester and Westmarland 2005). Generally, there is nothing to suggest that women always and unequivocally see prosecution as the right way forward: many simply want the abuse and violence to stop; and they want advice rather than their partner's arrest or prosecution. Indeed, it has been argued that the penalization of men (their arrest, prosecution and punishment) may make matters worse because the criminal justice system has a brutalizing effect (Carlen, 1992, Hudson 1998). We know that there is very little support for the idea that increased penalties reduce criminal behaviour (von Hirsch et al. 1999) and, while it should be acknowledged that there is some evidence that programmes can make a difference (for example, Scourfield and Dobash 1999, Featherstone et al. 2007), some programmes do not take men on court orders and, in any case, the evidence suggests that programmes are more effective where men *wish* to be involved rather than when they are *required* to be involved (McNeill et al. 2010). Notwithstanding some good work in this direction, the continuing limitations and ambiguities of criminal justice approaches – as highlighted above – suggest that there is every reason to explore alternative ways of dealing with men's violence against their partners, restorative justice included.

Since 2010, we can observe a shift in policy direction with an increased focus on ending violence against women and girls (Home Office 2010). Moreover, even though violence against women became a policy priority at the turn of the millennium, with the Labour Government introducing the *Domestic Violence, Crime and Victims Act 2004* which provided more protection to intimate partner violence victims by criminalizing breaches of non-molestation orders, it has been argued that progress has been slow (Howe 2006). A number of writers have argued that this is because the criminal justice system does not and cannot challenge the patriarchal structures which both underlie and sanction men's violence towards women, particularly violence against their female partners (see, for example, Howe 2006, 2008 and Smart 1989, 1995 on the links between local and global agendas).

In recognition of women's vulnerabilities in matters relating to prosecution, there are Independent Domestic Violence Advisers and other specialist intimate partner violence services available to provide support alongside Victim Support and Witness Services in some areas. Further, in some parts of England and Wales, intimate partner violence cases are heard in Specialist Domestic Violence Courts which represent a partnership approach to intimate partner violence by the police, prosecutors, court staff, the probation service and specialist support services for victims. Members of the Witness Service are able to arrange pre-court familiarization visits if desired and can accompany the witness into court to give support. If the witness has had support from other agencies, a member of that support service (for example, Women's Aid or an Independent Domestic Violence Adviser) may also accompany the witness into court.

But while there has been an increase in 'successful' prosecutions of intimate partner violence by the Crown Prosecution Service in England and Wales, with steady increases in convictions, there are still a good number of cases which do not proceed at court because of victims' retraction of their evidence or victims' non-attendance at court (Crown Prosecution Service 2010). There are a number of different reasons for this happening, but some of this may be ambivalence about prosecution as the right way forward. All this points to the possibility of restorative justice as a way of dealing with violence against women.

The Prospect of Restorative Justice for Dealing with Intimate Partner Violence

Restorative justice is not the panacea that was first anticipated in its rediscovery and application to the Western world, but it has proved to be most promising in its effects (as many chapters in this volume show). Nevertheless, the Consultation Paper *Restorative Justice: The Government's Strategy* (Home Office 2003) which posed pertinent questions about restorative justice and intimate partner violence revealed strongly polarized responses. Some intimate partner violence specialists were very much against the use of restorative justice, while proponents thought that it could be beneficial in some cases. The arguments against the use of restorative justice revolved around a perceived risk of re-victimization, power imbalances and the seriousness of intimate partner violence. Accordingly, the *Best Practice Guidelines for Restorative Justice Practitioners* did not offer agreement that restorative justice might be used in intimate partner violence, nor was there mention of restorative justice in the *Code of Practice for Victims* launched in 2006 (Home Office 2006).

Despite this conclusion to the Consultation Paper, an extensive review of research findings by Sherman and Strang (2007) showed the following results:

> Across 36 direct comparisons to conventional criminal justice (CJ), [restorative justice] has, in at least two tests each: substantially reduced repeat offending for some offenders, but not all; doubled (or more) the offences brought to justice as diversion from CJ; *reduced crime victims' post-traumatic stress symptoms and related costs; provided both victims and offenders with more satisfaction with justice than CJ; reduced crime victims' desire for violent revenge against their offenders*; reduced the costs of criminal justice, when used as diversion from CJ; reduced recidivism more than prison (adults) or as well as prison (youths) (2007: 4) (emphasis added).

In terms of *victim* benefits, two randomized control trials in London showed that restorative justice reduces post-traumatic stress; in four it showed that restorative justice reduces the desire for violent revenge; and in four it showed that victims prefer restorative justice over criminal justice (Sherman and Strang 2007). Linked to this, and unsurprisingly perhaps, is the conclusion that the emotional power of the process of bringing perpetrators and victims together can prompt change in terms of empathy for each other and, for the perpetrator, a change in attitude that can result in desistance from crime. The evidence here suggests that restorative justice works best when it involves offences which have an affective dimension (violent offences, for example).

To add to this, Tim Newell, a prison governor, wrote about the impact of restorative justice practice in prison and pointed to promising conclusions with respect to violent perpetrators (Newell 2007). Interestingly, Leibmann and Wootton (2010) were commissioned by Her Majesty's Prison Cardiff in the UK to investigate the possibilities of restorative justice for intimate partner violence to see whether or not there was scope to develop further programmes in prisons. Their review covered a range of existing intervention programmes (including the Freedom Programme for Men, the Integrated Domestic Violence Abuse Programme based on the Duluth Model, and the Healthy Relationships Programme). They also looked at voluntary sector led work and revealed, for example, that the Hampton Trust (2013), which works across Hampshire and the Isle of Wight to resolve violence and conflict, runs family group conferences to enhance family strengths in dealing with violence, including intimate partner violence. Other initiatives such as the Warwickshire Domestic Violence Support Service (Huckle 1998) have certainly included elements of restorative justice, but one project which has restorative justice at its heart is the *Daybreak Dove Project* which was set up in 2001 in Basingstoke and Deane (Hampshire). The project takes referrals for and from any family – using the broadest interpretation of intimate partner violence possible, where there is at least one child. The project involves family group conferences and, certainly between April 2006 and March 2007, there were reports by Hampshire Constabulary of success in terms of reducing crime reports about intimate partner violence (Liebmann and Wootton 2010).

On the other hand, *Respect*, which is the UK membership association for domestic violence perpetrator programmes and associated support services had earlier stated that 'Couples work, anger management, mediation and restorative justice are not appropriate responses to men's abusive behaviour to women' (Respect 2004: 16). However, there is no amplification of this statement within the *Statement of Principles and Minimum Standards of Practice.* Instead, emphasis within the statement suggests an agenda of responsibilization: 'men must be held responsible for their actions' – with the implicit assumption that restorative justice would facilitate avoidance of this.

Conclusion

A number of critics have raised concerns about the use of restorative justice for intimate partner violence (see, in particular, the chapter by Julie Stubbs in this volume). In my view, these are all answerable. For example, although it might be thought that women are unlikely to be able to assert their needs through restorative justice processes, 'kith and kin' or broader 'communities of care' might be mobilized to provide a forum in which victims can make clear the impact of violence against them and many women, for a range of reasons, wish to remain with their partners and not see them punished within the criminal justice system. What restorative justice processes envisage is encouraging women to make choices about their futures from a range of options which best suit them.

In summing up then, established criminal justice practices and the law have not speedily, convincingly or uniformly succeeded in ensuring women's safety and there are some promising results from empirical studies relating to the use of restorative justice in the context of violence. At the same time, there are a number of objections to using restorative justice, although many of these criticisms can be challenged and, even where there is widespread scepticism, there has been surprising support for restorative justice (from victim advocates, for example; see Victim Support 2010).

Needless to say, restorative justice is not a suitable option in all cases at all times. Many of the discussions about restorative justice are idealistic and, while empirical evidence on its usefulness for dealing with violence against women is very promising, there are consistent cautionary caveats about the need to take into account the specificities of individual cases, careful planning, and cultural perspectives. At the same time, it is also important to take account of women's preferences and the weight of evidence here, with the above caveat, is that female victims of men's violence see practical potential in restorative justice. But what is essential here is that restorative justice means more than symbolic reparation and that it delivers effective and safe outcomes.

Notwithstanding slow and ambivalent progress in England and Wales, there is now recognition that restorative justice may be a very useful addition to the panoply of provision for victims of intimate partner violence. How far this has come through involvement in international debates and exposure to international evidence and through practitioner-led initiatives is not clear. Non-governmental organizations have certainly played a key role in shaping policy (Women's Aid, Refuge and the Zero Tolerance Trust included). Feminist activism has also played a significant role in prompting debate, even if there has been ambivalence or opposition to restorative justice from some quarters. Some of the impetus for change in England and Wales has clearly come from European developments. Thus, *Section 7* of the new Victims' Code indicates that:

> The police must ensure that they provide the entitlements to adult victims of crime: the police must, where appropriate, offer or direct victims to information on restorative justice and how they can take part, assessing suitability based on the particular sensitivities of the case and/or the vulnerability of the victim, and ensure that safeguards are in place to ensure the victim is not re-victimized, particularly for victims of domestic or sexual abuse or violence (Ministry of Justice 2013).

Further, the Code implements relevant provisions of the European Union (EU) Directive (2012/29/EU) which establishes minimum standards on the rights, support and protection of victims of crime, Directive 2011/92/EU which combats the sexual abuse and sexual exploitation of children, and Directive 2011/36/EU which prevents and combats the trafficking of human beings.

Moreover, late amendments which led to the Crime and Courts Bill 2012 and the resulting Crime and Courts Act 2013 added 'meeting the needs of victims' to the aims of restorative justice and allows the courts to defer sentence for restorative justice in order to give practitioners time to find out if all parties consent to it (House of Lords Hansard column 1440–43). Slow, sure, but promising progress.

How long intimate partner violence will remain a priority is perhaps open to question in light of the election of regional Police and Crime Commissioners in November 2012, whose role it is to identify policing priorities, alongside tensions between national and local government in terms of resources. The policy-making process in England and Wales is inescapably inherently political. This highlights the need to think about cultural specificity in trying to understand developments.

The steps taken to enshrine restorative justice as a possible response to intimate partner violence within both law and policy are hugely significant, but there is further to go in ensuring sustainable resourcing for restorative justice practice. There is also further to go in terms of evaluating strategies and practices in whole-scale rather than piecemeal fashion. It is also to be hoped that this will not be a case of two steps forwards and three steps backwards in the context of government attempts to reduce expenditure. There have been ongoing attempts to measure the costs of intimate partner violence (Walby 2009), but the human cost of not facilitating restorative justice as a response to intimate partner violence may be greater.

References

Association of Chief Police Officers. 2011. *Restorative Justice Guidance and Minimum Standards*. Available at: http://www.acpo.police.uk/documents/criminaljustice/2012/201208CJBARJMinStd.pdf.

Bush, T. and Hood-Williams, J. 1995. *Domestic Violence in a London Housing Estate*. Home Office Research Bulletin, No. 37, 11–18.

Carlen, P. 1992. Criminal Women and Criminal Justice: The Limits to, and Potential of, Feminist and Left Realist Perspectives, in *Realist Criminology*, edited by R. Matthews and J. Young. London: Sage, 51–69.

Crown Prosecution Service. 2010. *Violence against Women Crime Report 2009–10*. London: CPS Management Information Branch. Available at: www.cps.gov.uk.

Department of Health, Social Services and Public Safety Northern Ireland. 2005. *Tackling Violence at Home – A Strategy for Addressing Domestic Violence in Northern Ireland*. Available at: http://www.dhsspsni.gov.uk/tackling_violence_strategy.pdf.

Department of Health, Social Services and Public Safety Northern Ireland. 2008. *Tackling Sexual Violence and Abuse – A Regional Strategy*. Belfast: Department of Health, Social Services and Public Safety.

EU. Directive 2011/36/EU. *Preventing and Combating the Trafficking of Human Beings*. Available at: http://europa.eu/legislation_summaries/justice_freedom_security/fight_against_trafficking_in_human_beings/jl0058_en.htm.

EU. Directive 2011/92/EU. *Combating the Sexual Abuse and Sexual Exploitation of Children*. Available at: http://eur-lex.europa.eu/LexUriserv/LexUriserv.do?uri=OJ:L:2011:335:0001:0014:EN:PDF.

EU. Directive 2012 29/EU. *Establishing Minimum Standards on the Rights, Support and Protection of Victims of Crime*. Available at: http://eur-lex.europa.eu/LexUriserv/LexUriserv.do?uri=OJ:L:2012:315:0057:0073:EN:PDF.

Featherstone, B., Rivett, M. and Scourfield, J. 2007. *Working with Men in Health Care and Social Care*. London: Sage.

Hampton Trust. 2013. Available at: www.hamptontrust.org.uk/key-issues/domestic-abuse.

Harwin, N. 2006. Putting a Stop to Domestic Violence in the United Kingdom: Challenges and Opportunities. *Violence against Women*, 12, 6, 556–68.

Hester, M. and Westmarland, N. 2005. *Tackling Domestic Violence: Effective Interventions and Approaches*. Home Office Research Study 290. London. Home Office.

Home Office. 2003. *Restorative Justice: The Government's Strategy*. London: Home Office.

Home Office. 2005a. *Domestic Violence: A National Report*. London: Home Office.

Home Office. 2005b. *National Domestic Violence Delivery Plan*. London: Home Office.

Home Office. 2006. *Code of Practice for Victims of Crime*. Available at: http://webarchive.nationalarchives.gov.uk/+/homeoffice.gov.uk/documents/victims-code-of-practice.html.

Home Office. 2009. *Together We Can End Violence against Women and Girls: A Consultation Paper*. London: Home Office.

Home Office. 2010. *Call to End Violence to Women and Girls*. London: Home Office.

Home Office. 2011a. *Crime in England and Wales 2010 to 11: Crime Statistics from the British Crime Survey*. Available at: https://www.gov.uk/government/publications/crime-in-england-and-wales-2010-to-2011.

Home Office. 2011b. *Call to End Violence to Women and Girls: An Action Plan*. London: Home Office.

House of Commons, Home Affairs Committee. 2008. *Domestic Violence, Forced Marriage and 'Honour'-Based Violence*. Sixth Report of Session 2007–08. Vol. 2: Oral and Written Evidence. Available at: http://www.publications.parliament.uk/pa/cm200708/cmselect/cmhaff/263/263ii.pdf.

House of Lords, Hansard 1440–43. 2013. *Crime and Courts Bill 2012* (Royal Assent given 25 April, 2013).

Hoyle, C. 1998. *Negotiating Domestic Violence*. Oxford: Clarendon.

Howe, A. 2006. New Policies for Battered Women: Negotiating the Local and the Global in Blair's Britain. *Policy and Politics*, 34(3), 407–27.

Howe, A. 2008. Violence against Women: Rethinking the Local-Global Nexus in Feminist Strategy, in *Women, Crime and Social Harm*, edited by M. Cain and A. Howe. Oxford: Hart Publishing, 37–55.

Huckle, W. 1998. *Mediation and Domestic Violence: The Process or the Principle*. Workshop at Mediation UK Annual Conference, Sheffield, June, 1998.

Hudson, B. 1998. Restorative Justice: The Challenge of Sexual and Racial Violence. *Law and Society*, 25, 237–56.

Kelly, L. 1999. *Domestic Violence Matters: An Evaluation of a Development Project*. Home Office Research Study No. 193. London: Home Office.

Liebmann, M. and Wootton, L. 2010. *Restorative Justice and Domestic Violence/Abuse*. A Report commissioned by HMP Cardiff 2008 but updated in April 2010. Available at: http://www.rjc.org.uk/resource/restorative_justice_and_domestic_violenceabuse/#.UXocjc0f8no.

Matczak, A., Hatzidimitriadou, E. and Lindsay, J. 2011. *Review of Domestic Violence Policies in England and Wales*. London: Kingston University and St George's, University of London, 1–28.

McNeill, F., Raynor, P. and Trotter, C. 2010. *Offender Supervision: New Directions in Theory, Research and Practice*. Cullompton: Willan Publishing.

Ministry of Justice. 2012. *Restorative Justice Action Plan for the Criminal Justice System*. Available at: https://www.gov.uk/government/uploads/

system/uploads/attachment_data/file/162277/restorative-justice-action-plan.pdf.pdf.

Ministry of Justice. 2013. *Draft Code of Practice for Victims of Crime (published in accordance with section 33 of the Domestic Violent Crime and Victims Act 2004)*. Available at: https://www.gov.uk/government/uploads/system/uploads/attachment_data/file/182037/victims-code-consultation.pdf.

Mirrlees-Black, C. 1999. *Domestic Violence: Findings from a New British Crime Survey Self-Completion Questionnaire*. Home Office Research Study No. 48. London: Home Office.

Newell, T. 2007. Face to Face with Violence and its Effects: Restorative Justice Practice at Work. *Probation Journal*, 54, 227–38.

Respect. 2004. *Statement of Principles and Minimum Standards of Practice for Domestic Violence Perpetrator Programmes and Associated Women's Services*. Available at: http://www.respect.uk.net/data/files/old_site/Respect%20Statement%20of%20Principles%20and%20Minimum%20Standards%20of%20Practice%202004.pdf.

Restorative Justice Council. 2013. Available at: www.restorativejustice.org.uk/news/rsqmconsultation/#.UXmFr80f8no.

Scottish Government and the Convention of Scottish Local Authorities. 2009. *Safer Lives: Changed Lives. A Shared Approach to Tackling Violence against Women in Scotland*. Available at: http://www.scotland.gov.uk/Publications/2009/06/02153519/0.

Scourfield, J. and Dobash, R. 1999. Programmes for Violent Men: Recent Developments in the UK. *Howard Journal*, 38, 128–43.

Sherman, L. and Strang, H. 2007. *Restorative Justice: The Evidence*. London: The Smith Institute.

Smart, C. 1989. *Feminism and the Power of Law*. London: Routledge.

Smart, C. 1995. *Law, Crime and Sexuality: Essays in Feminism*. London: Sage.

Strang, H. 2002. *Repair or Revenge: Victims and Restorative Justice*. Oxford: Oxford University Press.

Tyler, T. and Lind, E. 1992. A Relational Model of Authority in Groups, in *Advances in Experimental Social Psychology*, edited by M. Zanna, vol. 25. San Diego, CA: Academic Press. 115–91.

United Nations (UN) Women. 1995. The United Nations Fourth World Conference on Women, Beijing, China – *Action for Equality, Development and Peace: Platform for Action*. Available at: http://www.un.org/womenwatch/daw/beijing/platform/plat1.htm.

Victim Support. 2010. *Victims' Justice: What Victims and Witnesses Really Want from Sentencing*. London: Victim Support.

von Hirsch, A., Bottoms, A., Burney, E. and Wikström, P-O. 1999. *Criminal Deterrence and Sentencing Severity*. Oxford: Hart Publishing.

Walby, S. 2009. *The Cost of Domestic Violence Update 2009*. Lancaster University. Available at: www.lancs.ac.uk/fass/doc … /Cost_ofdomestic_violence_update.doc.

Walklate, S. 2004. *Gender, Crime and Criminal Justice*. 2nd edition. Cullompton: Willan Publishing.

Welsh Assembly Government. 2005. *Tackling Domestic Violence: The All Wales National Strategy*. Cardiff: Welsh Assembly Government.

Welsh Assembly Government. 2010. *The Right to Be Safe*. Cardiff: Welsh Assembly Government. Available at: http://www.wiga.gov.uk/english/equalitypublications/welsh-assembly-government-the-right-to-be-safe.

Chapter 11

Restorative Practice with Family Violence

Julia Hennessy, Mike Hinton and Natalia Taurima

Introduction

We write this chapter from the joint perspectives of practice and management in social work, community work, corrections and restorative justice. Although from different backgrounds, each of us has the community's interest at heart and together we believe we can contribute to the debate on the practical aspects of using restorative justice for family violence. In particular, we aim to provide a practice perspective regarding the benefits and risks involved. To take this discussion forward, we address three key questions and include relevant case examples where applicable. These are:

- Can restorative justice be an effective and safe intervention for addressing family violence?
- What components need to be in place to ensure any risk is minimized?
- How can restorative justice processes assist in reducing the risk to vulnerable people and in the development of a safety plan?

Our aim is to add practitioners' perspectives but, in writing this chapter, we were informed by the practice guidance available in both New Zealand and England and Wales (since Julia Hennessy has considerable experience of and expertise in both jurisdictions). These are, respectively, *Restorative Justice in New Zealand: Best Practice* (Ministry of Justice 2004) and the *Best Practice Guidance for Restorative Justice Practice* (Restorative Justice Council 2011). Both sets of guidelines refer to family violence, but it is suggested in the New Zealand document that restorative justice processes should only being undertaken '*in appropriate cases*' and family violence is referred to as '*sensitive and complex*' in the England and Wales document. Both place a high priority on the specialized skills level and knowledge of facilitators, safety and participants' fully informed consent before participating in a restorative justice process. There are some slight differences in emphasis, however. Although both documents refer to risk assessment processes, the later England and Wales guidelines formalize this by including them in its guidelines (Restorative Justice Council 2011). The England and Wales document also cites the importance of continuity in the handling of cases by the facilitators whereas the New Zealand document states that participants *may* require some form of follow-up after the conference (Ministry of Justice 2004: 17). The England and Wales document (Restorative Justice Council 2011) also specifies compliance with child protection legislation and regulations whereas the New Zealand document refers specifically to restorative justice not being a substitute for the criminal justice system (Ministry of Justice 2004: 27). In both documents, therefore, there is awareness of broad contextual issues.

Can Restorative Justice be an Effective and a Safe Intervention to Address Family Violence?

Through our collective experience, we have found that restorative justice can be used safely in family violence cases. However, we qualify this by emphasizing that this is based on *our* experience. Using the guidelines and developing our own, we have invested considerable effort in ensuring that participants are thoroughly willing, prepared and supported in the 'before', 'during' and 'after' phases of the process. In this chapter we share some of the cases which have provided us with opportunities to develop increasingly effective and safe practice.

In New Zealand, having a restorative *hui* (discussion/meeting) before the restorative process can provide a starting point for an effective intervention. The use of a restorative process cannot stand in isolation and be deemed successful without effective follow-up programmes or courses, monitoring and the implementation of programmes that address all of the harm and its implications.

Facilitating a *hui*/conference that deals with family violence can work well, but it depends on the information available to the facilitators, the *whānau* (family) involved, their level of support and how thorough the facilitators are. The preparation for these *hui* can be intense and detailed to ensure that all aspects such as seating, eye contact, body language, support for both parties and the possibility of intimidation are addressed prior to the meeting. Furthermore, these factors must be monitored by the facilitators throughout the *hui*.

When the referral is received, a brief assessment of the information is made to establish whether or not it concerns family violence. Once this is confirmed, good practice requires the facilitators to then make contact with relevant local service providers who specialize in this field (Ministry of Justice 2004: 19). The nature of the offence and the complexity of the issues that surround family violence make it essential that this expertise is available to assist the facilitators to ensure the meeting is safe for all parties. A family violence expert and practitioner can then work together to ensure that any manipulation by the perpetrator is detected. This will ensure the process and participants are supported appropriately, thus enabling them to express themselves clearly and to contribute to the development of a plan that ensures safety, full involvement and ownership by all parties. This is especially important if the couple intend to remain together and/or when children are involved. The secondary function of the family violence expert is to ensure that all present, including the facilitators, are fully conversant with what constitutes family violence, the misuse of power and intimidation and its impact on victims. (For a different perspective on power in intimate relationships, see Chapter 18 by Anne Hayden.)

Trust is an important factor, often not discussed, but nevertheless essential to participants' feelings of safety and confidence in the facilitators and the restorative process. Trust can be built in many ways including meeting face-to-face pre-conference. Also helpful is having a female and a male facilitator present at a pre-conference meeting when the needs and requirements of the victim are heard; the facilitators being available to answer participants' questions; and not having participants wait too long before the conference. If a victim has to wait with the perpetrator for a prolonged period, it can cause anxiety and further stress. On occasions, when it is a difficult case, it is necessary to have participants arrive separately and wait in separate rooms before the conference starts. It is important, therefore, that the facilitators work through these steps carefully.

Having a pre-conference meeting with the perpetrator and his/her family or support is just as crucial so that they, too, are aware that the meeting will take place in a safe environment. They need to know that they will have the opportunity to be heard, to apologize, and to be part of a process which will explore options, including any rehabilitation s/he has undertaken or that is required.

Case One

This case involved a young couple, where the victim was *Pākehā* (a person of predominantly European descent) and the perpetrator was Samoan. The perpetrator was very jealous and controlling of his partner. Due to his last attack on her, she sustained injuries to her head and was also on anti-depressants for anxiety and depression. The facilitator worked with the victim, her sister and her mother, meeting and communicating with them several times as the victim was often forgetful due to her injuries. Through this communication, a connection was built. The facilitator asked the victim and her sister to prepare in writing what they wanted to say to the perpetrator. To assist with her anxiety about how the conference would be run, the perpetrator was asked who would be attending the conference to support him, to ensure his supporters understood the role they had at the *hui*. This included the possibility of challenging the perpetrator if there were any instances of him minimizing his behaviour. By the time the conference was organized, the victim, her sister and their mother were prepared to meet the perpetrator as they all had a lot to say.

The co-facilitator and the perpetrator developed a rapport, the perpetrator sharing with him information about his past, the violence he had endured and witnessed as a child, his violent behaviour and his abuse of alcohol. In light of this information, the co-facilitator managed to talk to the Pacific Liaison Officer who was able to confirm that he would work alongside the perpetrator to support his acceptance into a 'living without violence' programme and an alcohol and drug programme. Through this process with the co-facilitator, the perpetrator was able to think about his offending, his inclination to behave violently and the consequences of his offending. This ensured that the perpetrator came to the conference prepared to listen, to take responsibility and to change.

The *hui* was a success, not only due to the amount of time taken in preparation, but also due to both parties being willing to listen. The family was very angry at the perpetrator and articulated this. The perpetrator was very respectful to the victim's mother and sister. At the end of the conference, the victim's mother and her sister expressed their support for the perpetrator and accepted his apology. They were content with the actions he was undertaking to deal with his violence.

What Components Need to Be in Place to Ensure any Risks Are Addressed?

As outlined above, preparation and understanding the dynamics of all of the participants and the *whānau* are critical. Guidance from experts also helps to ensure any risks are identified and decisions are made about how to manage and address these in advance. Aspects of preparation for all conferences that are especially important for family violence cases are:

- The venue must be comfortable and acceptable to both parties.
- Participants need to know that they can stop the conference at any time.
- Facilitators must ensure that both parties have consented voluntarily and have not been coerced into participating.
- Perpetrators should be advised that any undertakings they make are realistic – for example, saying they will pay reparation of $10,000 might not be appropriate for someone on an unemployment benefit.
- Perpetrators are advised to think about what they are prepared to do to make good the harm and victims are advised to consider what they would accept from the perpetrator before the conference.
- Perpetrators need to know that the victims and family may be very emotional.
- Perpetrators need to know that, if the conference is held pre-sentence, there are no guarantees that the court will follow the recommendations of the conference.

Cultural dynamics and cultural diversity can play a large part in how the conference should be facilitated in New Zealand. This is where understanding people's differences, beliefs, values and acknowledging and working within those parameters is very important. If a facilitator knows what these cultural differences are and is able to address all aspects of the parties' cultural diversity in an inclusive non-threatening manner they are better equipped to provide the opportunity to repair harm in a manner that best suits all participants. Importantly, it is worth noting that cultural dynamics and diversity can include but are not specific to ethnicity. There are times when two European nationalities or a European and a non-European are involved in a conference. In these situations, a process which is most comfortable for both parties should be used.

Cultural diversity and dynamics between Europeans are just as important as between *Māori* and *Pākehā*: for example, Croatian and Serbian are both European but they are culturally different, as are the English and the Scots. One practical way in which cultural differences can be seen in New Zealand is in the use of *karakia* (prayer) at the beginning of a meeting which is often considered to be a part of *tikanga* (protocol) *Māori*. On the other hand, this could be regarded as the result of the colonization of *Māori* and the adoption of religious practices which have evolved through time to become a cultural dynamic relating to *Māori*. Another way cultural diversity can be demonstrated is in bringing *kai* (food) to share when the conference stops for a break. Similarly, when *Māori* visit a *marae* (meeting house), they take a *koha* (gift), usually money, which is customary behaviour for *Māori* but may not always be understood by non *Māori*.

The same applies with venues. If the victim and the perpetrator are comfortable in a *marae* then it appropriate to hold the restorative justice conference there. But if this does not suit any of the parties another venue must be used. If there is any concern over venue the victim's wishes are prioritized. The perpetrators' agreement to the victims' venue requirements is a step towards taking responsibility for their actions. However, there are also other considerations. The following case example shows that the process needs to allow plenty of time for reasons relating to medical factors concerning the parties.

Case Two

The victim and perpetrator are sister and brother. Both have been through the mental health services. Currently the perpetrator (the brother) is spiralling out of control due to not taking his medication and the abuse of alcohol and illicit drugs which fuel his tendency to act violently. The victim (his sister) had pulled her life together and was currently employed. On the day in question, they had both been at home when the perpetrator assaulted her. The impact of the assault was serious and required hospitalization. As the perpetrator was under the mental health services, the facilitators made contact with his primary caregiver, his mother, and included their *whānau ora* (programme to look after a family's well-being) social worker. The pre-conference meeting with the perpetrator was to allow him to familiarize himself with the facilitators. Due to his mental state the facilitators needed to work slowly so that they did not confuse or frustrate him.

The issue in this *whānau hui* (family meeting) was not only the violence but the damage caused by his offending to the whole *whānau*. The victim and perpetrator are obviously linked by *whakapapa* (genealogy) and their mother was asked to make a choice of who would live with her: her daughter and *mokopuna* (grandchild) or her son who was still under mental health services and unwell. This was the choice given to her by the criminal justice system in the form of a bail condition that the perpetrator could not associate with the victim, his sister. This was not, for him, a realistic option. The bail condition was breached as the mother refused to make the choice set out above. Instead, her daughter threw herself into her job and only came home once she knew her brother was settled, allowing her mother to continue to look after her son.

What also made this case more complex was that, prior to the conference, the perpetrator had justified his offending against his sister by saying she deserved it. He believed it was her fault that their father had died as a result of a violent incident in their home. In that situation, the daughter had called the police because her father was assaulting her. While being detained by the police, the father had died.

The conference ended with the perpetrator expressing remorse for his actions and the victim accepting his apology. While this seems straightforward and an expected outcome, the remorse of the perpetrator was highly questionable and his comprehension of what was right and wrong could be called into question. The conference outcomes for the professionals involved, however, were much more significant as they gained a better insight into the needs of the victim and the perpetrator as well as a clearer understanding of the family dynamics that had not really been considered until this point.

The victim remained unsure of the perpetrator's sincerity and, while she was able express in the conference how she felt, she was not convinced that her safety and that of her family was ensured. She still had some major concerns about her brother.

A point of interest from this case is that this was regarded as a 'normal' offence – referred from the District Court by the presiding judge. On this occasion, however, the facilitators had invited a judge who specialized in mental health to observe the conference. Afterwards, the judge expressed major concerns that the criminal justice system had paid so little regard to the perpetrator's mental health. The judge did not, however, have concerns about the case being referred for a restorative justice conference.

This case highlights some of the complexities that often occur in family violence situations and how they offer learning opportunities to professionals working in the criminal justice system. There are often issues around addictions, mental health, and intergenerational violence, each of which needs special consideration.

How Can Restorative Justice Processes Assist in Reducing the Risks to Vulnerable People and in Developing a Safety Plan?

As already mentioned, the preparation and planning prior to a conference with all parties is like a brainstorming session between facilitators. It is essential that they understand the community and, in particular, the families they are going to be working with. They also need to be familiar with the services available in that community to use as part of the outcome or safety plan or throughout the process. It is also important that the method and approach used is one that all participants will respond to. If facilitators are working in a community with a large cultural and ethnic mix, it is up to the facilitators to educate themselves on the variances of the culture and the implications of these for the conference. Vulnerability is shown in different ways by different cultures.

Case Three

The charge was assault with intent to injure and was the result of an altercation between a brother (the perpetrator) and his brother-in-law (the victim) which resulted in the victim being stabbed, just missing his heart. In this case, the most vulnerable persons were the victim's wife/ the perpetrator's sister and the perpetrator's mother/the victim's mother-in-law.

The perpetrator's sister was desperate to communicate with her brother but was fearful of any repercussions since the criminal justice system had forbidden both she and her husband any association with the perpetrator. She was caught in a dilemma because she wanted to support her husband, but she also wanted to see her brother. Other vulnerable people were the *tamariki* (children) of both these men, who, as first cousins, were divided by a fight that stemmed from alcohol and an out of control uncle/father. What further complicated this matter was that the perpetrator's father was also responsible for intergenerational violence and sexual abuse within the family and was later charged and incarcerated for these offences. This was not due to any disclosures at the restorative justice conference.

A number of interventions and strategies were used when dealing with this *whānau* to ensure that the sister was safe at all times and that the mother was able to engage with both *whānau* without any incrimination. These included a *hui* within the *wharenui* (meeting house), the inclusion of a *kaumātua* (respected elder) and *karakia* before and after the *hui*. Once the victim and perpetrator had spoken and listened to each other, they were able to embrace as *whānau* and share *kai*, which, for *Māori*, is an important part of the healing process. The agreed safety plan was that the *whānau* would collectively take some responsibility for moving on so that the victim's wife would be happy and the children of both families could grow up knowing each other. Also relevant is that one family was moving overseas a week after the conference.

The facilitators must thoroughly plan a conference before it takes place. No conference should be a template and every conference needs to be managed according to its own specific characteristics, considerations and needs. When it is done this way, an opportunity for restoration is provided. The *mana* (status, spiritual power) of a victim is restored, the *mana* of a *whānau* name is restored, and perpetrators are provided with an opportunity to restore their *mana*. This is the beauty of restorative justice.

Conclusion

Thus, in relation to the three questions we set out at the beginning of this chapter, from our experience we believe that restorative justice processes can be effective and safe interventions for addressing family violence provided key participants are willing, thoroughly prepared and supported, they trust the facilitators and experts in family violence are enlisted throughout the process. In addition, the components set out under our second question must be complied with as minimum requirements for safe conferencing, while meeting cultural needs. Restorative justice can be an ideal forum for obtaining collective input into and agreement on a safety plan which can reduce further risk to vulnerable people, particularly victims and children.

In conclusion, the three cases discussed in this chapter give an indication of the diversity and complexity of situations which can come to a restorative justice service provider. They also demonstrate very clearly the responsibility held by facilitators to enlist the help of family violence experts, an aspect which cannot be over-emphasized. It is also important for practitioners, academics and policy makers alike to remember that one of the major attributes of restorative justice is that it provides hope: restoring hope that the situation can get better, that victims and perpetrators can get help, and that the cycle of intergenerational violence can end.

References

Ministry of Justice. 2004. *Restorative Justice in New Zealand: Best Practice.* Wellington: Ministry of Justice.

Restorative Justice Council. 2011. *Best Practice Guidance for Restorative Justice.* London. Available at: www.restorative.justice.org.nz.

Chapter 12
A Pacific Perspective on Restorative Justice: The Power of Saying 'Sorry'

Marie Ropeti

Introduction

A definition of restorative justice from a Samoan perspective encapsulates 'relationship' in all its meanings. One of the most significant concepts in the *Fa'a Samoa* (Samoan Way) is that people conduct their lives according to the unwritten principles of the space between two people '*va*', which, in its simplest form, means the maintenance of relationships between people, between *aiga* (extended family), between villages, between districts and, finally, between people themselves. It embraces culture, spirituality, gender arrangements and the healing of relationships.

Examples of these systems include extended families, churches, the traditional *matai* (chief) system and the community. Samoans are keen to seek ways where people can work together to seek positive outcomes for victims and perpetrators, especially within the Samoan context. The aim of this chapter is to identify the values of *ifoga* (submission ceremony seeking forgiveness) as complementary to those values that are essential to healthy, equitable and just relationships. It cannot be emphasized too strongly that process and values are inseparable in restorative justice, because the values determine the process and the process makes the values visible.

Different cultural and ethnic communities may employ different processes in order to actualize common restorative values and achieve similar restorative outcomes. The Samoan culture is a social system in which the *ifoga* values and processes are displayed. Unless we understand the Samoan culture as such a social system we will not understand why *ifoga* is important in reconciliation. For Samoans the use of *ifoga* is very common and has been used in many criminal cases to resolve conflicts. This chapter offers a brief description of the *Fa'a Samoa* and *ifoga*. It explores the impact of *ifoga* in the social system that determines how Samoan people act and what they believe is possible. It gives a glimpse of how restorative justice can change the landscape of criminal justice.

Fa'a Samoa

Fa'a Samoa is an all-encompassing concept that dictates how Samoans are meant to behave. It refers to the obligations that Samoans owe their family, community and church and sense of Samoan identity. The concept of respect is very important. You must always respect your elders; this includes those older than you, *matai*, ministers, politicians, doctors and teachers. This unquestioning demand for respect is taking its toll in modern Samoa. The younger generation, which is invariably better educated than its predecessors, constantly finds itself trying to balance the demands of a conservative Samoan society with its knowledge of the world, increasingly gathered from overseas education and experience. This has led to one of the highest suicide rates in the world (Cote 1997). *Fa'a Samoa* is evident in the legal system which is actually two separate systems, a Western style system administered by a police force and justice department and a traditional system administered at a village level. The two systems do occasionally come into conflict with one another but generally things work smoothly enough (*Samoa Observer* 1997).

Matai System

The word *matai* means chief and is an honour that is bestowed upon someone. The role of the *matai* is very complex and interwoven deep into the fabric of Samoan culture and history. *Matai* have family, civic, political and, prior to the arrival of the European, religious duties to perform. A *matai* title can be given to either men or women, although you will find far more men with titles than women. It is usually given to someone in acknowledgement for services that have been rendered. A family might give a title to a relation who has been able to support them through hard times or a village might give a title to someone who has done something of benefit to the village as a whole. Until recently only *matai* could vote in parliamentary elections, but, even today, only *matai* are eligible to seek parliamentary office. Furthermore, there are different ranks in the *matai* system.

Within each village every family has a *matai* who is a member of the *Fono* (council) and represents the interests of the family. The *Fono* is responsible for administering justice within the village and can pass down a wide range of judgements upon a perpetrator. The leader of the *Fono* is called the *ali'i*. The *ali'i* was considered to be far too important to be bothered with actually discussing people's problems and so the position *tulafale* (talking chief) arose. The *tulafale* acts on behalf of the *ali'i* at social occasions, ceremonies and in discussions with other villages and external bodies (Vaai 1999).

Aiga

In Samoa, the *aiga* (extended family) is all important. Every village is composed of several *aiga* and the larger the *aiga*, the more important it is and the more power it can wield in village affairs. This usually leads to healthy competition between *aiga*. Samoan families are generally large; it is not unusual for there to be 12 or more children. Traditionally, members of the family would work the land that was allocated to them by the *matai*, but now it is increasingly common for families to encourage their children to work in Apia so that they can earn a wage. There are now more Samoans living outside of Samoa than in the islands themselves. Most of these send money back to their family on a regular basis (Samoa Economy 2013).

Religion

Religion is one of the most important aspects of Samoan culture, to the extent that it is incorporated in Samoa's motto: '*Samoa is founded on God*'. Like most of the other Pacific Islands, it was neither governments seeking colonies nor traders looking for new opportunities who were responsible for most of the early contact. It was the churches seeking to introduce Western philosophies and standards of morality for the benefit of Indigenous peoples. However, there is a rule in every Samoan village that the church and the village council do not interfere in each other's business.

The arrival of Christian missionaries in the early 1800s saw the rapid spread of Christian ideals and education through the introduction of mission schools, the translation of scriptures and hymns into the Samoan language, and the training of local pastors. The missionaries accepted and utilized the *ifoga*. Indeed, its importance became enhanced. As quarrelling and aggressiveness were discouraged, it became all but obligatory for an offended person to accept the abasement of the *ifoga* with its accompanying compensation as a sincere Christian humility. This was sufficient to heal the wound or breach caused by an offence.

Central to the *ifoga* is the Christian element of forgiveness. John William, a pioneer missionary from the London Missionary Society, arrived in Samoa in 1830 and was instrumental in effecting some change to the Samoan culture. The concept of forgiveness was emphatically taught, simultaneous to the widespread conversion of the villagers with the result that Christianity altered the nature of *ifoga* to some extent. Prior to the Christian era, the execution of the perpetrator's *aiga* during an *ifoga* ritual was justified if their apology was not accepted by the victim's *aiga*. However, through Christian teachings, the punishment of death for serious offences was abolished. In many *ifoga* today, the minister of the church goes with the *ifoga* party in an attempt to induce the receiving party to accept the *ifoga* peacefully and quickly. Today in Christian Samoa, it is extremely rare for an act of *ifoga* to be rejected. The extent and strength of Christian values has had a major influence in the acceptance of *ifoga*. A refusal to accept a traditional apology from the wrongdoers would be considered un-Christian, unforgiving and in profound, spiritual terms, a repudiation of Jesus Christ's sacrificial act through which he died to forgive the sins of mankind.

Ifoga

Ifoga is a centuries-old formal traditional submission ceremony involving the perpetrator (Pratt 1911: 49). In this form of exchange, one group submits to a ritual and public humiliation in return for forgiveness by the perpetrator's family (Milner 1976: 82–3). The *ifoga* demonstrates remorse by begging for forgiveness from the victim and their *aiga*. The ceremony is significant both as a social and an economic activity because the successful performance of the *ifoga* prevents the escalation of socially and economically disruptive inter-group conflicts.

Ifoga as a submission ceremony is considered an act of surrender and true repentance. A serious crime committed involving a death or near death and any crime involving major injuries to the body is considered severe (Stair 1983: 96). For such cases a very important part of the submission is the use of a *toga* (fine mat) covering his/her head demonstrating respect for the family of the abused. A fine mat is a unique and a special material, made from a pandanus tree, which has been hand-woven. It is the most valued possession of the Samoan culture. It is also used for many occasions such as weddings, funerals, festivals, dances, higher rank gatherings and other traditional events.

The exchange of speeches and gifts acknowledges the damage done to the social honour of the offended person or party and how it is restored by the ceremony. The Samoan society has a comprehensive set of procedures aimed at managing conflicts. Disputes within families are typically resolved in mediations between representatives of various sides of the extended family that are led and directed by the *matai* leader of the extended family. Mediations usually take place after the *matai* have informally canvassed the opinions and possible solutions with those involved at the centre of the matter. Their speeches remind those involved of the harm caused to the group's reputation. The availability of a basis for saving face provides the opportunity and need to protect the group's reputation from those who could capitalize on its misfortune and also provides another motive for a resolution.

Disputes between families within a village have serious social and economic consequences for villages generating similar concerns. When minor issues, often between individuals and households, escalate, other larger entities may be drawn into the conflict. Where villages become divided for long periods of time, economic and social cooperation is also made more difficult and the well-being of its constituent families can be compromised. *Matai* from the village council, which is composed of the chiefs of all families, typically mediate in these matters. This body has the authority to prevent, and a vested interest in preventing, the escalation of intra-village disputes. Unresolved conflicts bring their ability to manage their village into question and can make the village, their influence and their authority a matter of public discussion.

Contemporary society has, however, brought changes, often with less positive outcomes when it comes to a dispute. More recent forms of disputes occur frequently as larger numbers of unrelated people routinely come together in sports events, work places, nightclubs, markets and on public roads. Conflicts periodically arise between unrelated individuals, often as the result of motor vehicle accidents, workplace disagreements and nightclub brawls. Unlike disputes within families and villages, involving perpetrators who are known to one another and unfolding over time, these events typically develop suddenly and cannot be monitored and managed. In these situations, the perpetrators may have no common interests or associations that mediators might invoke as the basis for reconciliation.

These days, a mere apology may not be considered a big deal, but an apology with a fine mat gives formality and sincerity to the occasion because of the importance of its value to the Samoan people. The involvement of a high chief *matai* may be indispensable depending on the seriousness of the crime. If the offence is severe, the high chief *matai* of the perpetrator's village will have to perform the *ifoga*. When the high chief is involved, sometimes he/she would take with him/her the lower ranked chiefs of the village for security.

The Act of Ifoga

The perpetrator and the village high chief quietly get up long before the sun rises without any kind of prompt or announcement and make their way to the village, carrying with them the finest of fine mats. The perpetrator or the high chief will then kneel and bow down to the ground covering himself/herself with the very fine mat sitting in front of the family's house or at the open space where major village functions take place. Usually this is on sand, dirt or on the sharp coral rocks that decorate the front of many houses in Samoa. They will stay with no food or water and in all weathers, be it the scorching heat or pouring rain for as long as it takes for their apology to be accepted, which could take hours.

If the apology is not accepted by the victim's family, this village high chief or the minister of the village will often step in and accept the apology on their behalf, essentially forcing forgiveness. Samoan wisdom is usually good about acknowledging the advantages of peace over war. With this acceptance, the perpetrator who has spent hours under the fine mat is invited, along with his/her family, into the house of the victim's family. The victim's family would speak to demonstrate the sincerity of their forgiveness. The traditional *ava* drink (a ceremonial beverage shared to mark a formal occasion) and prepared food will be served by the victim's family. After the encounter with the victim's family, the perpetrator and family are released with the promise that no further retribution will be sought.

The *ifoga* remains an essential part of Samoan culture as a demonstration of sincere remorse and respect. The court and the victim's family may consider using a mediator based on the victim's family acknowledgement of *ifoga*. Where else in the world can crimes of murder be forgiven with a fine mat and a sorrowful heart? The *ifoga* demonstrates humility as Samoa's most prized possession. Forgiveness brings peace.

Challenges of Ifoga

Stewart's research into *ifoga* (1975: 183) confirmed that, in practice, the outcomes were largely restorative. All those involved participated (though this was true for only about half the victims) and agreed with decisions, and the decisions focused largely on the repair of harm and the reintegration of perpetrators. However, there were some notable departures from good practice. For example, while some victims felt truly involved in the decision-making, restrictive/punitive outcomes were noted in some *ifoga*, with the rehabilitative and integrative aspects of *ifoga* falling well short of the needs of the victims and the perpetrator.

In Samoa today, *ifoga* continues to provide a vehicle for reconciliation in circumstances where other means of reconciliation are unavailable and in which quick, decisive and public actions are required to prevent escalation. But the return of Samoans who have lived abroad and the pervasiveness of mass media have increasingly encouraged people to think of themselves as members of non-traditional communities, such as youth, women, gay, disabled or transgendered people and union members. This trend has led in turn to discussions of the interests and rights that attach to membership of these social categories, appropriate means of advancing their interests, and the ability of traditional institutions to reflect and represent them. There is now more broad-ranging discussion of these issues than previously. The same forces have produced an increased focus on individual rights defined in universal conventions.

When, for instance, a young, well-educated woman was raped in a village in Savai'i, the rapist's family immediately performed an *ifoga* that was accepted by the young woman's family. While banishment of the man, the gifts and apology and its acceptance resolved matters between the families and alleviated tension within the village, it did little to resolve the victim's sense of personal violation and hurt. Against the advice of the chief *matai* in her family who considered the matter closed, the young woman sought redress for personal violation to her as a woman. A charge was laid with the police and the alleged rapist was subsequently tried, convicted and imprisoned for the rape. Discussions about her decision revealed divided opinions. Some construed her actions as an affront to her family and specifically to its chief *matai*, who had already accepted the apology on her behalf. In taking this action, she was seen to be publicly challenging their authority and, specifically, their right to determine the seriousness of an affront to one of their members and the appropriate remedy – to accept an apology and to effectively end the matter.

Others judged her decision appropriate and reasonable. They argued that the *ifoga* had resolved the matter of the affront to the honour of one family by another and had restored relations between the families involved. While they accepted the restorative element of the *ifoga*, they argued that its effect was confined to the restoration of relations between communities. It did not, they argued, resolve the dispute between the woman and the man.

Samoan village rejected ifoga of banished family

Culture should never be used as an excuse for undermining the application of justice or used to invoke 'soft' options in response to offending. In the midst of significant changes when culture is shifting dramatically, people often feel something is wrong but cannot identify what it is. It is common to assume that such feelings, tensions and anxieties provide a sufficient basis to initiate change in a culture. The following case presents us with an example.

A former cabinet minister and his family were ordered to leave the village of Vaimoso Apia, Samoa (*Samoa Observer* 2009) after a traditional apology or ifoga presented by the family of the perpetrator to the village was rejected. Preceding events were as follows.

Thirteen years earlier, the perpetrator was ostracized because he called a village meeting without the right authority to do so. Recently, village spokespersons stated that he took part in the bestowal of the village Paramount title on three persons. Again as the perpetrator, especially one married into the village, he acted beyond his authority. He was also accused of brandishing a gun over a land dispute. More recently, the perpetrator was banished from Vaimoso for 'unfounded' statements he made to the media concerning the reason for his ostracism in 1999.

The perpetrator refused to leave. The village council then decided to mete out a punishment called '*mu le foaga*', where one's house and belongings are burnt. Fortunately, ministers of religion and the police intervened, after which the matter was referred to court. The Vice President of the Land and Titles Court advised both parties to review and reconcile the matter.

'You are making the Head of State sad,' he said. 'The Head of State is a son of the village; you should reconcile and renew.' The perpetrator was ordered in court to apologize to the village, which he did. But the village did not accept his apology. Vaimoso's high chief requested the court to allow the village more time to discuss its advice, which the court accepted. While the villagers met in Vaimoso after leaving the Land and Titles Court, the perpetrator's *aiga* presented an *ifoga*.

But after the family and three ministers sat in the blistering sun for almost two and a half hours waiting for a response, the spokesperson for Vaimoso said the *ifoga* had been rejected. The ultimate outcome was for the perpetrator, his wife and children to be banished from the village of Vaimoso. It was clear that the spokesman only responded because he respected the ministers who were present. He apologized to them for the decision of the village explaining it was not a rejection of them but a rejection of the perpetrator. If the ministers had not been present they would not have responded at all and just let the perpetrator bow his head all day.

The role of the church in the village is to assist its parishioners when in trouble. Obviously this was the case for the ministers and the perpetrator in Vaimoso. But it did not mean that the village had to accept the perpetrator's *ifoga*. The perpetrator knew that the usual way was to leave the village and then instigate reconciliation later on. The point of the rejection was simple. For 13 years this man had not had the humility to offer his *ifoga*, only finally doing so because the court told him to. This is not true *ifoga*.

Police, the court and ifoga

The police and courts constrain the rights of communities to resolve matters with the performance of the *ifoga*, continuing to investigate and prosecute offences even when informed that an *ifoga* has been performed and accepted. Even privileged members of society whose families have performed *ifoga* have been charged by the police. For example, after the family of a pastor who killed a child in a motor vehicle accident performed an *ifoga* on his behalf, the pastor was tried, convicted and fined. Macpherson and Macpherson (2005: 125) commented: 'This is not to say that the courts ignore the significance of the ifoga, which is recognised as part of the legal system of Samoa.' They cited Sir Guy Powles (2004) who described the *ifoga* as:

> A legal process within the customary law domain of Samoa's dual legal system. It is a process based upon Samoan law which preceded European contact with the islands, and which is preserved by the independence constitution of Samoa 1962, and recognised today by the formal courts (Powles 2004: 2, cited in Macpherson and Macpherson 2005: 125).

In court proceedings, lawyers routinely report *ifoga* and other forms of reconciliation offered to the court and ask to have these taken into account by the court. Magistrates also routinely ask, usually in cases involving violence against the person, whether or not reconciliation has been attempted, and they may take any reconciliation by families into account in sentencing. In some cases, these petitions have resulted in reduced sentences.

In other families, a further discount would be acknowledged if the dispute was within a single *aiga* extended family, the remorse was genuine, *matai* or senior family members took some responsibility and there were good prospects of permanent reconciliation. However, judicial discretion is exercised in determining whether or not the apology is genuine and whether either the withdrawal of charges or a sentencing discount is appropriate, a factor borne out by recent decisions where the court has set aside requests to have *ifoga* considered as mitigating factors.

In the recent past, senior members of the Samoan Government, the Samoan Supreme Court and the Samoan Law Society have expressed interest in the alternative dispute resolution systems being devised and promoted by the Fiji-based Pacific Judicial Education Program. This excludes lawyers and employs three sets of procedures that can provide faster, less expensive and less public resolution of disputes outside the courts (*Samoa Observer* 2004). If these systems are adopted and established, they may provide an additional and less expensive option to the *ifoga*.

There are clearly limitations in traditional dispute resolution procedures with respect to social and individual affirmation. The challenges are prompted by a number of factors: growing individualism and egalitarianism combined with other social and political changes have constrained the ability of traditional institutions to resolve disputes. In these circumstances, the court necessarily becomes an adjunct to traditional processes *ifoga*. However, restorative justice reflects a philosophy practised by Indigenous peoples for thousands of years which, in my view, should underpin appropriate modern processes (Consedine 1995).

Where restorative processes form an unbroken tradition as in Samoa, they may exist independently of the criminal justice system and provide a culturally oriented alternative to deal with disputes, other than those legislated as offences (Ministry of Justice 1996). In these circumstances, the courts are likely to become increasingly significant sites for the resolution of disputes about social honour. It is possible that the *ifoga* will continue to exist alongside civil and criminal actions as at present and judges may continue to take the performance of *ifoga* into account in sentencing decisions. If this occurs, the role of the *ifoga* will have changed substantially. It will no longer be the sole form of dispute resolution in such cases, but an adjunct to the process which will be played out, not in one place at one time, but at several places at different times. Thus the parties to the dispute will calculate what is to be exchanged for what in one context and, later, the perpetrator and the court will determine what is to be exchanged for what in another context. This has obvious implications for the *ifoga*.

Ifoga and Samoans in New Zealand

Samoans have emigrated to New Zealand since the turn of the twentieth century (Connell 1983). Today, Samoa and New Zealand-born Samoans play an increasingly important part in New Zealand's multicultural society. Previous research by the Polynesian Advisory Committee of the Vocational Training Council (1985) has found that the Western Samoan community in New Zealand has attempted to transmit its traditional Samoan values and social structures to the New Zealand context. This transmission of culture has not, however, been without modifications and concessions (MacPherson and Pitt 1974).

In New Zealand, Samoans are holding fast to their language, God, cultural practices, customs and beliefs. Established Samoan communities have organized themselves around their churches, where the church congregation becomes akin to a Samoan village. The difference, however, lies in the fact that, because these church-centred communities comprise people from different villages, a power struggle amongst *matai* of that congregation to assert their status exists. This struggle can spill over into ceremonial observances like the *ifoga*.

Because of proximity, the importance of blood *aiga* and the concept of village (as it exists in Samoa) are predominantly lost in the Samoan communities in New Zealand. This does not mean that the *ifoga* becomes lost as a custom for Samoan people there. The dynamics of the *ifoga* as performed in New Zealand are vastly different from that performed in Samoa; however, the same spirit of genuine apology underlies it.

Restorative processes in a traditional justice environment can achieve the goals set out in restorative philosophy of fairness, responsiveness, participation, accountability, forgiveness, healing and reintegration. Furthermore, at least within New Zealand, the use of a restorative approach is an effective alternative to the use of the harsh and punitive responses that are so often damaging to all who are directly involved and to the health of the wider society. *Ifoga* in Samoa is very different. In Samoa, customary practices survive alongside the introduction of modern Western justice systems. However, the customary practices display both restorative and highly punitive elements. The demands of *ifoga* can be harsh compared to that of the diversionary restorative practices that have emerged in New Zealand. Nevertheless, *ifoga* is an example of how customary practice can moderate the impact of the traditional Western justice system in ways that allow consideration of both compensation for victims and an emphasis on forgiveness and can lead to restoring the balance of relationships within the wider community.

A Newspaper Report of a Case in New Zealand

> New Zealand's court system should 'educate itself' on the Samoan ritual of ifoga forgiveness when sentencing Samoans for violent crime, says a community leader, Fa'amatuainu Tino Pereira. On Monday, a Samoan minister and his wife were sentenced to two years in prison after admitting 22 counts of assault, neglect and cruelty over two years against eight adopted or foster children in their care.

That ifoga had occurred and family differences resolved the 'Samoan way' was a key part of submissions made to the judge by family members at the sentencing. Fuimaono Tuiasau, for the mother, said that in three family meetings the couple had apologised 'for the pain and suffering they had endured' and asked the children for forgiveness. At the last one, following a passionate plea, one of the children accepted on the others' behalf.

Mr Pereira, who chairs the Samoan Advisory Council, said the use of ifoga was not really appropriate in this case because it involved children. Nevertheless, it should not be disregarded by judges. The court system needed to look to other ways of sentencing, he said. Ignorance of the ritual in courts threatened its existence. It could be a basis for judges to consider alternatives to prison, and look to sentences which might benefit the Samoan community. Ifoga was traditionally used in cases of extreme violence, Mr Pereira said. The chief of the perpetrator's family would go to the home of the victim's family and kneel, for up to a day, before forgiveness occurred or he was killed. But, such killings happened rarely now.

The two-year jail sentence was an appropriate deterrent, said the judge. Sentencing, Judge Craig Thompson said he took into account that ifoga had occurred to reconcile the family, but he viewed it as parallel to the legal process (*New Zealand Herald*, 27 July 2000).

Case Study

A Samoan dancing group travelled to New Zealand in 2005 to fundraise for the village church. The group of 20 young men and women, led by four matai, was hosted by a church in West Auckland. During the time of their four weeks stay, performances were held every night around Auckland and members of the group enjoyed meeting families and friends they had not seen for a long time. During one performance, a man from the host church assaulted a man from the dancing group. The man from the dancing group was badly injured, needing hospitalization. The police were called but no complaint was laid. On Sunday morning, as members of the host church arrived for worship, they were met with an *ifoga* at the front of the church. The dancing group from Samoa with the four *matai* were all sitting on the ground bowing their heads with the injured man (who had by then discharged himself from the hospital) under the fine mat. The minister and elders of the host church were taken aback and asked what was happening. After speeches of welcome and the begging for forgiveness from both sides, everyone went into the church for more deliberation. After the service of worship, the host church provided a shared lunch.

As it turned out, the man who assaulted the member of the dancing group was very angry because he was told that the man from Samoa had been sleeping with his wife. When the *matai* from Samoa heard what had happened, they quickly sent word to the injured man, who was still hospitalized at that time, not to say anything to the police. He was asked to find his way to the church early the next morning.

After deliberations and the two communities coming together in a form of reconciliation, there was no need to take this case any further. The injured man was returned to the hospital for more treatment and the church at West Auckland paid his hospital fees.

Conclusion

Ifoga as a concept is a form of restorative justice and must be integrated within the current system unless it is to appear as some inferior form of justice. If restorative justice were introduced, it should be an integral part of the criminal justice system, partly in order to get consistency and fairness, but also as a means of holding hearings and conferences out in the community, away from the formal and perhaps intimidating atmosphere of courts and government departments. If established properly, *ifoga* would help us get away from our heavy reliance on the courts and would make perpetrator /victim-initiated restorative justice a reality.

Restorative justice is about changing the way in which we view crime. It is about identifying the damage caused to relationships within the family and other members of the community. It also provides opportunities to repair that damage. It is about challenging the premise of fixing blame in order to exact retribution and focusing instead on the responsibilities and obligations of all those concerned to make good the damage, restore right relationships and bring about reconciliation. This cannot be achieved unless the current criminal justice system takes on board these fundamental changes in philosophy. For this reason it is essential that restorative processes such as *ifoga* are integrated and not kept outside the criminal justice system (New Zealand Catholic Commission for Justice and Peace 1995).

Incorporating restorative justice programmes as part of the criminal justice system may make it more effective. Not only does this mean that existing resources can be used, reducing the possible expense of implementing the programmes, but it also gives the programmes legitimacy that will encourage perpetrators and victims to take advantage of them.

References

Connell, J. 1983. *Migration: Employment and Development in the South Pacific.* Noumea: South Pacific Commission.

Consedine, J. 1995. *Restorative Justice: The Healing Effect of Crime.* Christchurch: Ploughshares Publications.

Cote, J.E., 1997. A Social History of Youth in Samoa: Religion, Capitalism, and Cultural Disenfranchisement. *International Journal of Sociology*, 38, 217–34.

MacPherson, C. and Pitt D. 1974. *Emerging Pluralism: The Samoan Community in New Zealand.* Auckland: Longman Paul.

Macpherson, C. and Macpherson, L. 2005. The Ifoga: The Exchange Value of Social Honour in Samoa. *The Journal of the Polynesian Society*, 14(2), 109–34.

Milner, G.B. 1976. *A Dictionary of the Samoan Language.* London: Oxford University Press.

Ministry of Justice 1996 *Restorative Justice. A Discussion Paper.* Available at: http://www.justice.govt.nz/publications/publications-archived/1996/restorative-justice-a-discussion-paper-1996.

New Zealand Catholic Commission for Justice and Peace.1995. *Submission 84* to Ministry of Justice Call for Submissions on Discussion of Restorative Justice 1995. Available at: www.catholicjusticeauckland.org.nz.

New Zealand Herald, 27 July 2000.

Polynesian Advisory Committee of the Vocational Training Council. 1985. *Understanding Polynesians.* Wellington: Vocational Training Council. 7.

Pratt, George. 1911. *Pratt's Grammar and Dictionary of the Samoan Language.* Apia: Malua Printing Press.

Samoa Economy. 2013. *CIA World Factbook.* Available at: https://cia.gov/library/publications/the-world-factbook.

Samoa Observer, 23 November 1997. Available at: www.samoaobserver.ws.

Samoa Observer, 15 June 2004. Available at: www.samoaobserver.ws.

Samoa Observer, 14 March 2009. Available at: www.samoaobserver.ws.

Stair, J.B. 1983. *Old Samoa or Flotsam and Jetsam from the Pacific Ocean.* Papakura: McMillan.

Stewart, W.J. 1975. Ifoga: The Concept of Public Apology, the Family and the Law in American Samoa. *Journal of International Law and Economics*, 10, 183–96.

Vaai, Saleimoa. 1999. *Samoa Faamatai and the Rule of Law.* The National University of Samoa, Le Papa- I Galagala, Apia: National University of Samoa. Available at: digitalcollections.sit.edu/cgi/viewcontent.cgi?article=1635andcontent

PART V
Restorative Justice and Family Violence – Research Findings

Empirical evidence about whether or not it is appropriate to use restorative justice to help couples and their families who are experiencing family violence is key to making restorative justice more acceptable. At present, academic critics, policy makers and victim advocates are limiting its use because they state that there needs to be empirical evidence to substantiate that it is not detrimental to victims. As long as critics maintain this stance, service providers and practitioners are reluctant to take the risk. This creates a 'catch 22' situation whereby there are minimal opportunities to obtain empirical evidence.

This part contains four chapters comprising largely previously unpublished empirical studies. These include Venezia Kingi's qualitative data from victims and perpetrators of family violence who participated in restorative justice and from key informants (Chapter 13) and Anne Hayden's commentary on the views of victims and perpetrators of intimate partner violence who had not experienced restorative justice on the feasibility of using it in such cases (Chapter 14). Gale Burford and Joan Pennell provide in Chapter 15 a brief literature review and then an in-depth case study about fathers, family violence and restorative justice; and in Chapter 16 Kathleen Daly and Dannielle Wade describe their research on sibling sexual violence and restorative processes.

Much of the previously published research literature presents the views of practitioners and academics. This part focuses on the voices of victims and perpetrators. These are an important contribution to the debate on restorative justice and family violence and thus go some way towards filling a gap and take us closer to the possibility of using restorative justice processes to deal with family violence.

Chapter 13
The Use of Restorative Justice in Family Violence: The New Zealand Experience

Venezia Kingi

Introduction

This chapter contributes to the ongoing debate about the potential of restorative justice processes to deal with conflicts within families by presenting the findings of some New Zealand research (Kingi et al. 2008). The aim of this research[1] was to review the delivery of restorative justice processes in family violence and to describe the experience of and outcomes for victims and perpetrators who participated. By asking perpetrators about family violence, it is possible to assess the extent to which they recognize the harm caused by their actions and whether or not they are committed to changing their behaviours as a result of the restorative justice process. Seeking the views of victims, on the other hand, enables us to gauge whether or not they perceived that changes had actually happened. The research involved interviewing 19 victims and 19 perpetrators who had taken part in face-to-face restorative justice processes delivered by community providers at five New Zealand sites[2] during the period January 2005 to June 2006. Eleven of the victims and perpetrators were involved in the same incident and so comparisons can be made between their respective perspectives.

Sample Characteristics

Most of the 19 victims were female (16) and most of the 19 perpetrators were male (14). There were similar proportions of *Māori* and New Zealand European participants (each made up approximately half) though a few participants identified

---

1 The review was part of a larger project being undertaken by the New Zealand Ministry of Justice to further investigate the nature, extent and effectiveness of the use of restorative justice processes in family violence.

2 The five sites were chosen on the basis of the volume of family violence cases handled by restorative justice service providers and included two in the North Island (Mangere and Levin) and three in the South Island (Nelson, Christchurch and Timaru). One was an Indigenous provider, three involved community panels and three were pre-sentence. One was pre-trial diversion.

as Pasifika (four) or 'other' (five). Participants were mainly under the age of 40 and similar proportions were employed or receiving benefits (approximately one-half). There were no same-sex couples.

The nature of the relationships between the victims interviewed and 'their' perpetrators was mainly that of a current (10) or ex-partner (5). Other relationships included siblings, children, parents and in-laws. The most serious offences were, in order of frequency: male assaults female, common assault, threatening act/behaviour, conspiracy to commit murder, assault with intent to injure, grievous bodily harm and wilful damage. Relationships between the perpetrators interviewed and 'their' victims were similar. Again, most were either current (seven) or ex-partners (six). The most serious offences were, again in order of frequency: male assaults female, common assault, threatening behaviour, arson and assault with intent to injure.

Views of Victims and Perpetrators

The primary focus of this chapter is to describe how victims and perpetrators experienced restorative justice panels/meetings for offences involving family violence and their views on the suitability of such processes for dealing with family violence. We consider each step of the restorative justice process, starting with the preparatory stages, through the meeting process to the outcomes or agreements decided at the meeting.

Safety

The safety of participants at the restorative justice meetings was of paramount concern to the facilitators. The providers' consideration of safety issues began with their assessment of the suitability of the perpetrators and victims to take part in a restorative justice process. If the facilitator had any safety concerns, the meeting would not go ahead. An additional safety element introduced by one provider was the presence of a police representative and, at another, the presence of support people for both the victim and the perpetrator was mandatory. At a third site, all participants were required to sign an agreement saying that they would abide by the rules set down for the meeting. There was a specific protocol setting out the areas to be discussed with the victims and perpetrators prior to the restorative justice process taking place. The facilitator's experience and ability was considered crucial when dealing with family violence referrals. If the victim said she or he felt unsafe, the facilitator would stop the meeting and the perpetrator would be returned to the court to be dealt with there.

Approximately one-third of victims (six) said that they had been asked whether or not they had any concerns for their safety if they attended a meeting.[3] They

3 Another three victims (two women and one man) said that this was not an issue for them and five could not remember whether or not this had been discussed.

were also asked if they had been informed how their safety would be addressed during the meeting. Only three said that there had been a direct reference to this. What was discussed rather were the conditions under which the meeting could be curtailed and having support: 'At any point if I felt it was getting out of hand I could take a break or leave.' However, this did not mean that all victims had concerns; most assumed that they would be safe. Only two victims remembered any discussion of their safety when arriving at or after the meeting. One had been asked 'Do you think there will be any trouble afterwards?' Six (four women and two men) said that in their case there was 'no reason to discuss this'.

Even fewer perpetrators (three) said they had been asked if they had concerns for their safety. Perpetrators were asked if they had been told about any safety 'ground rules' governing the meeting and eight said that they had. These were basically: 'Zero tolerance of any abuse of any type' and 'If it got out of hand it was over.'[4]

Ten perpetrators and six victims remembered discussing with the facilitator at the preparation stage what the perpetrator could do to 'repair the harm'. This was described as 'Very briefly about the types of things people can do.' One of the female perpetrators also commented on the hurried nature of the process 'It wasn't very informative. Everything was real fast.' And as a female victim explained, 'you could be given all the information necessary yet still not be prepared'.

The Meeting

First impressions Victims and perpetrators were asked what they thought the restorative justice meeting was trying to achieve. Common understandings were that the meeting was designed:

- to talk about what had happened incorporating both points of view;
- for the perpetrator to realize the impact of what s/he had done and be made accountable;
- to come to some resolution over the offending – to repair the harm and to help the perpetrator and victim so that this would not happen again.

Victims and perpetrators were also asked how they felt when they first went into the meeting. Approximately half of all victims (13) and perpetrators (11) reported feeling anxious, nervous or apprehensive. However, a few (five victims and four perpetrators) said that they had felt positive or hopeful about what was going to take place.

4 Three perpetrators (two women and one man) said that this was not an issue in their cases, three said there had been no direct reference to safety rules and four could not remember being told about this.

Participation Victims and perpetrators were asked various questions about their meeting. It is clear from the data that, for most victims and perpetrators, the restorative justice meeting was a positive experience. Almost all understood what was happening and felt involved. For example, one victim said 'Oh yes I think it really does aim at the victim.' However, another who said that she had only felt 'partly' involved was angry at how she had been treated:

> There were times when I felt totally not involved. [They were] talking about [perpetrator] rationalising and minimising his behaviour. It made me really angry. I began to think who is this focussed on? It was more to do with [perpetrator's] recovery than mine and I was just the witness.

Victims and perpetrators, in the main, felt that they had been treated with respect. Only one female victim had anything negative to say: 'I wasn't treated as the victim, not at any stage.' Similarly, almost all victims and perpetrators had had the opportunity to say what they wanted. Most perpetrators also thought that they had been given a chance to explain their actions. One man who did not said: 'They had a preconceived idea I'm negative, a bad person. Nothing I could say made a difference.' Most victims felt able to articulate the effects of the offence on them; one woman explained: 'I was able to say what I wanted to say and how I felt without getting too stressed out.'

Perpetrators generally felt they were treated fairly and most said that they had felt ashamed of what they had done. One man said poignantly: 'Watching my mother cry was hard to handle. It made me feel ashamed for what I had done.' Only two perpetrators felt that they were dealt with as if they were 'a bad person'. On the other hand, if those saying that this had happened 'to some extent' are added, more than a quarter (five) of the perpetrators (four men and one woman) felt that they had been treated in this way. The following is illustrative of what they said: 'In some bits I did. I felt guilty when I was explaining my actions. It felt like I was being made out to be a caveman type of thing – bop her and take her back to the cave.'

Only one victim and one perpetrator said that someone dominated the discussion. Few victims or perpetrators said that they were too scared to say what they really felt but two victims said that they felt unsafe emotionally. One explained: 'You've been frightened, your senses are heightened, you can misconstrue what is said.' One of these women also reported feeling too scared to say what she really felt. She explained: 'You feel subdued, you have to be polite and keep it civil.'

Some perpetrators (nine) and victims (seven) said that they had support with them at the restorative justice conference and almost all of these victims and perpetrators said that this had been helpful. Only four victims and three perpetrators said that they would have liked more support. The same numbers (eleven) of victims and perpetrators said that someone (usually a supporter, the facilitator or a panel member) spoke up for them in the meeting. The lack of support was not always a negative factor. 'It wasn't needed. The panel were supportive in that they heard what we had to say and talked to us about [our] emotions ... I appreciated that.' One male perpetrator described the meeting as evoking – 'a bit of everything – happiness, sadness, crying – it was quite an emotional thing.'

Impressions at the end of the meeting When asked how they felt by the end of the meeting, most reported feeling relieved and positive about the experience. The following quotes exemplify their comments:

> I left thinking, man, I've got a lot to do! Let's get into it; I want to get it done.

> You've got to want to acknowledge yourself as the offender and that you have done wrong and who the victim is and you need to make serious changes.

> I was quite happy and relieved that we'd gone through that. It had been dragging on. It had happened about two months before.

However, some victims (three) were dissatisfied with the process and others (three) had concerns about what would happen next. In the words of one: 'I felt bewildered – thought what was that about? I was expecting some back and forth and talking things through. It didn't happen.' In a case where the meeting broke down, the victim said 'I felt furious.' And a female perpetrator commented: 'I was left flabbergasted; feeling as if things weren't fully resolved. We were made aware that if we wanted to stop the meeting that was fine but it was just the way it was done.'

Whether or not the meeting had had a productive outcome, victims' feelings towards the perpetrator had rarely changed. Several said they were 'still angry' and even those who had forgiven the offender to some extent had not forgotten what had happened: there was still a lack of trust. The remarks of one female victim sum up how these victims felt: 'I had a really horrible taste in mouth. But I play the game, he was really happy but I stewed on it. I'm still not over it. I felt that was over the top and he got away with it as usual.'

Perpetrators viewed things somewhat differently. One example: 'I didn't have as much animosity towards her as I did previously. I got to see it from her perspective. I don't think her feelings had changed. I was appreciative she had supported this instead of me going to jail.' One young man, who had committed a serious offence against members of his *whānau*, had this to say: 'I felt sad for them [victims] because of the pain I'd caused. I realized I needed to change if I wanted a chance of reconciliation.'

Good and bad features of the restorative justice meetings Victims and perpetrators were asked to identify any 'good' or 'bad' features of the meeting. Their opinions were, in the main, positive. Sixty-three per cent of victims (12) said that there were no 'bad' features.

By far the most common 'good' features identified were the open dialogue and the healing process that occurred in a non-judgemental environment. The following quote from one female victim illustrates the sort of comments made: 'It was relaxed. I was tense. When we went in we were embarrassed by our actions and why we were there. We were frightened we might get judged. But it was okay. It was nice to have people there from the community that I knew.' Being able to meet the perpetrator in a safe supportive environment was also mentioned by victims as a good thing. They appreciated that people were willing to offer help and that the perpetrator could be made accountable without going to prison. Some victims also spoke positively of the facilitators or panel members.

The most commonly mentioned 'bad' features were victims feeling unsupported or being made to feel that they were to blame for the offending, or that the meeting did not achieve anything – there was no resolution. One victim did not like the venue and another felt pressured to contribute. She remarked: 'You shouldn't feel pressurised to respond if you weren't confident responding. It put you on the spot sort of. I had a little bit to say but it was like they were expecting more.'

As with the victims, perpetrators mentioned 'bad' features of the meeting less frequently than 'good' features. However, four perpetrators reported things that they were unhappy with and these included: the meeting not resolving anything; not being given a chance to speak without interruption; and being made to feel bad. One male perpetrator was angry about the process and commented: 'I was not supported, made to feel bad, not treated with respect.' He also said that the meeting had no 'good' features.

By far the most common 'good' features identified by perpetrators were that the meeting had enabled them to put things right or provided a starting point for this by allowing them to meet with the victim. The next most commonly mentioned were 'feeling supported', being 'treated with respect' and the fact that the process had been 'well organised'.

Approximately half of the victims and the perpetrators said that overall they were 'very satisfied' with the meeting. Most participants said that they were satisfied to some extent, although perpetrators (16) were more likely than victims (14) to report this. In fact, two victims (one man and one woman) said that they were 'very dissatisfied' with the meeting. One remarked: 'It made me feel worse.'

The Agreement

Reaching agreements The restorative justice meetings held for family violence in three of the sites resulted in agreements which perpetrators were required to complete before the disposition of their case, whereas in two sites a report was provided for the sentencing judge, who could choose to incorporate all or part of the agreement into the perpetrator's sentence. In community panel diversion referrals, a report went to the police prosecutor who could withdraw the charges if the agreement was fulfilled by the perpetrator.

Fourteen victims and fourteen perpetrators had taken part in restorative justice processes which resulted in 'formal' agreements: an agreement or resolution had been reached at all of these meetings. In most cases, the people identified as coming up with the details of the agreement were the panel and the facilitator. In the words of one respondent: 'They came up with ideas as we went along. We had the chance to agree.' All victims and perpetrators said that they could remember at least some of what was in the agreement and that they had understood what needed to be done. However, the following remark made by a female victim signals that in some cases such 'collaborative' processes may be unintentionally coercive:

> I felt a bit swept along. I had to go along with it – trying to come up with all the answers to turn the situation around. I was probably a little self-sacrificing for the greater good; to heal him and us. It was not what I needed. He was not made accountable; I put my own needs aside.

Agreements reached at these restorative justice meetings consisted of a variety of tasks. They were, in order of frequency: attendance at programmes (twelve), relationship counselling (ten), community work (six), a social activity (five), reparation (four), apologies (four), donations (two), not to act violently (two) and work for the victim (one). The facilitators undertook most of the monitoring of the perpetrator's compliance with the tasks in their agreement. None of the perpetrators had failed to undertake the required components of the agreement, although some were still involved in programmes or community work at the time of their interview. However, sometimes the social activities that were suggested as a way of 'repairing the harm' were impossible to undertake for those on limited incomes.

Views of agreements and outcomes More than two-thirds of victims said that the perpetrator had apologized to them at the meeting. Similarly, most perpetrators said that they had apologized at this stage. Apologies were usually accepted. Perpetrators (13) were more likely than victims (six) to say that they had understood how the victim felt about the violence. However, one perpetrator who admitted he had not been able to understand made the following comment: 'To be honest no I didn't. I know what had happened – she did say to me, that because she feels safe around me it hadn't damaged her. But she was quite upset. It's hard to put yourself in someone's place.' Despite this fact, almost two-thirds of victims said that they felt the perpetrator had been made accountable for what s/he had done. However, five (two men and three women) categorically stated that this was not the case. In the words of one victim: 'Not at all. And the worst part about it was after that meeting they withdrew the charges and I never got told why.' Although some victims felt that the perpetrator had made up for what s/he had done, others were less sure. And almost half (seven women and two men) stated unequivocally 'no' when asked this question.

Good and bad features of the agreements Victims and perpetrators were specifically asked to identify the 'good' and 'bad' features of the agreement. All victims and all but one of the perpetrators had something to say about 'good' features. Most often mentioned by victims and perpetrators were attendance at a programme or involvement in counselling. Reaching an agreement was referred to by three victims and one perpetrator. Receiving apologies was mentioned by three victims and being able to apologize was mentioned by one perpetrator. One victim said it was good 'that the perpetrator did not go to prison'; one offender said that he and his ex-partner 'were friends again'; and, as another offender remarked, 'It brought closure and created a starting point to move on.'

Only a few victims (five) commented on the existence of any 'bad' features in the agreement. These were: that the perpetrator got off too lightly ('He would come home from community work and talk about how cushy it was'); it did not reflect the victim's concerns; and, in one case, it made things worse ('Him having to pay me a set amount of money (for medical expenses) fired it up and made things worse.') Even fewer perpetrators commented on 'bad' features in the agreement.

Perpetrators (13) were more likely than victims (9) to say that the agreement was 'about right'. Three female victims felt that it was 'too soft'; as did one female offender who commented: 'I should have been put onto a programme to change my behaviour.' One male victim said it was 'too harsh': 'By that stage [the incident] had all been forgotten.'

After the Meeting

Satisfaction with the restorative justice process Seventeen of the victims and 16 of the perpetrators said that they were pleased they had taken part in the restorative justice meeting. One perpetrator said he was 'partly' pleased he had participated. The female and male victims who disagreed were frustrated that there had been no formal outcome or had thought that the meeting would have been more constructive. The female victim stated: 'I suppose, part of me felt it was good but part of me felt it was a waste of time. Apart from him apologizing, that was pretty much all that happened.'

All perpetrators and 16 victims said that they would recommend restorative justice processes to other victims and perpetrators to deal with family violence. Two victims said they would 'partly' recommend it. In fact, almost four-fifths (79 per cent) of victims said that they would take part in the process again should the need arise. A further two said it would 'depend on the circumstances'. However, three female victims said that they would deal with things differently if there was a 'next time'. As one put it: 'I wouldn't even bother calling the cops. I would walk out the door and go. I did it to set boundaries. I don't want to see him in jail; it just makes things worse.'

Eleven victims and the same number of perpetrators said that as a result of participating in the meeting they now felt 'better' about the incident. It had enabled them to deal with the issues and get closure. Eight perpetrators said they felt 'no different' and that they still felt bad about what had happened.

Similarly, five victims said that they felt 'no different' about the incident and that they were still not happy about what had happened. Two said they felt 'worse'.

In one case, the meeting had broken down and, in the other, the victim had not been happy with the outcome of the meeting.

Taking responsibility for the offending Victims were more likely than perpetrators to think that the perpetrators still needed help to address their violent behaviour. Most perpetrators said that they had got help or were involved in the process of getting it. Yet clearly victims still thought this was an issue. In fact, only two victims said they felt 'more safe' as a result of taking part in the restorative justice meeting. However, most said that safety was not an issue for them either because they no longer had a relationship with the perpetrator or they had 'never felt unsafe'. Others said that they felt 'no different', but that they were wary of the perpetrator.

Perpetrators were asked whether or not taking part in the restorative justice process had helped them take responsibility for their violence. The majority said that it had. Victims were asked whether the violence or abusive behaviour had stopped since the restorative justice meeting. Six said that it had. Another seven said that the violence had 'partly' stopped. They usually mentioned that it had changed in nature – it was no longer physical but there was 'lots of psychological stuff'. Five could not comment as they no longer had any contact with the perpetrator. Another victim said that she had finished the relationship because the violence did not stop.

Perpetrators were also asked what they had learnt about the effect of their behaviour as a result of participating in the meeting. Some said that they had learnt nothing new – they had always known it was wrong. However, others admitted that being confronted with their actions had had an effect. In the words of one: 'I still feel like an idiot for losing it. She was really scared and I was really angry. I felt sick about it.' Eleven perpetrators said that what they had learnt about their behaviour had affected their views of the use of violence or abuse. In most cases it was: 'a wake-up call', 'something that I know is not right' and 'I needed to change.' Two referred to lives characterized by violence and one woman reflected: 'I feel like violence has been part of my life for a long time. I've been sexually and physically abused. I grew up believing violence was a part of life – that's how you gain respect, but really you're only gaining fear.'

Appropriateness of restorative justice for family violence Finally, both victims and perpetrators were asked if they thought restorative justice meetings were a good way to deal with family violence. Their responses were mainly in the affirmative. All victims thought that such processes worked in the case of family violence although some qualified this. In the words of one: 'Yeah except for if there are people who are more violent, there should be more security. Someone who can contain the offender or it could get ugly.' Perpetrators held similar views. Again, in the words of one: 'Yes for the first one, it wouldn't work if it was an ongoing thing. Couples need to be given the opportunity if they want to stay together.'

Perpetrators' behaviour subsequently Victims were asked how the perpetrator had taken responsibility for his/her violent behaviour since the meeting. Approximately two-thirds had positive comments to make in this regard. The following is illustrative of what they said:

> He paid for his own counselling for eight sessions. He is trying – there's no more denials, he's more honest about things. He can't pretend there's not a problem and he's working through it. It was his whole upbringing – counselling started to open a can of worms – he's trying to heal himself. This thing brought it out into the open.

Five victims did not think the perpetrator had taken responsibility for the behaviour.

Perpetrators were also asked how they had taken responsibility for their behaviour since the meeting. More than three-quarters reported the strategies they now used. They included 'anger management', 'walking away' and 'time out'. One man explained: 'I guess thinking about relationships in general and if they don't work out control your behaviour and not to over react when things are beyond your control.'

Nature of current relationship between victims and perpetrators Victims were asked how their relationship with the perpetrator had been since the restorative justice meeting. Ten said that the relationship had improved. It was 'Really awesome. We just get along so much better.' However, one woman qualified her response: 'It's been all right but we both put lots of effort in.' Five said that it was something like the following: 'Up and down; some brilliant moments and some disastrous moments.' Three reported that they no longer had a relationship with the perpetrator.

Similarly, perpetrators were asked how their relationship with the victim had been since the restorative justice meeting. Twelve said that the relationship had improved although two qualified this: 'It got worse, then better' and 'It's functional now.' Four said that there was no longer a relationship. One remarked: 'It determined where our paths were heading and we both realised they were heading in different directions.' Two others said that it was 'too soon' to tell.

Views of Matched Victims and Perpetrators

Victims and perpetrators commonly view family violence differently, particularly in relation to any apologies given and remorse shown. They may also have different reasons for taking part in the restorative justice processes. This section explores the responses made by the 11 'matched' (that is, involved in the same incident) victims and perpetrators to some of the questions they were asked about the restorative justice process and outcomes.

All agreed that they would recommend the restorative justice process to others to deal with family violence. However, one victim qualified this as 'only for couples wanting to work on their issues.' Approximately three-quarters said they were pleased that they had taken part in the restorative justice process. Where there were different views, victims were more likely to have reservations than perpetrators. One male victim said that he was not pleased that he had taken part.

Perpetrators and victims also mostly agreed on the extent to which they needed information or support after the meeting. Where there was disagreement, the victims rather than the perpetrators said they would have liked more. One victim would have liked information on relationship counselling and the other wanted to be kept informed about whether the perpetrator had completed the tasks in the agreement.

Although almost two-thirds of the victims and perpetrators agreed that the perpetrator's apology had been accepted, there was some disparity in the views of the remaining third. Most responses varied in the degree of acceptance (that is, 'partly' versus 'yes'). However, in one case, the victim disagreed with the perpetrator who thought that his apology had been 'partly' accepted.

There was less agreement between victims and perpetrators as to whether the perpetrator had understood the effect of the violence on the victim. However, in one case, both the victim and the perpetrator agreed that s/he had not understood. Intuitively, one would imagine that the perpetrators said that they understood the victims' feelings and that the victims would disagree with this. This was so in three cases. In another two, however, it was quite the reverse. That is, the victims thought the perpetrators understood how the violence had affected them when, in fact, the perpetrators reported the opposite.

Similarly there was some disparity in the views of victims and perpetrators in relation to whether or not the perpetrator had been able to make amends for the offending. Victims were more likely to say that this had not happened, whereas perpetators were more likely to say that they had made amends to some degree or that it was not an issue.

In addition, more than half of the victims and the perpetrators had somewhat different views on how they felt about the violence now. However, there was no clear pattern. For example, in two cases, although the victims said that they felt 'better', the perpetrators said that they still felt bad about what had happened. In contrast, in a further two cases, the victims (one man and one woman) felt 'worse' and the perpetrators felt 'no different' (although this does not imply that they were not aware of the effects of the violence).

The area where there was the least agreement between the victim and the perpetrator was whether or not the perpetrator still needed help to address his/her violent behaviour. Victims were more likely than perpetrators to say that the perpetrator still needed help. Seven out of the eight victims who disagreed with 'their' perpetrator reported this. Perpetrators reported that they had dealt with the problem.

Nine of the 11 matched victims and their perpetrators agreed about the nature of their relationship since the restorative justice meeting. Six thought that the relationship had improved, one said that 'it was a work in progress' and two concurred that there was no relationship between them now. There was no pattern with the other two victims and perpetrators. In one case, the victim thought that the relationship was better, whereas the perpetrator considered the victim still to be angry with her. Conversely, in the other case, the perpetrator said that the relationship had improved and the victim said that there was no relationship between them now.

Conclusion

Notwithstanding their individual experiences, all perpetrators and most victims said that they would recommend restorative justice processes to other victims and perpetrators to deal with family violence. Approximately 80 per cent of the victims said that they would take part in the process again should they need to. All participants generally agreed that restorative justice meetings were a good way to deal with family violence, although some qualified this by saying it depended on those involved and the circumstances relating to the violence.

Family violence spans the continuum from less serious offences (such as wilful damage) to the most serious offences (such as rape and murder). The offences that participants in this review were involved in included those in the less serious to medium seriousness range in that they had not resulted in serious injury or required the victim's admission to hospital. Based on the findings of this review, particularly participants' levels of satisfaction with the processes and outcomes, it appears that the use of restorative justice processes is appropriate in such cases.

The dynamics of family violence are complex and the nature of the close and often ongoing relationship of the victim and the perpetrator further complicates this issue. The extent to which family violence can be addressed through a restorative justice meeting is likely to be only a small proportion of the many offences victims endure at the hands of the perpetrator. Zehr (2002) posits that restorative justice processes can provide a way of looking at offending which emphasizes the repair of harm and the offender's accountability, something that conventional court processes infrequently do. The findings of this research concur and indicate that restorative justice meetings for those who want to continue their relationships – be they partners, siblings or parents – combined with perpetrators' participation in violence intervention programmes, may lead to positive change. Similarly, restorative justice meetings may enable those who no longer wish to be in a relationship to gain some resolution and end the relationship on amicable or, at the very least, civil terms. This may be particularly relevant where there are children involved. However, findings from this review do suggest that in some cases collaborative processes may be unintentionally coercive and that victims put their needs aside 'for the greater good' to heal the family. Facilitators need to be aware of the potential for this and do what they can to prevent it.

Nevertheless, some points of consensus appear to be emerging: the importance of victim-centred processes; the need for well-resourced sustainable restorative justice programmes; facilitators trained and skilled in the dynamics of family violence/gendered crimes; the importance of comprehensive preparation and initial vetting processes; the availability of therapeutic programmes to address issues of violence; and last, but definitely not least, the safety of victims before, during and after the process. The findings of this research allow us to state that restorative justice processes, as one of a suite of potential responses to intimate partner and other forms of family violence, should continue to be offered.

References

Kingi, V., Paulin, J. and Porima, L. 2008. *Review of the Delivery of Restorative Justice in Family Violence Cases by Providers Funded by the Ministry of Justice*. Report prepared for the Ministry of Justice. Wellington: Ministry of Justice.

Zehr, H. 2002. *The Little Book of Restorative Justice*. Intercourse, PA: Good Books.

Chapter 14
Perpetrators' and Victims' Views of Restorative Justice and Intimate Partner Violence

Anne Hayden

Introduction

This chapter reports on research (Hayden 2010) which was conducted in New Zealand to examine the non-reporting of intimate partner violence to the police and to explore whether or not the use of restorative justice would increase reporting. The research was motivated by the awareness that couples experiencing intimate partner violence had few options open to them besides remaining in the situation or reporting the violence to the police and facing uncertain consequences.

Methodology

The research involved in-depth interviews, auto-ethnography and observation in two New Zealand courts that specialized in intimate partner and family violence. It comprised a small sample of non-randomized victims (eight) and perpetrators (six) who had experienced intimate partner violence, and 15 key informants who worked in the field of intimate partner violence (including victim advocates, judges, men's group leaders, restorative justice practitioners and cultural advisers). This chapter focuses only on the views of the victims and perpetrators. None had participated in a restorative justice conference and few had any knowledge of it. Therefore, research participants were given a scenario of a co-facilitated model where the victim and perpetrator each had support people, were taking part voluntarily, and the conference was held in a safe place.

Findings

Views on Non-Reporting

Of the eight victims, four had reported the intimate partner violence to the police. Only two of them were satisfied with the police response and one of these had experienced his intimate partner violence and reported it in the UK. Thus, only one of the eight victims was confident in or satisfied with the New Zealand criminal justice response to their experience. Despite the fact that half of them had reported the violence to the police, all victims gave reasons for not reporting. One victim became so adjusted to the behaviour that she became helpless and less able to talk about it:

> It was really mental rather than physical. I was never physically assaulted in any way … There [was] nothing to [report]. I supposed I wasn't valued as a person or my opinions weren't valued, and the person I was with set out, mainly in verbal [abuse] and in action, but not aggressive action, to demoralise me or belittle my position in the relationship.

A Chinese victim, despite her partner's harassment after she had taken out a protection order, was fearful that reporting him again would cause further loss of face for him and consequently would exacerbate the situation. Another victim, who knew what was happening was wrong, rationalized:

> [I]t was more threats, intimidation, emotional abuse, verbal abuse … If there had been a lot of real physical violence, then it [would have] been different. You know sometimes I'd think, you know, give me a good punch. I['d] have the scar, the black eye, the broken nose, whatever, and then I could go, you know?

A male victim who had been a victim for a long time finally telephoned the police. Their response to him was to inform him 'to be a man and leave the house'. No further support or action was offered. Although there was further abuse after this, he did not report it. Another victim endured threats to himself, his staff and business for over a year before reporting his partner's violence. He recalled:

> [T]here were all sorts of threats hanging around and he would try and drive me out of my business … he would shout and scream and abuse me whilst I was consulting … he would equally bully and abuse my staff. He would bully me in front of clients … [once it got physical] my business was at risk, my income was at risk, [and] my staff were at risk.

Although not quite a consensus, the general view of participants about the criminal justice system's response to intimate partner violence was critical. It is arguable that these opinions would have created disincentives to use it. Statements by victims and perpetrators included the following:

- I have little faith in the jury system.
- This is a huge machine that sometimes is not doing what it should be.
- It is very confrontational … more attacking victims.

- It is unfair the domestic violence court treats men like feral beasts who must be controlled.
- The family court is gender-biased.
- The courts believed the lies of victims.

General Views of the Restorative Justice Process

No victims or perpetrators ruled out the possibility of using restorative justice for intimate partner violence. One victim and one perpetrator were enthusiastic. The victim, who was Chinese, considered it would be especially appropriate for ethnic families. If she went through the same experience again, she said she would use restorative justice. The perpetrator, an Iranian whose partner had physically fought against his wish to leave her, said that, had restorative justice been available, he would have used it without reservation.

Twelve participants – five perpetrators and seven victims – were provisionally positive about the use of restorative justice. The most reluctant of the participants who were provisionally positive was a perpetrator who had subsequently worked as a stopping violence group leader under the auspices of a victim agency. He said his reasons for this involvement were: 'After I attended the [stopping violence] programme … for her my apology in a way is to do this [leading a stopping violence programme] for a living now … Back then I didn't even have the capabilities that I do now.' However, he would only have participated in a restorative justice process if his partner had wanted to. Three perpetrators saw the benefits of restorative justice as being the possibility of it serving both parties rather than the interests of one. Of these, one hoped it would be constructive in promoting the care of the children; another stressed dealing with both sides of the conflict; and the third stated that the meeting needed to have clear objectives and to serve both parties. Another perpetrator felt it was important that the process was voluntary.

One victim who at the time of the research was using the criminal justice system felt a bit ambivalent about the restorative justice process, saying that she would feel nervous and would not like to face her ex-partner again. However, she added that she would consider it if he had to sit and listen and had no speaking rights. Another said he would go but would worry that it would be like a court. The second most enthusiastic victim about restorative justice generally had a partner with a borderline personality disorder and so she felt that it would not have been appropriate in her case. Another victim considered attending a restorative justice conference in the early stages of the abuse would be better.

Fraser, whose partner had made numerous false allegations to the police, commented that, if his partner knew there was going to be an automatic restorative justice conference, she might have thought twice about being abusive. He considered that the process needed to be compulsory to ensure that she and others would attend. Fraser also favoured a follow-up conference:

> It wouldn't have to be as formal; it wouldn't even have to be a collective meeting; it could be done individually. Where the parties could meet facilitators individually or be given the option ... [for] a debrief [about] ... what's happened and how it's been, whether they are satisfied with the outcome, whether both parties have lived up to expectations and in terms of the victim, with the victim dissatisfied with what has transpired and what steps the other party has made. And in terms of the perpetrator, it would be a good opportunity for them just to reiterate the changed behaviour and their remorse and their willingness to continue to accept responsibility for their behaviour.

Two others said it depended on their partners being willing or mature enough to discuss their problems. Another victim considered ethnically appropriate facilitators to be important and qualified their attendance on the facilitators being *kaumātua* (male elder) or *kuia* (female elder) or had tried to get one to attend. The Chinese victim observed that restorative justice would be better than the present processes through the criminal justice system because:

> Restorative justice is a very good platform, especially in the Asian culture because ... [of the] shame aspect of it. You report the man; the woman gets chastised by the community because ... the woman brings shame to the family. So if you have a process like restorative justice, when it is two-sided, where you have trained people who can equalise the power ... If I had known of restorative justice and if [it] was available, it would have been a marvellous way [to deal with the abuse].

Both victims and perpetrators raised the issue of labelling, suggesting that negative labels had the potential to be detrimental to the process and/or the safety of either party. In the words of one perpetrator: 'If the emphasis is on 'you're the perpetrator, and you're the victim,' then I think it is going to be destructive and get people's backs up.' A victim echoed this, saying: 'In a restorative justice conference it's no longer a perpetrator and a victim, it's Jane and Rich.' The perpetrator from Iran regarded restorative justice as more appropriate for dealing with intimate partner violence because of the complex dynamics of violence, especially when it is two-sided. Another perpetrator said: 'It would be a very positive thing if the emphasis is on dealing with all aspects of this relationship ... [Support people] can help this couple with the education, the relearning and monitoring of how to relate to each other.' A victim agreed: 'Give them both a chance where they're not all powerful [and in] control and dominant. That's been stripped away ... it would also then give the perpetrator an opportunity to look at themselves [to] see the consequences of their actions, and hopefully ... motivate them to change their behaviour.' Thus, in this way, both parties could take steps to correct their behaviour.

Views on Safety

Safety was discussed in terms of psychological/emotional and physical safety (for more information, see Hayden 2012, 2013). Fear of retribution was raised by four victims and by one perpetrator. Victims tended to focus on what would happen after the conference. For example, one victim commented that it was one thing being in a controlled situation during the conference, but she was concerned that she would be punished afterwards for speaking out. A perpetrator expressed concern about the reaction of extended families to what they might have learned at the conference, which could put the perpetrator back where he started. A male victim's concern was emotional safety, noting the difficulty that can arise from revealing things to friends and family rather than to strangers.

Measures that could be taken to make the process safer appeared to be influenced by ethnicity and/or prior experience of intimate partner violence. For example, the Iranian perpetrator considered it necessary to have two security guards present and for each participant to be body searched before the conference to avoid any risk. One victim, whose partner was a gang member, on the other hand, saw the information the facilitators had as an important safety factor. Another victim felt it would be good to have someone with her as she left the conference. Other criteria relevant to participants' safety included perpetrators' maturity and willingness to compromise. Here, too, the importance of monitoring outcomes was stressed to ensure that any agreements reached were followed through. One victim put it this way:

> The mere fact of ... being asked to document things would be enough to reinforce the events of that restorative justice conference ... I would imagine that promises would have been made. And I'd like to, being a victim, see that those promises are being kept. And if they were not kept, it was documented.

Possible Gains for Victims and Perpetrators

Some victims and perpetrators saw restorative justice as a possible catalyst for change, accountability, re-education on how to relate to one another, and an opportunity for open and honest discussion in relative safety. One perpetrator believed it was a way in which perpetrators could realize that other people were concerned about them. The same perpetrator thought facilitators could tell the couple how they were relating to each other. In addition, victims considered restorative justice could help their partners understand the effects of intimate partner violence; the process could enlighten the victims about why they had stayed in the situation; the abusive partner could demonstrate changes in their behaviour since the incident; and promises could be documented.

A restorative justice process could provide opportunities for facilitated and supported negotiation on important issues like finance, child custody and safety. The following examples illustrate the deep concern felt by participants about these matters. One victim commented:

> The only negotiation I will do is a financial one. If he puts money into my solicitor's trust account [to pay his share of the mortgage], signs the documents, then I might think of dropping the first charge [against him] and [reduce the charge from male assaults female to common assault].

A perpetrator negotiated with his alcoholic partner that the protection order against him would stay in place, provided he had custody of the children; three victims had negotiated promises from their partners to desist from further abuse.

A Chinese victim, Brenda, considered participation in a restorative justice process could have given her partner a way of dealing with his violent behaviour without losing face. She explained:

> I'm going to quote Chinese [quotes in Chinese] It means … This person is up on stage, the perpetrator, and you've painted him in a corner as a bad guy and everybody in the audience has seen him. He can't come down from the stage gracefully. The thing is he knows he's wrong. But to keep his face he has to do this thing … But if you can do it in an oblique way … to let him step down from the stage gracefully, then everybody wins. Whereas the Western way is confrontational, it destroys the family, it doesn't allow for reconciliation, it causes loss of face which means that the man is forced to, in fact a lot of times I think … the fact that I went into refuge … I forced him to [do] that. To save his face, to redeem his face, he had to fight and to try to make me wrong. So we get caught up and I regret it, I regret it. That I took that path; and that was a Western path, the Western education in me. But the Chinese woman in me realized that I was doing it very, very wrong … [I could have] used restorative justice as a means of facilitating, and I would use reconciliation in the widest sense of the word … reconciliation does not mean [necessarily] that the woman goes back to the man. Reconciliation … of the issues … it could be that one of the outcomes is that you live separately, recognizing that 'you are the father, you are the mother. Let's negotiate a way to continue the parenting' before it even goes into the court, [the perpetrator] goes to jail, [or is] throw[n] … in the cell for a night, for 24hrs or for 36 hrs.

Facilitators' Skills and Knowledge Base

All the participants in the research recognized the importance of various factors relating to facilitators. These included: gender appropriateness; having a balance between theoretical and practical experience; the need for routine monitoring and debriefing; having friendly and sensitive personalities; common sense; culturally appropriate behaviour; and education/experience in the National Network of Stopping Violence and/or National Collective of Women's Refuge. They suggested that facilitators needed to be fair and to have integrity. They also needed skills which enabled them to guide the process; to intervene as necessary; to identify and ask relevant questions; and to have cultural safety awareness. It was important for them to rely on evidence rather than on hearsay; to model appropriate behaviour; and to be able to direct participants to appropriate agencies for help. One perpetrator, for example, felt facilitators should be sufficiently skilled to make recommendations if necessary, to treat participants fairly, and to set out clearly the next steps for the perpetrator to follow so that s/he could change. Another saw the facilitators' role as being able to detect manipulation and to respond constructively, fairly and respectfully to all parties, while another commented that it was necessary for facilitators to tell couples that they had the power to make the necessary changes rather than have them imposed from outside.

A victim stated that facilitators needed to uphold respect and to show that they could handle even the most difficult situations. She thought they also had to be careful about how they asked questions of the participants. With the help of suitably trained facilitators, restorative justice was seen as a possible catalyst for change, accountability, and an opportunity for open and honest discussion. One victim reflected on the benefits of having an open and honest discussion with his partner 'without there being ... any screaming or shouting ... [in] a safe environment to talk.' Another commented that she would '[gain] that support, that trust, that I'm safe ... the environment is safe for all of us, and confidentiality is the biggest.'

However, it was also noted that the background of facilitators could put them in positions where they could inadvertently influence the conference process or outcome. One concern expressed by three perpetrators and two victims was that the process could be manipulated. A perpetrator put it this way: 'The concept is rather easily open to abuse if the people running it have wacky values, for ... example accepting accusations of domestic violence without any proof that violence has actually occurred.' Other concerns raised around the possibility of manipulation were: getting a lighter sentence or avoiding conviction; insufficient focus on the needs of victims; and one party having an agenda alien to the concept of restorative justice (for example, a vengeful victim or a ruthless perpetrator). Thus the research findings suggest a perception that restorative justice processes could be vulnerable to abuse by perpetrators, victims *and* facilitators.

The Restorative Justice Process

Most participants who commented on whether or not the restorative justice process should be voluntary said that they preferred non-compulsory involvement as this would encourage people to attend. They considered that making the process compulsory would be likely to lead to resistance by the person compelled to attend. There was also general recognition that the earlier the process took place in the development of intimate partner violence, the better the outcome was likely to be. One perpetrator, however, who had experienced considerable difficulty in the courts with child access and custody, felt that the process should be compulsory. He considered restorative justice offered an opportunity to pressurize his partner to pay constructive attention to childcare and, secondly, to ensure undertakings at the conference were carried out.

What happened before a restorative justice conference was discussed with participants. This related, firstly, to what occurred at a personal level for the individuals concerned and, secondly, to the pre-conference process used by facilitator(s). A male victim said that he did not think it would be appropriate to have a conference on the day or week following the incident, because people needed time for reflection. Time was also needed for abusers to accept that their behaviour was inappropriate and to demonstrate new behaviour. As previously discussed, maturity was considered another important factor. Like victims, perpetrators said that they needed to be properly prepared. One commented that perpetrators needed to be prepared for the likelihood that they could feel defensive which would be counterproductive.

Expectations of a Restorative Justice Conference

Participants were asked what they would expect from their partner at a restorative justice conference. The way they interpreted this question was up to them. Participants' responses were then categorized into 'positive', 'provisionally positive' and 'negative'. Four victims and four perpetrators conveyed that they had positive expectations of their partner. Three victims gave provisionally positive responses and two victims and one perpetrator gave negative responses. The positive responses centred on the following expectations: improved communication between the parties; the perpetrator's accountability; acknowledgement of wrongdoing by the perpetrator; being equally committed to the process; having the ability to self-reflect; demonstrating that they wished to improve their behaviour; and a restorative justice conference was perceived to be a better process for managing concerns around parenting.

Because he knew his partner had the best interests of their children at heart, one perpetrator trusted that they would reach the right decision at a restorative justice conference, whether or not they remained together. A male victim said he would want his partner to be totally willing to commit to participating. He expressed the view that there was no point in dragging somebody along who was not willing to listen. Other victims felt that the way their partners or former partners responded depended on how well the facilitator managed the conference and their ability to get their partners involved in the discussion.

Examples of participants expressing negative expectations of their partner were as follows:

- He would not go.
- There would just be a traumatic experience … anger, sadness, probably some fear about what would happen as a result of a [restorative justice conference].
- Attack a little bit.
- My ex-partner's unwillingness to compromise would make it a waste of time.

One perpetrator felt quite strongly that the use by restorative justice practitioners of terminology such as 'offender' or 'perpetrator' would have a negative impact. He described the embarrassment at being required to stand in the dock for judicial monitoring for the counselling which he and his partner were undergoing at his request. Therefore, he considered it important for facilitators to recognize mutual conflict, looking at both sides, rather than assign each party to either the 'victim' or 'perpetrator' role.

Other more general comments relating to expectations included: it was better to have expectations of oneself than to have expectations of one's partner; and unrealized expectations of reconciliation could have a negative impact on perpetrators.

Conclusion

To sum up, using restorative justice for intimate partner violence was supported by the majority of the participants in this research. They agreed that the present criminal justice system in New Zealand is having little impact in its attempts to reduce the incidence of this type of offending. Few chose to involve the criminal justice system and, of those who did, few were satisfied with it. This indicates that an acceptable alternative means of dealing with these situations is required. Most participants in the study were positive about the prospect of restorative justice. As pointed out by both victims and perpetrators of different ethnicities, cultural needs presently not met by the criminal justice system could be met at a restorative justice conference. The study examined the extent to which restorative justice might improve reporting of intimate partner violence to the police. The research found that, of all participants, almost four-fifths considered that restorative justice would increase the reporting of intimate partner violence and all participants saw the potential of using restorative justice for dealing with intimate partner violence. Many also wished they had had the option of restorative justice earlier in the development of the intimate partner violence they had experienced or perpetrated.

References

Hayden, A. 2010. Why Rock the Boat? Non-Reporting of Intimate Partner Violence. PhD thesis, Auckland University of Technology.

Hayden, A. 2012. Safety Issues Associated with Using Restorative Justice for Intimate Partner Violence. *Women's Studies Journal*, 26(2), 4–16.

Hayden, A. 2013. The Promises and Pitfalls of Restorative Justice for Intimate Partner Violence. *Internet Journal of Restorative Justice*, 1(1), 1–38. Available at: http://www.rj4all.info/content/IJRJcontents.

Chapter 15

Taking a Fresh Look: Fathers and Family Violence

Gale Burford and Joan Pennell

Introduction

The intersection of the intimate partner violence and child protection systems offers unique opportunities for reconciling the often conflicting aims of ensuring safety and well-being for mothers and their children while engaging with men in the aftermath of their violent behaviour. This is accomplished through the use of a restorative justice approach that adopts community-centred child and family practices (Burford and Hudson 2000, Pennell and Anderson 2005) while using protective measures as needed (Braithwaite 2002), embraces both families' and children's rights in a framework of family engagement (Pennell et al. 2011), and draws from theories associated with gender-inclusive feminism (Pennell and Kim 2010). Gender-inclusive feminism positions family, community and culture at the heart of children's and women's safety and responsible fathering. Such approaches are based on both the rights of the child to be connected to their families and the rights of families to have their culture respected. The approaches seek to increase and improve the engagement of fathers and mothers in the lives of children. This is based on the simple assumption that things go better for children when the adults in their lives are cooperating in the children's best interests but also takes into account managing the risks associated with men's behaviour when they have been violent while recognizing how important fathering and mothering are in child development and well-being (Featherstone 2010a, 2010b, Scourfield et al. 2012). In short, we acknowledge both the high levels of injury and positivity of which men are capable with their children and other members of their families. The nexus of family violence and children's protection sheds light on fathers and fathering without, as Featherstone (2010b) says, erasing the importance of mothers and mothering and thereby takes a position that advances gender inclusiveness and family support.

Fathers and Fathering: Interpersonal Violence and Child Protection

The need for interventions that bring fathers and paternal family members to the table in child protection grows, along with other important reforms, out of several important threads in child protection (Nelson 1984, Waldfogel 1998) but also out of the work of gender-inclusive feminist leaders. It also, of course, grows from critiques of state power by Indigenous groups (for example, Ministerial Advisory Committee 1988) and feminist legal scholars (Goodmark 2011). Historically, it is mothers who have been the primary subjects of children's protection investigations and interventions to the exclusion of fathers (Brown et al. 2009, Featherstone 2010a, Featherstone et al. 2010, Goodmark 2004/5, Malm et al. 2006, 2008, McBride et al. 2005, Morris and Featherstone 2010, Strega et al. 2008). At the same time that fathers have been systematically excluded from services, considerable research on the important role that positive parenting by fathers plays in the lives of children has mushroomed (American Humane Association 2007, Arendell 2010, Daniel and Taylor 2001, Featherstone 2009, Lamb 2010, Marsiglio and Roy 2012, Rosenberg and Wilcox 2006).

Fathering and Child Safety

Goodmark (2004/5) has argued that batterers' accountability has been so hard to achieve in child protection systems for a wide range of reasons. These include workers' fear of batterers and their avoidance of the uncertainty associated with having to manage the risk of involving the batterer in investigations, assessments and case plans particularly if the men are step-parents.

Mothers who want to protect their children but at the same time do not want to leave their abuser find themselves in a bind. Fathers are labelled either 'good' or 'bad' without full assessment, are barred from involvement by mothers or by service providers who organize all their work around mothers, and/or simply find it easier to be uninvolved because of their own reluctance, disinterest or uncertainty about how to parent (Scourfield et al. 2012). This has the effect of blocking off relationships with members of the paternal side of the family who often have a great interest in being involved. When fathers have been violent, professionals are often left uncertain about how to involve paternal relatives without increasing the risk to abused women or their children. The task is to help the family to rebuild or make new connections that will enlist family members including non-kin or 'like family' supports in strengthening their capacities for informal helping and long-range connections for the children (Adams and Chandler 2002, 2004, Burford 2009, Pennell and Burford 2002, Pennell et al. 2011).

Restorative Justice Theory and Practice with Family Violence

Importantly, both authors of this chapter have long expressed caution about the use of restorative justice in situations of family violence unless there are children with ties to both the abuser and the abused and to their extended family (Burford and Pennell 1998). At the same time, we acknowledge that restorative justice theories, especially as they conceptualize the victim (Bolivar 2010), have developed considerably in relation to a multiplicity of goals and a range of evaluation strategies and methods. Some approaches to working with family violence are located in statutory settings, while others are part of far more community-led initiatives. Some are more clearly aimed at therapeutic or healing goals, sometimes depending on high levels of trained professional facilitation, while others give greater emphasis to peer support, democratic deliberation and fair processes (Coker 2002, Fernandez 2010, Fredrick and Lizdas 2010, Gal 2011, Hamel 2008, Kim 2010, Mills et al. 2012, Waldegrave 2000).

It is in children's welfare that protocols for using restorative justice approaches for engaging family groups to address interpersonal violence have been developed, trialled, evaluated and found to be safe (Burford et al. 1995, Pennell 2005, Pennell and Burford 2000, 2002, Pennell and Francis 2005) and their use is expanding (McCrae and Fusco 2010, Weigensberg et al. 2009). The development of wider 'think family' policy and research frameworks (Morris et al. 2008) which focus on including fathers and the wider extended family have fostered these developments. Family engagement approaches share in common placing the non-abusing family members, including mothers, in the circle and organizing meetings with their leadership in mind. These practices need to be developed hand-in-hand with a range of services including gender specific supports for engaging fathers (Scott and Litshak 2012), evidence-informed treatments (for example, trauma and substance abuse), and concrete supports for kin caregivers who become involved as caregivers, often at great expense (Crumbley and Little 1997, Doolan et al. 2004, Farmer and Moyers 2008) and at risk of increased violence toward themselves by the teenage children (Day and Bazemore 2011).

An Example from Vermont

We have chosen a case example from Vermont which we believe illustrates many of the significant issues that conspire to exclude fathers while at the same time shows how one family, once they were able to have a family meeting, were able to exert influence over the plan for their family. Importantly, the year during which the events in this example played out, the state child welfare agency in Vermont was in the second year of a major effort to transform its system. This was towards families' engagement and restorative justice practices in planning for children's protection and youth justice earlier in the process (Burford 2013). An important part of this was the engagement of fathers and extended family relatives, both paternal and maternal, through the families finding strategies and family engagement meetings, including family group conferences and family safety plan meetings. Vermont's family safety plan meetings are carefully facilitated throughout by a contracted person who is not otherwise involved with the family and the discussion is organized around a consultation framework which explores the family's strengths, risks, challenges, safety and next steps (Lohrbach and Sawyer 2004,). The meetings emphasize the social worker making a clear, specific and respectful statement near the beginning of the meeting about the child protection concern which brings the state into the family's lives. This is seen as a crucial difference between using family engagement strategies in statutory versus non-statutory matters. Family group conferences are modelled after New Zealand's approach which aims to bring together as many family members as possible with careful preparation and the use of strategies to empower the family group to provide leadership.

The family safety plan meeting discussed below happened over a year from the time the case was opened through a traditional investigation. In 2012, nearly 60 per cent of the family meetings (combined for family safety plan meetings and family group conferences) held in Vermont included someone from the paternal side of the family (including fathers) while nearly 100 per cent included maternal family (including mothers). While data on paternal involvement were not captured prior to 2012, this is in all likelihood an increase in fathers' and paternal families' involvement, given the deliberate efforts in the state to engage fathers. Written practice guidance has been developed in the state for engaging fathers in both family safety plan meetings and family group conferences along with protocols for holding meetings when there has been violence in the family (Vermont Department of Children and Families 2006, 2008, 2012a, 2012b).

The following example is drawn from separate interviews with Marie, a young teenage mother, and her mother, Monica. Henri is Marie's child. Isaac is Monica's husband and Marie's stepfather. Importantly, the interviews are the only information available about the case; hence, only Marie and Monica's perspectives are represented. For reasons of confidentiality, pseudonyms are used and the identities of the family members are masked. The research protocols were approved by the University of Vermont Institutional Review Board.

The Report of Suspected Intimate Partner Violence and Child Abuse

Isaac and Monica brought Marie to the hospital where they were involved in the admissions process and remained during the delivery of her baby and for the visiting hours afterwards. Isaac and Monica were in the hospital room visiting Marie and Henri when a social worker arrived and said she wanted to interview Marie alone. Monica and Marie both observed that all they ever knew of the report was that someone at the hospital had contacted the child welfare agency saying they thought Isaac might be violent.

Investigation and Case Planning Response

Marie said the social worker:

> Sat down on the edge of my bed, kicked everybody out of my room, took my baby out of my room … introduced herself as being from [the child welfare agency] and that they 'were here to help' … [and that I should] 'answer as honestly as you can because if you are not 100 per cent honest with me and we

> do find out we can say that you are – she didn't say it in a threatening way but I took it that way – She said that I would be looked at as an 'unreliable source to talk to', and that I would be 'inconsistent with what I was saying'.

Marie's description fits the practices associated with a worker who is carrying out an investigation being mindful that the information she collects may need to stand up in court. During the interview, Marie says that she told the social worker of an incident that happened at home during the time she was pregnant which had frightened her. Both Monica and Marie believed it was this incident that was used as the basis, along with social worker's confidence in the person who had made the report, to take both Henri and Marie as a minor child into the custody of the state within a few hours of Henri's birth.

Both Monica and Marie maintained that the only reason hospital personnel were concerned was because Isaac is black and that one of the nurses had something 'personal' against him. Monica said that Isaac was interviewed as part of the investigation and asked for his explanation of the event that had happened at the house but after that he was never again permitted to be involved until the family meeting. Monica summed it up by saying: 'My husband has never been able to say anything since the beginning other than when they investigated.' She said that she and Isaac experienced the investigation as 'confrontational' and as their being 'under attack'. The case plan required that there would be no contact of any kind between Marie and her mother and Isaac and that Monica and Isaac could have no access or contact with little Henri.

As a black man and a stepfather, Isaac may well have been viewed with suspicion from the beginning. He was living in a bi-racial relationship in a predominantly white state. Also influential perhaps was Monica's history of childhood abuse and her prior relationship with a man who had abused her child. The fact that Marie was abused by her biological father and had become pregnant at a very early age could well have been regarded as Monica's responsibility. By the time Marie was forced to describe damaging details about her parents, a context had been constructed by the investigator and appeared to have fuelled the decision to take Marie into the custody of strangers at a time when she most needed the guidance and support of her own family.

After her discharge from the hospital, Marie was admitted to the first of several foster homes where she and Henri lived, but with the state maintaining separate legal custody status for them. The state allowed Henri's teen father and his parents to have unsupervised contact with the baby, but contact was forbidden between Marie and the baby's father and his parents. Marie's recollections revealed that she felt most of the burden was on her:

> I couldn't see my baby's father for the longest time. For no reason. We've never done drugs, we've never drank alcohol. We were just two teenagers who thought they were in love who made very … We're not together any more. And I shouldn't blame … but I kind of blame that on the situation that I'm in. I mean

> [long distance away] … It's just hard. We're really young and it takes a lot to keep a relationship together especially at this young age.

Marie denied that intimate partner violence had happened. She recounted:

> I just answered her [the social worker] probably in more detail than I needed to … I was very scared … I had just barely had a child … And she asked me … she told me at first that I 'needed to be honest' … She asked me … if there was drugs or alcohol … if there was any violence and I said, 'no'. And she told me that what … she had heard from [the person who reported] that my stepfather was violent towards my mother. And the only thing that I could think about was [the incident that happened once while Marie was pregnant].

Marie maintained ever since that:

> My words were kind of twisted and so I was in [the child protection agency] custody and because it was my words, which it wasn't. Unfortunately I … and then I was hearing that if I tried to change my words … every time I said 'no that's not what I said', 'You're being inconsistent with what you're saying. Babies need consistency'. So I was scared to lose my son. I didn't know what to do. I was just like 'whatever'. I will do whatever you want me to do to just take care of my child.

Marie second-guessed what she thought the social worker wanted to hear balanced against her own priorities. Denied the release of explaining or telling their 'family story', Monica, Marie and Isaac were left to individually try to insert their feelings and views around the process of interrogation. Importantly, they set out on a course of compliance thinking that if they were perceived as cooperating with expectations they would be believed and able to re-unite.

Goodmark (2013) points out that cooperating with authorities in criminal justice responses to intimate partner violence does not guarantee safety for women and often jeopardizes their safety. To that, we would add that cooperating with forensic investigative child protection responses that isolate women and children from actively influencing the context in which they want to have their experiences and needs understood often has the same effect. It is not a guarantee of safety for mothers and it all too frequently jeopardizes the permanency and well-being needs of the children.

Trauma as a Complicating Factor in Risk Assessment

Both Monica and Marie said the investigation and subsequent events left them traumatized. In Monica's words, it was 'almost like having your child and your grandchild kidnapped in one day … We set up the crib and she went to the hospital and didn't come home'. Marie said one of her greatest concerns throughout was that her baby was not getting to know his grandparents, Monica and Isaac.

Monica and Marie both believed that the way they appeared to the social worker during the investigation and after was confounded by their own histories of trauma. Marie said she had lived with her biological father when she was younger and that he was abusive to her. She connected that abuse to the fear which she felt in seeing the incident involving her stepfather. In her words: 'I didn't really know yet what was abuse and what wasn't. So when I saw that [the incident in her home] just flashbacks happened in my head and I reacted.' She asserted that Isaac instantly recognized her reaction and took steps to show that the incident between him and Monica was not what it appeared and he 'apologized at the time and the incident was finished'. She says that she has maintained ever since that it was the only incident she ever witnessed involving Isaac and that she believes it was 'a regular argument with my mother and I just took it that way ... He did not do anything.' For her part, Monica disclosed: 'I've got post-traumatic stress ... I was raised in a family where they could write a horror story about my childhood. Honestly I am one of those kids.'

Yet once their case had been characterized with the language of 'intimate partner violence', both Marie and Monica found that it became impossible to shift the emphasis onto what they believed were their needs. In Monica's view:

> On paperwork in court it never comes up that [the child welfare agency] investigated my family and said that they didn't find any reason to substantiate the claims and that even [the worker] herself said that she knew it wasn't a case of abuse – it was more a case of I was having trouble with my teenager and having control over that. But then in court it's right back to the abuse stuff ... We're always feeling like we're gonna have to be constantly proving something and if for some reason someone doesn't like us, well there's another person on the state's side to say 'no'. They took my child without a good reason.

According to both Monica and Marie, this situation went on for over a year before a referral was made for a family meeting.

Featherstone (2009) discusses the importance of using the terms 'father' and 'mother' to infuse a gender equity perspective into all discussions and believes that terms like 'parent' and 'child' mask important differences of fathers, mothers, daughters and sons by lumping them into categories that make their needs less visible in the realities of practice. Ferguson and Hogan (2004) offer rich descriptions of the ways that totalizing, overly positive and overly negative, constructions of a father can 'float around in the system' and get used as justification for workers excluding them or simply failing to persist in reaching out to them. The result often leaves mothers holding all the responsibility for what has happened and to make all the changes or just the opposite to make the father into 'the good parent' and diminish the mother.

Referral to Family Safety Plan Meeting and Planning for the Meeting

Marie and Monica both felt hopeful on their separately learning that their social worker had finally made a referral for a family meeting. They were never quite sure what prompted the referral for a family meeting although they both knew that 'another kind of family meeting' that was to 'include other people' and 'more people' had been discussed for some time. This meeting would be 'something different than the usual case planning meetings' that were attended by only Marie and the professionals. Marie and Monica wanted the meeting to happen and each felt that at last their individual efforts might be paying off. However, both were at first confused by the names of the meeting. Initially they were told the meeting would be a family group conference but then it was changed to a family safety plan.

When she first heard the name of the meeting, Monica reacted:

> [I] had some issues with it just because it's about a *safety* plan and part of the accusations that were made was that there was some sort of violence or abuse in our home and there isn't and it was never substantiated and we have to keep over and over having to remind [the social worker] that it can't keep coming up in our paperwork and stuff because there is no real grounds for it. But at the same time I want to be able to visit my grandson and see my daughter … so I'm willing to agree to pretty much anything that they ask.

Despite Monica's and Marie's perception, a 'substantiation' of some kind had been made that allowed the state to take custody of both Marie and Henri and the social worker and court were evidently unyielding in the face of suggestions to lift the directive that there should be no contact of any kind. It is likely that the case was coming up for a 12-month review at which the worker would have been required by statute to show evidence of reunification efforts or to explain why termination of Monica's rights as a parent were not being considered. And so, no matter what the name of the family safety plan meeting was, Monica and Marie were relieved. Each thought a family meeting would help get past what they perceived to be a stalemate with the social worker.

Marie and Monica subsequently learned that Isaac was to be included. In Monica's view, even though she said she was worried: 'It was our chance, if they did attack us again [this time] we could, in front of more people, stand up for ourselves and say what our part is and our feelings and that's exactly what happened.' Isaac had never been 'able to defend our family … and say 'I would never abuse my children. I would never abuse my wife.'

Marie summed up her understanding of the purpose of the meeting as to 'get a good understanding on you know why I am in DCF custody, what steps do we need to take to get out of custody and so on.' In Marie's words:

> All I wanted to do was go home. There is absolutely nothing unsafe about my home. I mean there's always work that needs to be done with homes and

> families but it's just absolutely ridiculous to me that I am still in custody … It's unfortunate that I couldn't articulate myself at the time because, or understand really what was going on … That's why I chose to go to [residential group for young mothers]. I could not stand going from foster home to foster home to foster home. I didn't know these people. I did not know their rules. I did not trust my son around them.

Asked what was getting in the way prior to the meeting, Marie responded:

> Honestly. My [child protection] social worker … you know, not that she doesn't try to be open minded. She really does. But … I don't think she really got a chance to see the full picture. And she had a really hard time trusting everybody … No matter how hard I worked it wasn't really going anywhere … No matter how much I proved to my worker and my mother proved to my worker that we were really doing everything we were supposed to do, it wasn't really going anywhere. And I think that was kind of a roadblock, not that she didn't want to see us successful. She was just scared of 'what ifs?'. Like 'what if she went home and this happened?'

The Family Safety Plan Meeting

Rossner (2011: 169) points out that while 'the format and language [of restorative meetings] vary across the world … the common aim is a forum where families and communities have a direct role in creating justice.' While most readers would wish this meeting had happened much earlier in the process, it did serve its main restorative aim of allowing the family to be seen and understood as a family and to build a working partnership between the family and the state. In particular, Monica and Marie remembered the impact of the independent facilitator on the social worker's perception of the family as they talked through the difference between a fear and a risk, a step that is built into the family safety plan protocol:

> The lady [who facilitated the meeting] was quite helpful … because [the social worker] said her fear … we were talking about the risk factor and the fear and the lady who was running it helped [the social worker] realize there is a difference between a fear and a risk … and I saw [the social worker] kind of acknowledge that 'yeah, maybe it isn't so much a risk as it's a fear' based on what your paperwork says, but when there's no proof of that then it is a fear. The risk would be if something had happened … so she just helped clarify and I was so grateful for that.

The meeting changed the perception of Isaac in the family too. According to Monica, the meeting was not harsh or confrontational. On the contrary, the meeting was constructed to avoid argumentation and provocation and to make honest discussion possible. Monica was concerned about how Isaac would be perceived by others at the meeting:

> And even though you could hear his [Isaac's] tone wasn't as calm as mine … it also wasn't threatening … I was afraid 'Oh great. They're going to hear he's upset and they're not going to like him because of that or they're gonna judge him because of that', but … he was able to express himself and everyone remained calm and no one came back at him like 'You did' and 'You know you did' or 'You would' … And Marie was also able to say what she did say and she didn't say and we were all able to clarify on our side as a family … We felt better in the end that finally we were able to say again in front of [the social worker] and as a family what our side was … which we all feel [individually] we've been saying all along and haven't been heard.

In Monica's view:

> We all felt good because we all had emotions to share and feelings about how we felt throughout this whole thing and we were all able to express how we felt. Even [the social worker] was able to express how she felt in a non-threatening way. No one, I think, felt threatened or denied their feelings and the most important thing that we got out of it was that we were all able to say what needed to be said and no one said 'well you shouldn't feel like this'.

In short, the meeting provided a forum in which their past traumas could be separated out from the problems that were occurring at the time of the report of the abuse but also from an assessment of the current strengths and concerns about the family. Both Monica and Marie expressed satisfaction that the plan from the meeting recommended that they all attend counselling together, something they said they had been asking for all along, but were refused because the worker did not think it was safe for them to be in face-to-face contact.

While Marie was happy with the outcome, she still had reservations about the plan:

> I don't think we ever got a straight answer from [the social worker] on what she wants, but I think it's very clear in some ways that the plan was to you know just kind of start out meetings with my mother, prove to [the child welfare agency] over time, or actually I shouldn't say [the agency] but [the social worker], that it isn't what she thinks. You know it's not … My family is just a normal family. Basically prove that. And I think so far it's been going great. We still have our moments with her where we feel frustrated but we have to kind of see it through her eyes … She is letting me go to home visits. She is letting me see my mother.

This is not an unusual experience for family members involved with family meetings in statutory services where the mandate of the state to protect children and women necessarily gives the state the final say in approving plans (Ney et al. 2013). In this example, the social worker feared that family violence was re-occurring while according to the presumed victims, Monica and Marie, they continued to be affected by past trauma but had created a safe family with Isaac. The practice of engagement with families in situations where children and women appear at risk can act as a correction to social workers' preconceptions and agencies' aversion to risk. At the same time, if Monica, Marie and potentially Henri had been in danger, the state must not abrogate its role to treat violence against children and women as a crime. A gender-inclusive process was necessary in order to gain a full understanding of what had happened in the family. Restorative justice as practiced in family group meetings can serve as a way to challenge totalizing characterizations of fathers and men, especially those who are culturally marginalized, and to help social workers partner with families and collaborate with their professional colleagues to create balanced assessments and manage the risks involved. Safety in this view is the product of building trust and relationships. We end by quoting Marie's last word on the meeting: 'My son gets to be part of his grandparents' life.'

References

Adams, P. and Chandler, S.M. 2002. Building Partnerships to Protect Children: A Blended Model of Family Group Conferencing. *Family Court Review*, 40(4), 503–17.

Adams, P. and Chandler, S.M. 2004. Responsive Regulation in Child Welfare: Systemic Challenges to Mainstreaming the Family Group Conference. *Journal of Sociology and Social Welfare*, 31(1), 93–116.

American Humane Association, American Bar Association Center for Children and the Law and the National Fatherhood Initiative. 2007. *Literature Review: Non-Resident Fathers, Paternal Kin, and the Child Welfare System.* Colorado Springs, CO: US Department of Health and Human Services.

Arendell, T. 2010. *Co-Parenting: A Review of the Literature.* Available at: http://www.ncoff.gse.upenn.edu/content/co-parenting-review-literature.

Bolivar, D. 2010. Conceptualizing Victims' 'Restoration' in Restorative Justice. *International Review of Victimology*, 17, 237–65.

Braithwaite, J. 2002. *Restorative Justice and Responsive Regulation.* Oxford: Oxford University Press.

Brown, L., Callahan, M., Strega, S., Dominelli, L. and Walmsley, C. 2009. Manufacturing Ghost Fathers: The Paradox of Father Presence and Absence in Child Welfare. *Child and Family Social Work*, 14(1), 25–34.

Burford, G. 2009. Who's Regulating Whom? Challenges to Families in Looking after Their Children. *Communities, Children and Families Australia*, 4(1), 22–8.

Burford, G. 2013. Family Group Conferences in Youth Justice and Child Welfare in Vermont, in *Restorative Justice Today: Practical Applications*, edited by K.S. van Wormer and L. Walker. Los Angeles, CA: Sage, 81–92.

Burford, G. and Hudson, J. 2000. *Family Group Conferencing: New Directions in Community-Centred Child and Family Practice*. Piscataway, NJ: Transaction Publishers.

Burford, G. and Pennell, J. 1998. *Family Group Decision Making: After the Conference – Progress in Resolving Violence and Promoting Well-Being: Outcome Report* (vols 1 and 2). St. John's, NF: Memorial University of Newfoundland, School of Social Work.

Burford, G., Pennell, J. and MacLeod, S. 1995. *Manual for Coordinators and Communities: The Organization and Practice of Family Group Decision Making* (revised). St. John's, NF: Memorial University of Newfoundland, School of Social Work. (In English, French and Inuktitut.) Available at: http://faculty.chass.ncsu.edu/pennell/fgdm/manual/ index.htm.

Coker, D. 2002. Transformative Justice: Anti-Subordination Processes in Cases of Domestic Violence, in *Restorative Justice and Family Violence*, edited by H. Strang and J. Braithwaite. New York: Cambridge University Press, 128–52.

Crumbley, J. and Little, R.L. 1997. *Relatives Raising Children: An Overview of Kinship Care*. Washington, DC: CWLA Press.

Daniel, B. and Taylor, J. 2001. *Engaging with Fathers: Practice Issues for Health and Social Care*. London: Jessica Kingsley Publishers.

Day, S.E. and Bazemore, G. 2011. Two Generations at Risk: Child Welfare, Institutional Boundaries, and Family Violence in Grandparent Homes. *Child Welfare*, 90(4), 99–116.

Doolan, M., Nixon, P. and Lawrence, P. 2004. *Growing Up in the Care of Relatives or Friends: Delivering Best Practice in Family and Friends' Care*. London: Family Rights Group.

Farmer, E. and Moyers, S. 2008. *Kinship Care: Fostering Effective Family and Friends Placements*. London: Jessica Kingsley Publishers.

Featherstone, B. 2009. *Contemporary Fathering: Theory, Policy and Practice*. Bristol: The Policy Press.

Featherstone, B. 2010a. Engaging Fathers: Promoting Gender Equality, in *Gender and Child Welfare in Society*, edited by B. Featherstone, C. Hooper, J. Scourfield and J. Taylor. Oxford: Wiley-Blackwell, 173–94.

Featherstone, B. 2010b. Writing Fathers in but Mothers out!!! *Critical Social Policy*, 30(2), 208–24.

Featherstone, B., Hooper, C., Scourfield, J. and Taylor, J. 2010. *Gender and Child Welfare in Society*. Oxford: Wiley-Blackwell.

Ferguson, H. and Hogan, F. 2004. *Strengthening Families through Fathers: Developing Policy and Practice in Relation to Vulnerable Fathers and Their Families*. Waterford: The Centre for Social and Family Research, Waterford Institute of Technology.

Fernandez, M. 2010. *Restorative Justice for Domestic Violence Victims: An Integrated Approach to Their Hunger for Healing.* Lanham, MD: Lexington Books.

Fredrick, L. and Lizdas, K.C. 2010. The Role of Restorative Justice in the Battered Women's Movement, in *Restorative Justice and Violence against Women*, edited by J. Ptacek. New York: Oxford University Press, 39–59.

Gal, T. 2011. *Child Victims and Restorative Justice.* Oxford: Oxford University Press.

Goodmark, L. 2004/5. Achieving Batterer Accountability in the Child Protection System. *Kentucky Law Journal*, 93(3), 623–57.

Goodmark, L.A. 2011. *A Troubled Marriage: Domestic Violence and the Legal System*. New York: New York University Press.

Goodmark, L.A. 2013. *Another 'Troubled Marriage': Domestic Violence and the Failures of Legal Response*. New York: New York University Press Blog: From the Square. Available at: http://www.fromthesquare.org/?p=1549.

Hamel, J. 2008. Beyond Ideology: Alternative Therapies for Domestic Violence, in *Intimate Partner and Family Abuse: A Casebook of Gender-Inclusive Therapy*, edited by J. Hamel New York: Springer, 3–26.

Kim, M. 2010. Alternative Interventions to Intimate Violence: Defining Political and Pragmatic Challenges, in *Restorative Justice and Violence against Women*, edited by J. Ptacek. New York: Oxford University Press, 193–217.

Lamb, M.E. 2010. *The Role of the Father in Child Development.* 5th edition. Hoboken, NJ: John Wiley and Sons.

Lohrbach, S. and Sawyer, R. 2004. Creating a Constructive Practice: Family and Professional Partnership in High Risk Child Protection Case Conferences. *Protecting Children*, 19(2), 26–35.

Malm, K., Murray, J. and Geen, R. 2006. *What about the Dads? Child Welfare Agencies' Efforts to Identify, Locate and Involve Nonresident Fathers.* Washington, DC: US Department of Health and Human Services, Office of the Assistance Secretary for Planning and Evaluation.

Malm, K., Zielewski, E. and Chen, H. 2008. *More about the Dads: Exploring Associations between Nonresident Father Involvement and Child Welfare Case Outcomes.* Washington, DC: US Department of Health and Human Services, Office of the Assistance Secretary for Planning and Evaluation.

Marsiglio, W. and Roy, K. 2012. *Nurturing Dads: Social Initiatives for Contemporary Fatherhood.* New York: Russell Sage Foundation.

McBride, B.A., Brown, G.L., Bost, K.K., Shin, N., Vaughn, B. and Korth, B. 2005. Paternal Identity, Maternal Gatekeeping, and Father Involvement. *Family Relations*, 54, 360–72.

McCrae, J.S. and Fusco, R.A. 2010. A Racial Comparison of Family Group Decision-Making in the USA. *Child and Family Social Work*, 15(1), 41–55.

Mills, L.G., Barocas, B. and Ariel, B. 2012. The Next Generation of Court-Mandated Domestic Violence Treatment: A Comparison Study of Batterer

Intervention and Restorative Justice Programs. *Journal of Experimental Criminology*, 9(1), 65–90.

Ministerial Advisory Committee. 1988. *The Report of the Ministerial Advisory Committee on a Māori Perspective for the Department of Social Welfare*. Wellington: Department of Social Welfare.

Morris, K. and Featherstone, B. 2010. Investing in Children, Regulating Parents, Thinking Family: A Decade of Tensions and Contradictions. *Social Policy and Society*, 9(4), 557–66.

Morris, K., Hughes, N., Clark, H., Mason, P., Burford, G., Galvani, S., Tew, J., Lewis, A. and Becker, S. 2008. *Whole Family Approaches: A Literature Review*. London: Social Exclusion Unit/Cabinet Office.

Nelson, B.J. 1984. *Making an Issue of Child Abuse: Political Agenda Setting for Social Problems*. Chicago, IL: The University of Chicago Press.

Ney, T., Stoltz, J. and Maloney, M. 2013. Voice, Power and Discourse: Experiences of Participants in Family Group Conferences in the Context of Child Protection. *Journal of Social Work*, 13(2), 184–202.

Pennell, J. 2005. Safety for Mothers and Their Children, in *Widening the Circle: The Practice and Evaluation of Family Group Conferencing with Children, Youths, and Their Families*, edited by J. Pennell and G. Anderson. Washington, DC: NASW Press, 163–81.

Pennell, J. and Anderson, G. 2005. *Widening the Circle: The Practice and Evaluation of Family Group Conferencing with Children, Youths, and Their Families*. Washington, DC: NASW Press.

Pennell, J. and Burford, G. 1995. *Family Group Decision Making: New Roles for 'Old' Partners in Resolving Family Violence: Implementation Report* (vols 1–2). St. John's, NF, Canada: Family Group Decision Making Project, School of Social Work, Memorial University of Newfoundland.

Pennell, J. and Burford, G. 2000. Family Group Decision-Making: Protecting Children and Women. *Child Welfare*, 79(2), 131–58.

Pennell, J. and Burford, G. 2002. Feminist Praxis: Making Family Group Conferencing Work, in *Restorative Justice and Family Violence*, edited by H. Strang and J. Braithwaite. Melbourne: Cambridge University Press, 108–27.

Pennell, J., Burford, G., Morris, K. and Connolly, M. 2011. Introduction: Taking Child and Family Rights Seriously: Family Engagement and its Evidence in Child Welfare. *Child Welfare*, 90(4), 9–16.

Pennell, J. and Francis, S. 2005. Safety Conferencing: Toward a Coordinated and Inclusive Response to Safeguard Women and Children. *Violence against Women*, 11(5), 666–92.

Pennell, J. and Kim, M. 2010. Opening Conversations across Cultural, Gender, and Generational Divides: Family and Community Engagement to Stop Violence against Women and Children, in *Restorative Justice and Violence against Women*, edited by J. Ptacek. Oxford: Oxford University Press, 177–92.

Rosenberg, J. and Wilcox, B. 2006. *The Importance of Fathers in the Healthy Development of Children*. Washington, DC, U.S. Department of Health and

Human Services, Children's Bureau Office on Child Abuse and Neglect. Available at: https://www.childwelfare.gov/pubs/ usermanuals/fatherhood/fatherhood.pdf.

Rossner, M. 2011. Reintegrative Ritual: Restorative Justice and Micro-Sociology, in *Emotions, Crime and Justice*, edited by S. Karstadt, I. Loader and H. Strang. Oxford: Hart Publishing, 169–91.

Scott, K.L. and Lishak, V. 2012. Intervention for Maltreating Fathers: Statistically and Clinically Significant Change. *Child Abuse and Neglect*, 36(9), 680–84.

Scourfield, J., Tolman, R., Maxwell, N., Holland, S., Bullock, A. and Sloan, L. 2012. Results of a Training Course for Social Workers on Engaging Fathers in Child Protection. *Children and Youth Services Review*, 34(8), 1425–32.

Strega, S., Fleet, C., Brown, L., Dominelli, L., Callahan, M. and Walmsley, C. 2008. Connecting Father Absence and Mother Blame in Child Welfare Policies and Practice. *Children and Youth Services Review*, 30(7), 705–16.

Vermont Department for Children and Families, Family Services Division. 2006. *Family Group Decision Making Practice Guidance for Planning, Implementing, Training, and Evaluating (Child Welfare).*

Vermont Department for Children and Families, Family Services Division. 2008. *Family Group Decision Making Practice Guidance for Planning, Implementing, Training, and Evaluating* (Appendix A: Situations Involving Domestic Violence).

Vermont Department for Children and Families, Family Services Division. 2012a. *Engaging Fathers: A Position Paper.*

Vermont Department for Children and Families, Family Services Division. 2012b. *Family Safety Planning (FSP) Practice Guidance.*

Waldegrave, C. 2000. 'Just Therapy' with Families and Communities, in *Family Group Conferencing: New Directions in Community-Centered Child and Family Practice*, edited by G. Burford and J. Hudson. New York: Aldine, 153–64.

Waldfogel, J. 1998. *The Future of Child Protection: How to Break the Cycle of Abuse and Neglect.* Cambridge, MA: Harvard University Press.

Weigensberg, E.C., Barth, R.P. and Guo, S. 2009. Family Group Decision-making: A Propensity Score Analysis to Evaluate Child and Family Services at Baseline and after 36 Months. *Children and Youth Services Review*, 31, 383–90.

Chapter 16
Sibling Sexual Abuse: Offending Patterns and Dynamics in Conferences

Kathleen Daly and Dannielle Wade

Introduction

Debate on the appropriateness of conferences in cases of gendered violence[1] has been occurring since the mid 1990s (Braithwaite and Daly 1994). Critics are concerned with power imbalances of victims and perpetrators in face-to-face meetings and the potential for re-victimizing victims. Others see benefits, including a victim's ability to voice the story of her victimization and its impact, and to be validated and believed by others.

We see two problems with the debate. First, it ignores huge variability in victimization contexts and relationships. All types of gendered violence (physical, sexual or both) and all types of relationships (between adults, youths or children) are discussed as if they were the same. Second, there is little empirical evidence on actual practices and outcomes *or* on victims' experiences, which could inform the debate. With relatively few jurisdictions in the world using conferences in youth or adult cases of gendered violence, researchers have few sites to conduct research.

We advance the discussion by analysing a particular type of gendered violence, sibling sexual abuse, and by presenting new research on court and conference responses to it. After a review of the literature, we describe the character and range of sibling sexual abuse and what happens when cases go to court or conference. We highlight themes emerging from four conference case studies and present one case in some depth. We find that many of the critics' concerns with conferences are not relevant to sibling abuse cases, but the cases do raise other concerns.

Sibling Sexual Abuse

Sibling sexual abuse is defined differently, depending on a therapeutic or legal frame of reference (Stathopoulos 2012: 3). Age differentials (typically a three

1 The term *gendered violence* refers to all forms of partner, family, and sexual violence. The gendered pattern of male perpetrator-female victim is most typical, although other dyads occur.

to five year gap) were once used, but today the emphasis is placed on power imbalances between siblings (McVeigh 2003: 117).

The prevalence of sibling sexual abuse is not known, but it is believed to be the most common form of intra-familial sexual abuse, occurring three to five times more often than father-to-daughter sexual abuse (Ballantine 2012: 56, Stathopoulos 2012: 8). In research on over 13,000 sibling abuse incidents reported to the police in the United States, 71 per cent of victims were female and 92 per cent of perpetrators were male. The most common dyad was brothers abusing sisters, but 25 per cent were brothers abusing brothers (Krienert and Walsh 2011). Researchers believe that sibling sex offences are less likely to be reported to the police; and, if reported, they are less likely to move further into the criminal justice process to prosecution, conviction or sentencing (Ballantine 2012: 56–7, Rayment-McHugh and Nisbet 2003).

Sibling sexual abuse is called an 'opportunistic' form of abuse because of the physical proximity of siblings (Stathopoulos 2012: 1); however, it is secretive, ongoing and can continue for many years. The shame associated with it leads to denial or minimization by parents or guardians. Some researchers in the 1980s believed it was harmless, a form of childhood experimentation, but researchers now emphasize its negative effects on victims (Doyle 1996, Laviola 1992, Panagakis 2011, Phillips-Green 2002, Rudd and Herzberger 1999). These include distrust of others; anger towards the sibling and parents; intrusive thoughts about the abuse; suicidal thoughts, self-harm or suicide attempts; low self-esteem; difficulties having intimate or physical relationships in adulthood; mental health problems (for example, post-traumatic stress disorder, anxiety, conduct disorder, depression and eating disorders); and substance abuse. Complicating matters further, some abusive siblings may themselves have been physically or sexually abused.

Disclosure is a key problem. Abused siblings worry that if they disclose, they will be disbelieved, blamed for the abuse, punished by their parents or create family conflict. Some believe that they are responsible for the abuse and do not want to see their sibling punished (Carlson et al. 2006, Doyle 1996, Laviola 1992, McVeigh 2003, Panagakis 2011).

Recent Australian commentary has proposed that referral to therapy may be the most optimal response for an offending youth (as well as for victims and relevant family members), compared to a criminal justice response alone (Kambouridis 2012, O'Brien 2010, Stathopoulos 2012). Likewise, a victim's ability to disclose offences and be supported by parents has a positive bearing on recovery (Stathopoulos 2012: 14). Both points are relevant when we compare court and conference responses to sibling sexual abuse.

Debate on Conferences and Gendered Violence: The Negatives and Positives

Debate on the appropriateness of conferences typically centres on partner violence and analysts have in mind *adult perpetrators and victims*. Those who focus on sexual violence have in mind *adult perpetrators and child victims* (for reviews, see Cossins 2008, Daly 2008, 2012, Daly and Stubbs 2006, Koss 2000, Lewis et al. 2001, Ptacek 2005, 2010, Strang and Braithwaite 2002). With some exceptions (Daly 2002), few have pondered the dynamics of *youth perpetrators and child victims*, the dyad in sibling sexual abuse. The negative concerns are that, as an informal process, conferences may:

- reinforce power imbalances between victims and perpetrators and re-victimize victims;
- trivialize the offence or result in outcomes that are not serious enough;
- allow perpetrators to diminish guilt or shift blame to the victim;
- not promote perpetrators' accountability or be seen as a 'soft option'.

The positives are that conferences may:

- give victims (or a victims' representative) the chance to voice their story and to be heard;
- allow a victim's experiences to be validated and acknowledge that s/he is not to blame;
- create opportunities for family relationships to be repaired, if desired;
- encourage a perpetrator to take responsibility for their behaviour;
- provide an appropriate context for family, friends and other relevant community members to censure the offending behaviour.

Conferences are set in motion only after a person has admitted to offending. When we consider sibling sexual abuse and conferences as court diversion, the option of youth justice conferences may break a cycle of abuse by encouraging admissions. More perpetrators may admit, and victims and family members may be more likely to report offences to the police because they see a practical or positive outcome, not one that excludes a perpetrator from society or the family home.

Elements of Sibling Sexual Offending

The Sexual Assault Archival Study (SAAS) gathered information on all youth sex offences reported to the police over 6.5 years in South Australia (see Daly 2006, Daly et al. 2007b for background).[2] Of the 385 cases, 59 per cent were disposed in court, 31 per cent by a conference, and 10 per cent by formal caution. All the formal cautions and almost all the conferences were finalized by an admission ('proved'), but just over half (51 per cent) of the court cases were finalized with a proved

2 The SAAS dataset is a quantitative dataset of legal processes and outcomes. It does not have any interview material on victims' experiences of crime or views of justice.

(convicted) sexual offence.[3] Many assume that the court is a place that treats 'serious offences seriously', but the SAAS data show that it is equally a place where serious cases are dismissed or withdrawn. Of the 385 cases, 16 per cent were 'no-touch' public exposure or indecent behaviour offences; the rest were penetrative sex, oral sex or fondling over clothes ('touch' offences). We analyse only the 'touch' offences in all the following comparisons of sibling and other (non-sibling) cases.

Eighteen per cent of the 'touch' offences involved sibling relationships. Compared to other sex offences, sibling perpetrators showed more remorse during the police interview; they were more likely to make admissions to the police; and they were more likely to be referred to a conference. Victims in sibling cases were much younger (7.7 years) compared to those in other cases (12.6 years); and the victim-perpetrator age gap was wider (6.6 years compared to 2.6 years). Sibling offences were more likely to be ongoing, with multiple incidents over time: for 64 per cent of such cases the abuse was ongoing (compared to 23 per cent of non-sibling cases).[4] A perpetrator manipulating a position of trust was more frequent in sibling (83 per cent) than in other cases (45 per cent).

Legal and Therapeutic Responses to Sibling Cases

The SAAS data show that, of 'touch' sex offences reported to the police, sibling cases were more likely to be 'proved' (convicted) than others. One reason is that a higher share of sibling cases was finalized by a conference, but even those sibling cases that were referred to court were proved more often (72 per cent) compared to non-sibling cases (45 per cent).[5] Therapeutic responses were also more likely in sibling cases, with a higher share of perpetrators in sibling cases (68 per cent) taking part in a specialist programme for adolescent sex offenders (the Mary Street programme), compared to those in non-sibling cases (23 per cent).[6] The difference was also evident in the court cases. Thus, contrary to others, we find that sibling cases in South Australia were treated more seriously than other 'touch' sex offences, in both a legal and therapeutic sense.[7]

3 An additional four per cent were proved as a non-sexual offence and the rest (45 per cent) were dismissed or withdrawn.

4 Thus, the overall mean difference in duration of victimization was longer for sibling than non-sibling cases; but, of the on-going abuse cases only, the mean difference for the two groups was not significant.

5 Cases were 'proved' almost entirely because youths admitted offending or entered a guilty plea in court. 'Proved' means the same as 'convicted', but a youth's criminal history can be protected by recording a proved case 'without conviction', as occurs in most Youth Court cases in this jurisdiction.

6 Youths can and do participate in the Mary Street programme before going to a conference or court.

7 To be clear, the cases were treated 'more seriously' because youths in sibling cases admitted or pleaded guilty to offences more often than youths in non-sibling cases. One

SAAS Conference Cases

Of the 59 sibling cases in the SAAS dataset, 30 were finalized by a conference.[8] Offence elements in the conference cases were similar to all sibling cases: young victims (7.5 years), a large victim-offender age gap (6 years), a high share of offenders abusing a position of trust (77 per cent), and ongoing abuse (63 per cent). Of the 30 conferences, the victim attended in 10, always with a supporter.[9] Three conferences (10 per cent) had no victim or representative at all. With respect to outcomes, 83 per cent of youth were part of the Mary Street programme and an additional 10 per cent were referred to other types of counselling. In 90 per cent of cases, there were apologies (verbal, written or both), almost always after the conference. In all cases, offenders completed the agreement.

In-Depth Study Cases

The In-Depth Study assembled a detailed chronology for 14 sexual and family violence conference cases, drawing from the police report and interviews with victims (or their representatives) and the youth justice coordinators who ran the conferences (see Daly et al. 2007a, Daly and Wade 2012).[10] Five case studies of peer sexual violence and adolescent violence toward parents have been presented in previous articles (Daly and Curtis-Fawley 2006, Daly and Nancarrow 2010). Here we consider four case studies of sibling sexual abuse, which provide a deeper understanding of family and conference dynamics. Each case study is too detailed (ranging from 2,500 to over 4,500 words; see Daly and Wade 2012) to be given in full here or even as a short synopsis. Thus, we present one case and then summarize and discuss patterns across the four.

We chose to present Case 1, Ben (the perpetrator) and Sharon (his mother, who represented the victim) because the offending was especially serious and the case had other complex elements. This case and Case 2 had solo-parent households headed by mothers, who themselves had histories of being physically and sexually abused and who had a dual role in the conference of representing the victim and supporting the perpetrator. Their sons had also been physically or sexually abused and they were generally disengaged from the conference process. With the

reason is that it is more difficult for a youth to deny offending that occurs in close proximity to their parent(s), but there may well be other reasons.

8 An additional three cases were referred to a conference, but they did not go forward.

9 The victims who attended the conference were 9 years old, on average, at the time of offence.

10 The SAAS time frame was 6.5 years (January 1995 to 30 June 2001); the time frame for the In-Depth Study was 6 months (July to December 2001); thus, the SAAS and In-Depth Study conference cases do not overlap. Only the In-Depth Study contains interview material.

potential exception of the perpetrator in Case 3, whose adoptive father may have abused him, none of the other descriptors applied to Cases 3 and 4.

Case 1: Ben (14 years), Sharon (his mother) and Marie (8 years)

Ben is a 'weird and wacky kid', in the words of the police youth officer. He was physically abusive to both his younger sisters, Marie (8) and Claire (nearly 6). He told the youth justice coordinator that he liked to get his sisters in his dark closet until they screamed. On many occasions since Marie was 5, he has pushed his finger into her vagina when they were in the closet. Marie was very distressed by Ben's behaviour and Sharon said her daughter had several weeks of restless nights after disclosing it. Soon after Sharon's discovery, Ben was removed from the home and placed into foster care. During a pre-conference visit with Ben a week before the conference, the youth justice coordinator believed that Ben was not sorry for his offending; indeed, he reported that Ben had said he would hurt his sisters again. We infer from the file that Ben's father was abusive not only to Ben, but also to his sisters. Sharon blamed Ben's father for Ben's abusive behaviour.

After Sharon discovered the offence, she contacted a person at her Church and then someone at Family and Youth Services, who contacted the police. There were about six months between the disclosure of the offence and the conference.

The day before the conference, the police youth officer learned that, a year before, Ben had forced a boy at his school to give him oral sex. Ben was charged with rape, but it was later dropped. Had the officer known of this charge, the case would not have been referred for a conference. The people attending the conference were Ben, his Mary Street counsellor, his foster carer, and his mother Sharon, in addition to the youth justice coordinator and the police youth officer. The conference lasted 2.5 hours, including a 10-minute break before the conference agreement was finalized.

The female police youth officer was very strict towards Ben in the conference. She felt that she had to control her negative thoughts about Ben, believing that if he 'had raped before, he'd rape again'. The youth justice coordinator observed that Ben could be 'a bubbly kid', but that most of the time he would completely disengage from the conference. He also thought that Ben was 'controlling the information' in the conference. A major turning point was when Ben permitted his mother to read a statement he had prepared with his Mary Street counsellor. Up to that point, Ben made it clear to everyone at the conference that he had a written statement, but he had refused to read it. During a break toward the end of the conference, Ben's counsellor told him that it would be useful to share the statement. When the break was over, participants were discussing who should read the statement, but no one seemed like the right person. Then Sharon stood up and Ben allowed her to read the statement to the group. In his statement, Ben acknowledged that what he did was wrong and that he had to comply with visitation rules. From Sharon's perspective, this showed that Ben had 'grown', which was important to her. Although Sharon's role at the conference was to represent Marie and support Ben, she felt torn in this role. As the children's mother, she wanted 'to be there for both of them'. However, trying to do so 'really stretched' [her] 'to the limit ... But what could I do ... They're both my children, and I love both of them.'

The conference agreement had many requirements for Ben, including continuation of Mary Street counselling, attending school and a Just Consequences[11] programme, strict visitation rules, writing an 'acknowledgement' letter to Marie and Claire, and being placed on a good behaviour bond.

Assessing the conferences

The four conferences were intense, emotional and long, lasting on average two hours. We assess their dynamics against the 'negatives' and 'positives' listed above.

None of the young victims attended the conference; thus, the power imbalances and potential re-victimization that can arise from face-to-face meetings were not relevant in these cases. Difficulties can emerge, however, when mothers have dual roles of representing their victim daughter and supporting their offending son, as happened in Cases 1 and 2. The mother in Case 2 thought her son was trivializing the offence, but in no other case did this occur; nor in any case did offenders diminish their guilt or shift blame on to the victim. However, a significant finding from the case studies is that there was more to the story of abuse than was supplied in the police report or was said by anyone at the conference or during the interviews. The siblings' parents were typically unsure of the extent of the abuse; indeed, the most knowledgeable person seemed to be the youth's Mary Street counsellor. In one case, the youth agreed to lift the confidentiality restrictions on his Mary Street counsellor to share information, an outcome the youth justice coordinator termed 'a gift' to the victim's mother. Thus, in all cases, the youths' accountability at the conference was restricted to the offence(s) described in the police report. In a legal sense, this is appropriate (and it would be no different had the case gone to court), but it demonstrates the hidden nature of sibling abuse, even after it is discovered.

Ben's agreement was more onerous than others, particularly because he received a good behaviour bond, which is highly atypical in conference cases. In all cases, the youths were to continue counselling at Mary Street; and, except for Case 2, all completed their agreement. It is not clear what critics of conferences for sexual abuse cases (for example, Cossins 2008) would desire for 'more serious' outcomes.[12] From the SAAS data, sibling cases (whether referred to conference or

11 The Just Consequences program is similar to 'Scared Straight'. In South Australia, it was run by the Department of Corrections. It involves a structured discussion with prisoners who are close to being released and a group of young people and their parents. The general message is: *'don't do what I did'*. The Family Conference Team stopped using it in 2004.

12 Throughout her critique, Cossins (2008) has in mind adult, not youth, perpetrators which may explain her concern that conferences may appear to be *too lenient* a response.

court) were more likely to result in conviction ('proved') and to be referred to the Mary Street programme than other 'touch' sex offences.

In all four cases, the impact of the offence on the victim and victim's representative was brought forward. Victims were never blamed for the offences and offence seriousness was emphasized; however, the validation of victims' experiences was partial. This occurred, in part, because the full story of the abuse was never revealed; and, in part, because the victims were not physically present in the room to be acknowledged directly. Further, the conference's emphasis was more on censuring and stopping the youth's abusive behaviour than it was on validating the victim or the experience of victimization, although helping the victim (with counselling) was addressed. With the availability of the Mary Street programme, these conferences focused as much or more on therapeutic interventions for youths than on solely criminal justice responses; and there was both conference and parental support of victims. This type of response would be considered optimal by those in the practice sector (for example, Kambouridis 2012, Stathopoulos 2012), with the caveat that incorporating relevant family members in therapy is also desirable.

Repairing family relationships did occur and was an important positive outcome in three cases; in the fourth, it was not relevant because the households had split up and family members had moved interstate. Although all youths were encouraged to take responsibility for their behaviour, those in Cases 1 and 2 did so partially and were less engaged in the conference compared to the youths in Cases 3 and 4. The youths' Mary Street counsellors played an important role; in some cases, they facilitated information and relationship-building, but, in others, they could be overly protective of the youth.

During a three-year period following the conference, two youths stayed out of trouble completely (Cases 1 and 4), but two others amassed a substantial criminal history in South Australia, although no sexual offences were recorded. An analysis of general re-offending (that is, all types of offences) from the SAAS data found that the strongest predictor was previous offending and that youths charged with sexual assault of siblings and children were less likely to re-offend compared to those charged with peer assaults or 'no-touch' offences (Daly et al. 2013).

Conclusion

We conclude with these points. First, sibling sexual abuse is distinctive from other types of gendered violence: most victims are too young to attend and participate, and all parties are focused mainly on addressing the perpetrators' behaviour and ultimately on becoming reunited in the family home. Second, and relatedly, critics' concerns with 'power imbalances', a 're-victimization' of victims or outcomes not being 'serious enough' are not especially germane to these cases. However, one concern in these cases is that parents (typically mothers) may have a dual role of representing the victim and supporting the perpetrator. It is understandable that mothers, like Sharon, want to be there for both of their children, but this comes at a price of having a muted presence, voice or autonomy for victims in the conference. Third, the conferences displayed many positives, including bringing forward the impact of the offence on victims, censuring the offending, and facilitating a frank conversation among perpetrators and family members. Legal or justice aims were secondary to rehabilitative or therapeutic aims, specifically to prevent the youth from further offending. However, the cases demonstrated that the 'full story' of the abuse was often too painful, shameful, and confusing for siblings and family members to face up to completely.

References

Ballantine, M. 2012. Sibling Incest Dynamics: Therapeutic Themes and Clinical Challenges. *Clinical Social Work Journal*, 40, 56–65.

Braithwaite, J. and Daly, K. 1994. Masculinities, Violence, and Communitarian Control, in *Just Boys Doing Business? Men, Masculinities, and Crime*, edited by T. Newburn and E.A. Stanko. London: Routledge, 189–213.

Carlson, M., Maciol, K. and Schneider, J. 2006. Sibling Incest: Reports from Forty-One Survivors. *Journal of Child Sexual Abuse*, 15(4), 19–34.

Cossins, A. 2008. Restorative Justice and Child Sex Offences: The Theory and Practice. *British Journal of Criminology*, 48, 359–78.

Daly, K. 2002. Sexual Assault and Restorative Justice, in *Restorative Justice and Family Violence*, edited by H. Strang and J. Braithwaite. Cambridge: Cambridge University Press, 62–88.

Daly, K. 2006. Restorative Justice and Sexual Assault: An Archival Study of Court and Conference Cases. *British Journal of Criminology*, 46, 334–56.

Daly, K. 2008. Setting the Record Straight and a Call for Radical Change: A Reply to Annie Cossins on 'Restorative Justice and Child Sex Offences'. *British Journal of Criminology*, 48(4), 557–66.

Daly, K. 2012. Conferences and Gendered Violence: Practices, Politics, Evidence, in *Conferencing and Restorative Justice: International Practices and Perspectives*, edited by E. and I. Vanfraechem. Oxford: Oxford University Press, 117–35.

Daly, K. and Curtis-Fawley, S. 2006. Restorative Justice for Victims of Sexual Assault, in *Gender and Crime: Patterns of Victimization and Offending*, edited by K. Heimer and C. Kruttschnitt. New York: Routledge, 230–65.

Daly, K. and Nancarrow, H. 2010. Restorative Justice and Adolescent Violence toward Parents, in *Feminism, Restorative Justice, and Violence Against Women*, edited by J. Ptacek. New York: Oxford University Press, 150–74.

Daly, K. and Stubbs, J. 2006. Feminist Engagement with Restorative Justice. *Theoretical Criminology*, 10(1), 9–28.

Daly, K. and Wade, D. 2012. *South Australia Juvenile Justice and Criminal Justice Research on Conferencing and Sentencing Technical Report No. 5, In-Depth Study of Sexual Assault and Family Violence Cases, Part II: Sibling and Sexual*

Assault, Other Sexual Assault, and Youth-Parent Assault. Brisbane: School of Criminology and Criminal Justice, Griffith University.

Daly, K., Bouhours, B., Broadhurst, R. and Loh, N. 2013. Youth Sex Offending: Recidivism, and Restorative Justice: Comparing Court and Conference Cases. *Australian and New Zealand Journal of Criminology*, 46(2), 241–67.

Daly, K., Bouhours, B., Curtis-Fawley, S., Weber, L. and School, R. 2007a. *South Australia Juvenile Justice and Criminal Justice (SJJ-CJ) Technical Report No. 4: In-Depth Study of Sexual Assault and Family Violence Cases*. Brisbane: School of Criminology and Criminal Justice, Griffith University.

Daly, K., Bouhours, B., Curtis-Fawley, S., Weber, L. and School, R. 2007b. *South Australia Juvenile Justice and Criminal Justice (SAJJ-CJ) Technical Report No. 3 (3rd edition): Sexual Assault Archival Study (SASS), an Archival Study of Sexual Offence Cases Disposed of in Youth Court and by Conference and Formal Caution*. Brisbane: School of Criminology and Criminal Justice, Griffith University.

Doyle, C. 1996. Sexual Abuse by Siblings: The Victims' Perspective. *Journal of Sexual Aggression*, 2(1), 17–32.

Kambouridis, H. 2012. *Working with Sibling Sexual Abuse (Gatehouse Centre)*. Australian Centre for the Study of Sexual Assault Working With series. Melbourne: Australian Centre for the Study of Sexual Assault, Australian Institute of Family Studies.

Koss, M. 2000. Blame, Shame, and Community: Justice Responses to Violence against Women. *American Psychologist*, 55, 1332–43.

Krienert, J. and Walsh, J. 2011. Sibling Sexual Abuse: An Empirical Analysis of Offender, Victim, and Event Characteristics in National Incident-Based Reporting System (NIBRS) Data, 2000–2007. *Journal of Child Abuse*, 20(4), 353–72.

Laviola, M. 1992. Effects of Older Brother-Younger Sister Incest: A Study of the Dynamics of 17 Cases. *Child Abuse and Neglect*, 16, 409–21.

Lewis. R., Emerson, R., Dobash, R., Dobash, P. and Cavanagh, K. 2001. Law's Progressive Potential: The Value of Engagement for the Law of Domestic Violence. *Social and Legal Studies*, 10, 105–30.

McVeigh, M. 2003. 'But She Didn't Say No': An Exploration of Sibling Sexual Abuse. *Australian Social Work*, 56(2), 116–26.

O'Brien, W. 2010. *Australia's Response to Sexualised or Sexually Abusive Behaviours in Children and Young People*. Canberra: Australian Crime Commission.

Panagakis, M. 2011. Sibling Incest: An Exploration of Trauma, Impact, and Treatment. PhD thesis in Psychology, Azusa Pacific University, Azusa, California. Available from ProQuest Dissertations and Theses.

Phillips-Green, M. 2002. Sibling Incest. *The Family Journal: Counselling and Therapy for Couples and Families*, 10(2), 195–202.

Ptacek, J. (ed.). 2005. Special Issue, Feminism, Restorative Justice, and Violence against Women. *Violence against Women*, 11(5), 563–730,

Ptacek, J. 2010. *Restorative Justice and Violence against Women.* New York: Oxford University Press.

Rayment-McHugh, S. and Nisbet, I. 2003. Sibling Incest Offenders as a Subset of Adolescent Sexual Offenders. Paper to the Child Sexual Abuse: Justice Response or Alternative Resolution Conference, Australian Institute of Criminology, Adelaide, 1–2 May 2003. Available at: http://www.aic.gov.au/events/aic%20upcoming%20events/2003/abuse.aspx.

Rudd, J. and Herzberger, S. 1999. Brother-sister Incest – Father-daughter Incest: A Comparison of Characteristics and Consequences. *Child Abuse and Neglect*, 23(9), 915–28.

Stathopoulos, M. 2012. *Sibling Sexual Abuse.* Australian Centre for the Study of Sexual Assault Research Summary. Melbourne: Australian Centre for the Study of Sexual Assault, Australian Institute of Family Studies.

Strang, H. and Braithwaite, J. (eds). 2002. *Restorative Justice and Family Violence.* Cambridge: Cambridge University Press.

PART VI
Challenges and Opportunities

Applying restorative justice processes to family violence is a matter of concern for some practitioners and theorists as it is suggested that, even if restorative justice 'worked' for other offences, it cannot be used here because: there is not the anonymity associated with many other crimes; the offending is a violation of trust; the offending has often been the result of a prolonged exercise of power and control; and it may affect a number of people over time, including immediate and wider family members. Additionally, it is argued that restorative justice processes rely on perpetrators accepting that their behaviour is wrong, whereas perpetrators of family violence tend to blame other people, including the victim, for their offending. It is also suggested that restorative processes allow perpetrators to minimise their offending. Women who have been abused, for example, may be 'out-talked' by the other party and be afraid to disagree with their partner. Another concern is the perception that restorative justice is a means of dealing with a 'dispute' though violence within the family is clearly not a dispute which needs to be addressed and resolved. Julie Stubbs in Chapter 17 presents a considered account of these criticisms and concerns which are commonly directed towards the use of restorative justice for intimate partner violence and explores these issues in more detail.

Part VI is also about the importance of letting victims make the choices that suit them rather than professionals deciding for them. It has to be accepted, for example, that, although women do call the police, they may not want their partner arrested and/or prosecuted. Instead they want immediate protection and the violence to stop. Some victims of gendered violence also wish to continue their relationship with the perpetrator. These different relationships and victims' needs have to be considered in any legal response to such violence. Accordingly, the diversity of contexts and victims' wishes pose major challenges to both restorative and established criminal justice processes.

In Chapter 18, Anne Hayden discusses a number of the criticisms set out in Julie Stubbs' chapter and which appear more widely in the work of critics of the use of restorative justice processes in family violence. Because 'imbalance of power' is often cited as a major reason for not using restorative justice for these cases, she puts forward a different way of thinking about power in intimate relationships. She describes how it can be positive and negative and how it can be used by perpetrators and victims at micro and macro levels. Furthermore, she describes some of the implications this has for restorative justice practice and policy and her analysis presents an opportunity for further understanding the multiple dimensions of intimate partner violence.

In the concluding chapter, Heather Strang stresses: the need for rigorous research into the effectiveness of restorative justice with family violence in order to answer the many questions that surround this issue. She addresses the dynamics and implications of violence within the family; the development of restorative justice practice guidelines which have a wide-based consensus and are specific to the special needs of those living in violent situations; and the need for independent monitoring of specialized restorative justice practice and outcomes to enable continued improvement in practices. In this way, victims *could* be given another viable option to help them live peaceful and happy lives free from violence. And perpetrators *could* be given the opportunity to make amends for their behaviour and to address it in a more constructive manner.

Chapter 17
Gendered Violence and Restorative Justice

Julie Stubbs

Introduction

Reviews suggest that restorative justice 'works better with crimes involving personal victims ... with violent crimes more consistently than with property crimes ... [and] victims benefit, on average, from face-to-face restorative justice conferences' (Sherman and Strang 2007: 8). Why then is there such caution about using restorative justice for gendered violence? In this chapter I draw on research concerning gendered violence and restorative justice to argue that caution is well advised, and that generic models of restorative justice may be poorly equipped to deal with the needs of victims of gendered violence and entail risks. I also argue that restorative justice demands more from participants than conventional justice, which has implications for victims' safety and expectations of the victim's role.

Gendered Violence

'Gendered violence', such as intimate partner violence and sexual assault, arises from/within gendered social relations. Such offences reflect and contribute to the subordination of women (Ptacek 1999). Some scholars challenge the depiction of intimate partner violence as gendered and argue that there is gender symmetry in offending (Straus 2006), but this is highly contested (Dobash and Dobash 2004). There is agreement that female victims of intimate partner violence are more likely than men to experience fear, to be injured by their partner and to experience violence at separation and that most intimate partner homicides are committed by men (Dobash and Dobash 2004).

According to Miller and Mullins (2009: 34), recognition that 'gender relations order social life and social institutions in fundamental ways', 'structure life chances and opportunities' and 'generate and legitimate cultural norms of difference and inequality' has implications for restorative justice, especially in dealing with gendered violence. Achilles and Zehr (2001: 93) acknowledge that some developments in restorative justice have failed 'to take seriously the full implications of the philosophy and values they espouse' as in 'naively attempting to apply restorative approaches in highly problematic areas (such as intimate partner violence) without adequate attention to complexities and safeguards'. For instance, an incident based account of offending seems to underpin much of the restorative justice literature but is inadequate in understanding intimate partner violence and possibly other offences. Intimate partner violence is commonly recurrent, may involve physical, sexual and other forms of abuse and the perpetrator may exert considerable control over the victim through instilling fear of further violence. It typically involves the violation of trust by an intimate partner and perhaps also by family members and the community who have failed to protect the victim. Yet as Frederick and Lizdas (2003: 29) note, generic restorative justice approaches 'have not accounted for one of the chief characteristics of most domestic violence cases; the existence of ongoing danger occasioned by the victim's resistance to the batterer's authority and control'.

Debate continues as to whether restorative justice might be appropriate for gendered violence and, if so, what type and under what circumstances (Ptacek 2010, Strang and Braithwaite 2002, the special issue of *Theoretical Criminology* 2006 vol. 10 (1)). Some authors differentiate between types of gendered violence and their prospects for the safe use of restorative justice processes; for instance, Hopkins, Koss and Bachar (2004) distinguish date rape from ongoing intimate partner violence and see merit in adapting restorative justice for the former but urge great caution with respect to the latter.

What is Meant by Restorative Justice?

Assessing the merits of restorative justice in response to gendered violence is difficult because restorative justice is used to describe a diverse range of programmes and practices. While many schemes share a broad orientation to restorative justice, they differ in key respects.

Models of restorative justice vary between and within jurisdictions. For instance, in New South Wales, Australia, different forms of restorative justice are used to divert young perpetrators, inform sentencing for eligible adults, in Indigenous circle sentencing and with prisoners post-sentence where restorative justice has no influence on case outcome or parole (see contributors to Bolitho et al. 2012). Gendered violence offences are excluded from the first two programmes but may be included in the last. In England and Wales, programmes include warnings for young perpetrators, direct and indirect victim-offender mediation and conferencing schemes for adults operating in addition to conventional criminal justice and at various stages, such as between conviction and sentence, during a community sentence or pre-release for prisoners (Shapland et al. 2007). The Dove Daybreak programme deals with decisions concerning children in cases involving intimate partner violence but does not necessarily include perpetrators (Liebmann and Wootton 2008/2010: 18).

Restorative justice programmes that have been developed specifically for gendered violence, such as those described below, tend to differ from each other and from standard restorative justice in important ways. They are commonly hybrid models that blend restorative justice with therapeutic intervention and involve special expertise and considerable preparation and engagement with the parties.

RESTORE Arizona was a demonstration project for date rape and other first-time perpetrators of sex offences referred by prosecutors. Victims received support via a partnership with a sexual assault service. Perpetrators were diverted into an intensive, 12 month therapeutic programme and were required to participate in a restorative justice conference with the victim (or surrogate if the victim agreed to restorative justice but did not wish to participate), meet with a case manager, appear monthly before a community accountability board, complete psycho-sexual therapy and make a written apology to the victim (Koss 2010). Following successful completion, charges were dropped and perpetrators avoided sex offender registration.

By contrast, RESTORE NZ accepts referrals from courts following a guilty plea, where outcomes inform sentencing, and from the community where matters need not have been reported to the police. Importantly, perpetrators must accept responsibility. Not all cases proceed to a restorative justice conference. Two community experts, one for perpetrators and one for victims, assist a clinical team overseen by a psychologist to select appropriate cases, prepare the parties over a series of meetings, coach supporters, plan a restorative conference specific to the needs of the parties and monitor outcomes. The facilitator has specialist training in the dynamics of sexual violence (Jülich et al. 2010: 18–19).

Also in Arizona, the Circles of Peace/Circulos de Paz (CCP) programme for domestic violence is a court-referred restorative justice treatment programme designed as an alternative to batterer intervention programmes. Perpetrators attend weekly conferences for 26 to 52 weeks; facilitators use a 'transition framework' intended to bring about change. Victims (voluntary), extended family members and trained community volunteers participate in the conferences. Perpetrators who complete the programme have their matters dismissed by the court (Mills et al. 2013).

It is important to understand what advocates recommending restorative justice for gendered violence intend since the opportunities and risks, and the expectations of and upon victims, may differ depending on the approach. These differences also matter in assessing the possible implications of restorative justice research. Most evaluations have been of diversionary youth justice schemes but the research literature is growing concerning adult schemes, typically run in conjunction with criminal justice. Research suggests that results differ for different forms of restorative justice and for different kinds of people; for instance, a major England and Wales study of three schemes (Shapland et al. 2007) found more positive results for direct (conference or victim offender mediation) than indirect approaches (for example, shuttle mediation).

Low referral numbers in RESTORE NZ and RESTORE Arizona have limited the capacity for evaluation. In the former, research has focused on best practice principles and raised questions about how best to measure success (Jülich et al. 2010: 62–4). In the latter, researchers found that perpetrators developed empathy for victims over time (Bletzer and Koss 2012). A randomized controlled trial comparing CCP and the usual batterer intervention programme (BIP) found that CCP participants experienced less recidivism than BIP participants during all follow-up comparisons (Mills et al. 2013). However, statistically significant differences were only found for non-domestic violence re-arrests[1] and no significant differences in domestic violence re-arrests. Thus, CCP does no worse than the usual batterers' intervention programme and falsifies the belief that restorative justice cannot be used to treatment domestic violence crimes. However, this study did not examine other programme goals or restorative justice characteristics (Mills et al. 2013).

Restorative Justice and/or Criminal Justice?

Some advocates promote the benefits of restorative justice as if it provides a complete alternative to criminal justice. This is not achievable, since restorative justice is not a fact-finding forum but requires an accused person to accept responsibility for the offence (Daly 2006) and thus restorative justice does not attempt to overcome problems associated with the trial process. It is possible, on the other hand, that aspects of restorative justice could be introduced to shape the court process. For instance, Naylor proposed 'a collaborative court process ensuring a greater role for the victim, a more restorative sentencing regime, and a greater role for the judge to actively challenge attitudes to the offender and the community' (2010: 628). However, to some extent, the debate about whether or not restorative justice can or should replace conventional criminal justice commonly caricatures both positions (Hoyle 2010: 1–6). Achilles and Stutzman-Amstutz (2006: 218) caution against presenting an 'either/or' proposition since victims have benefited from some improvements in conventional criminal justice systems and those who are interested in restorative justice should not be asked to trade off opportunities afforded by conventional criminal justice. Most evidence about the use of restorative justice for adults is derived from schemes that are within the criminal justice system (Bolitho et al. 2012, Sherman and Strang 2007).

Community-based restorative justice programmes should be examined on their own terms rather than as a replacement for the criminal justice system. Community restorative justice schemes may increase opportunities (and risks) for parties to deal with offences or other harms but, like other modes of informal justice (Abel 1982: 278), dispute resolution (Field 2010) or therapeutic intervention undertaken voluntarily, will vary in their capacity to safeguard participants, encourage compliance, hold people accountable and give victims of crime the vindication they seek. They may offer particular risks in cases of ongoing violence. Community-based restorative justice schemes designed by Joan

1 The Mills study involved intimate partner violence and family violence cases. As such cases were considered to be 'domestic violence' under Arizona law, that term has been used in this context.

Pennell and colleagues in Newfoundland and North Carolina to respond to child protection issues and to offer safety planning for battered women (Pennell and Burford 2002, Pennell and Francis 2005) are seen as very promising (Ptacek 2010). They demonstrate the need for great care in designing specific restorative justice schemes related to family violence and the value of working in partnership with victim advocates and community organizations.

Restorative Justice as Victim-Focused?

There is no clear theoretical account of how or why restorative justice should benefit victims (Green 2007) but restorative justice is commonly said to be victim-focused and that, by putting harm at the centre of restorative deliberations, victims' interests will be served. However, restorative justice models differ in how central victims are to their design and practice (Dignan 2005). Bolivar (2010) analysed the various ways in which restorativeness for victims has been conceptualized in the literature (reparation, meeting needs, specific restoration of the damage, healing, empowerment) and found a mismatch between these concepts and the measures commonly used in evaluations (satisfaction, psychological symptoms, positive emotions). Achilles and Stutzman-Amstutz (2006: 219) note the opportunities afforded to victims by restorative justice but found that many programmes are perpetrator-focused, too often assume that they know what victims need or want, and that it is uncommon for victim advocates to be consulted or involved in planning restorative justice. While restorative justice guidelines often cite victims' safety as a key principle, Wemmers found that no study in her review had asked 'whether restorative measures respond to victims' need for security and to their fear of crime' (2002: 53). A related concern is that perpetrator-screening criteria for restorative justice encounters have not been 'victim oriented, research-driven, nor consistently applied' (Presser and Lowenkamp 1999: 335).

Victims' take-up rates in restorative justice vary substantially. Dignan (2005: chapter 5) reports rates from 14 per cent to over 80 per cent in different schemes. However, studies commonly report high levels of satisfaction with the process among victims who do participate. Some studies also measure satisfaction with outcome. Shapland et al. (2007: 26) found similar levels of satisfaction with outcomes generally among victims (75 per cent) and perpetrators (78 per cent) but found also that perpetrators were more positive than victims on several dimensions. Perpetrators were more likely than victims to say that, following the restorative justice conference, perpetrators now understood the harm caused (83 per cent compared with 60 per cent), restorative justice had solved the problems caused by the offence (51 per cent compared with 38 per cent), the perpetrator was now less likely to re-offend (79 per cent compared with 40 per cent) and that restorative justice was a good way to deal the offence (73 per cent compared with 64 per cent) (Shapland et al. 2007:37). Compared to the control group, 'conferencing did not seem to affect victims' process of recovery' (2007: 45), although 63 per cent of victims said that they felt better and 39 per cent said that they felt more secure (Shapland et al. 2007: 40). However, Dignan (2005: 42) has observed that research findings about the benefits of restorative justice for victims of crime are 'more equivocal regarding the part played by conferencing – as opposed to victim resilience, support from family and friends or simply passage of time – in contributing to any recovery.' Schemes are rarely funded to provide outcomes for victims, beyond any reparations or apologies that a perpetrator has the capacity or willingness to provide and some legislative schemes are limited to providing outcomes only for perpetrators (Daly and Nancarrow 2010: 171). The Newfoundland restorative justice model (Pennell and Burford 2002) was a rare example that generated additional resources to support families.

Which Victims?

Restorative justice tends to assume an idealized victim and may 'tacitly endorse victim stereotypes' (Green 2007: 183). Early studies of restorative justice did not examine gender issues, the experiences of racialized groups or whether or not victims' needs and experiences might differ according to the offence, victims' and perpetrators' characteristics or the relationship between the victim and the perpetrator (Green 2007: 183, Strang 2002: 209, Walklate 2006: 279). Victims may differ in the approach they take in reconstructing their lives and need different things at different times (Achilles and Stutzman-Amstutz 2006: 218). Victims of gendered violence (and others) commonly have both 'survival needs and justice needs' (Koss 2010). Survival needs such as 'safety, physical health, economic issues such as housing and employment, education or retraining, and immigration problems' (Koss 2010: 221) are typically not acknowledged in the restorative justice literature but may condition the capacity for, and timing of, participation in restorative justice processes. While some schemes invest substantial time and resources in preparing the parties for restorative justice (Koss 2010), that is not uniformly the case.

While some studies have found that victims of violence can respond well to restorative justice, others offer reason for caution. In a study of restorative justice for young perpetrators, Daly (2006: 141) found that the group of victims who exhibited high levels of distress were 'significantly more likely to be composed of female victims, personal crime victims (including those victimized in their occupational role or at their organizational workplace), violent offences, and victims and perpetrators who were family members or well known to each other'. After the conference, the high-distress group 'were far more likely to remain angry and fearful of perpetrators, and to be negative toward them', than the low-distress victims and, unlike other groups, the majority of the high-distress victims (71 per cent) said that they had not recovered from the offence one year later (Daly 2006: 141). While this may suggest the need for careful screening of cases for restorative justice, Pelikan (2002) found that among intimate partner violence victims in her study it was impossible to predetermine who was suited for restorative justice.

Victims' Choice

Victims' participation in restorative justice is voluntary and offers choices that are unavailable in conventional criminal justice. However, in the literature debating the use of restorative justice for gendered violence, women are largely constructed in one of two ways – as either too victimized to make choices or as active agents empowered through choice. Such a dichotomy is unhelpful; women's choices as they resist violence and attempt to find safety are constrained by the effects of gendered violence, by material circumstances and by cultural narratives and practices. The choice to participate is not adequate to ensure the safety and effectiveness of the process or outcomes.

'Voice' and Being Heard

Communication has been identified as a defining feature of restorative justice and as important to the parties. Sherman and Strang (2007: 29) say that victims crave a story of why and how the offence happened, while perpetrators crave to offer an explanation. Drawing on procedural justice literature, advocates often point to the importance of 'voice' and presume that telling their story is cathartic and empowering for victims. Shapland et al. (2007: 22) found that, among both victims and perpetrators, people differed in what they thought was important about the restorative justice conference; for victims, the most common response was being able to explain the effects of the offence (17 per cent). Meeting the perpetrator was the best thing for some victims (16 per cent) but the worst thing for others (10 per cent). For perpetrators, the best thing was being able to apologize (20 per cent) and being able to explain the offence (14 per cent).

As Wemmers and Cyr found, for victims 'voice is not just about expressing one's needs but also, and perhaps more importantly, about being heard' (2006: 122). Since popular discourses continue to trivialize offences like intimate partner violence or sexual assault and challenge the credibility of victims, there is reason for concern that victims' accounts may not be heard and validated. Research also indicates that perpetrators of intimate partner violence commonly minimize or neutralize their behaviour (Dobash et al. 1998). However, what appears to be minor may be much more significant when considered in the context of the coercion that is common in intimate partner violence (Stark 2007). For some victims, a word or gesture is enough to make them very fearful since it signals the likelihood of another beating and yet this may not be evident to others (Stubbs 2007). This suggests the need for facilitators and other participants to have a good understanding of gendered violence and raises questions about the wisdom of including offences of gendered violence in generic restorative justice schemes.

Responsibility

Restorative justice programmes require perpetrators to accept responsibility or at least not deny the offence. Shapland et al. (2007: 23) found that most people attending restorative justice conferences thought that 'they understood what the other party was saying' but victims were more sceptical about whether or not the perpetrator was sincere. However, apologies were given and accepted in most cases (Shapland et al. 2007: 25). Daly (2002) also found a mismatch between victims' and perpetrators' assessments of whether or not apologies were genuine. These findings are important since researchers have found that a feature of the minority of conferences that 'did not go well' was a dispute between victims and perpetrators about the facts of the offence, a failure by the perpetrator to take responsibility, making light of the offence or blaming the victim (Shapland et al. 2007: 47). Apologies are valued as an outcome of restorative justice, but may be particularly ill-advised in intimate partner violence contexts. Women face strong cultural expectations to accept apologies, but perpetrators of intimate partner violence commonly use apologies to placate victims only to re-offend (Stubbs 2007).

Within Project RESTORE Arizona, perpetrators were termed 'responsible persons' and required to successfully complete the programme before making an apology. Of 20 cases enrolled in the programme, 16 completed. A textual analysis of completed cases found that empathy for victims and acceptance of responsibility among perpetrators developed over time throughout the programme (Bletzer and Koss 2012). These findings suggest that standard restorative justice programmes, typified by a single event such as a conference, may not be sufficient to engender empathy for victims and responsibility among (some) perpetrators.

What Does Restorative Justice Ask of Victims?

As Crawford (2002: 123) notes, restorative justice asks participants to take on greater responsibility than in conventional criminal justice. Victims of gendered violence who participate in restorative justice processes, directly or indirectly, tell a personal story to the perpetrator and others with whom they may have ongoing relationships. Those who are able to speak effectively in their own interests, and also for their children, may find this empowering but '[t]he risks of speaking frankly in the RJ context are great' (Smith 2006: 186). For instance, 'as people negotiate relationships, they calculate the costs and rewards of compliance, conflict, disclosure, and relational commitment' (Heath and Jennings 2002: 215); and '[a]n unwelcome story … runs the risk of rejection, derision or reprimand' (Smith 2006: 186). Care also needs to be taken so that the high value placed on apology in restorative justice does not become an obligation or burden for victims (Stubbs 2007).

Conclusion

Sherene Razack has examined 'how relations of domination and subordination stubbornly regulate encounters in the classrooms and courtrooms' (1998: 10) and I remain concerned that the same may be true in restorative justice settings. The involvement of victims' supporters and community members cannot be relied on to challenge subordination and safeguard victims since communities are not necessarily benign, but are riven by inequality and may be intolerant or prejudiced (Dignan 2005: 179). Generic models of restorative justice may be poorly equipped to safeguard victims of gendered violence. A different approach is needed in which facilitators and participants fully appreciate the characteristics of gendered violence, avoid the risks of re-victimization which can arise when perpetrators minimize their offending or offer insincere apologies, and which can provide safe and meaningful outcomes for victims.

References

Abel, R. 1982. The Contradictions of Informal Justice, in *The Politics of Informal Justice*, vol. 1, edited by R. Abel. New York: Academic Press, 267–320.

Achilles, M. and Stutzman-Amstutz, L. 2006. Responding to the Needs of Victims, in *Handbook of Restorative Justice: A Global Perspective*, edited by D. Sullivan and L. Tifft. New York: Routledge, 211–20.

Achilles, M. and Zehr, H. 2001. Restorative Justice for Crime Victims: The Promise and Challenge, in *Restorative Justice: Repairing Harm and Transforming Communities*, edited by G. Bazemore and M. Schiff. Cincinnati, OH: Anderson Publishing.

Bletzer K, and Koss, M. 2012. From Parallel to Intersecting Narratives in Cases of Sexual Assault. *Qualitative Health Research*, 22(3), 291–303.

Bolitho, J., Bruce, J. and Mason, G. 2012. *Restorative Justice, Adults and Emerging Issues*. Sydney: Institute of Criminology.

Bolivar, D. 2010. Conceptualizing Victims' 'Restoration'. *Restorative Justice. International Review of Victimology*, 17, 237–65.

Crawford, A. 2002. The State, Community, and Restorative Justice, in *Restorative Justice and the Law*, edited by L. Walgrave. Cullompton: Willan, 101–29.

Daly, K. 2002. Restorative Justice: The Real Story. *Punishment and Society*, 4, 55–79.

Daly, K. 2006. The Limits of Restorative Justice, in *Handbook of Restorative Justice: A Global Perspective*, edited by D. Sullivan and L. Tifft. New York: Routledge, 134–45.

Daly, K. and Nancarrow, H. 2010. Restorative Justice and Youth Violence against Parents, in *Restorative Justice and Violence against Women*, edited by J. Ptacek. New York: Oxford University Press, 150–75.

Dignan, J. 2005. *Understanding Victims and Restorative Justice*. Maidenhead: Open University Press.

Dobash, R.P., Dobash, R.E. Cavanagh, K. and Lewis, R. 1998. Separate and Intersecting Realities: A Comparison of Men's and Women's Accounts of Violence against Women. *Violence against Women*, 4, 382–414.

Dobash, R.P. and Dobash, R.E. 2004. Women's Violence to Men in Intimate Relationships: Working on a Puzzle. *British Journal of Criminology* 44(3), 324–49.

Field, R. 2010. FDR and Victims of Family Violence: Ensuring a Safe Process and Outcomes. *Australasian Dispute Resolution Journal*, 21(3), 185–93.

Frederick, L. and Lizdas, K. 2003. The Role of Restorative Justice in the Battered Women's Movement. Minneapolis, MN: Battered Women's JUSTICE Project. Available at: http://www.bwjp.org/files/bwjp/articles/Role_of_Restorative_Justice_Battered_Women's_Movement.pdf.

Green, S. 2007. The Victims' Movement and Restorative Justice, in *The Handbook of Restorative Justice*, edited by G. Johnstone and D. Van Ness. Cullompton: Willan, 171–91.

Heath, R. and Jennings, B. 2002 *Human Communication: Theory and Research*. Mahwah, NJ: Lawrence Erlbaum Associates.

Hopkins, C.Q., Koss, M.P. and Bachar, K.J. 2004. Applying Restorative Justice to Ongoing Intimate Violence: Problems and Possibilities. *Saint Louis University Public Law Review*, *23*, 289–312.

Hoyle, C. 2010. The Case for Restorative Justice, in *Debating Restorative Justice*, edited by C. Cunneen and C. Hoyle. Oxford: Hart Publishing.

Jülich, S., Buttle, J. Cummins, C. and Freeborn, E. 2010. *NZ Project Restore. An Exploratory Study of Restorative Justice and Sexual Violence*. Auckland: Auckland University of Technology.

Koss, M. 2010. Restorative Justice for Acquaintance Rape and Misdemeanour Sex Crime, in *Restorative Justice and Violence against Women*, edited by J. Ptacek. New York: Oxford University Press, 218–38.

Liebmann M. and Wootton L. 2008/2010. *Restorative Justice and Domestic Violence/Abuse*. Wales: Home Office Crime Reduction Unit.

Miller, J. and Mullins, C. 2009. Feminist Theories of Girls' Delinquency, in *The Delinquent Girl*, edited by M. Zahn. Philadelphia, PA: Temple University Press. 30–49.

Mills, L., Barocas, B. and Ariel, B. 2013. The Next Generation of Court-Mandated Domestic Violence Treatment: A Comparison Study of Batterer Intervention and Restorative Justice Programmes. *Journal of Experimental Criminology*, 9, 65–90.

Naylor, B. 2010. Effective Justice for Victims of Sexual Assault: Taking Up the Debate on Alternative Pathways. *The University of New South Wales Law Journal*, 33, 662–84.

Pelikan C. 2002. Victim-Offender-Mediation in Domestic Violence Cases – A Comparison of the Effects of Criminal Law Intervention: The Penal Process and Mediation, in *Doing Qualitative Research' Forum: Qualitative Social Research 3, Art. 16*. Available at: http://www.qualitative-research.net/index.php/fqs/article/view/880/1919.

Pennell, J. and Burford, G. 2002. Feminist Praxis: Making Family Group Conferencing Work, in *Restorative Justice and Family Violence*, edited by H. Strang and J. Braithwaite. Melbourne: Cambridge University Press.

Pennell, J. and Francis, S. 2005. Safety Conferencing: Toward a Coordinated and Inclusive Response to Safeguard Women and Children. *Violence against Women*, 11(5), 666–92.

Presser L. and Lowenkamp, C. 1999. Restorative Justice: An Offender Screening. *Journal of Criminal Justice*, 27(24), 333–43.

Ptacek J. 1999. *Battered Women in the Courtroom: The Power of Judicial Responses*. Boston, MA: Northeastern University.

Ptacek J. 2010. Re-Imaging Justice for Crimes of Violence against Women, in *Restorative Justice and Violence against Women*, edited by J. Ptacek. New York: Oxford University Press, 281–86.

Razack, S. 1998. *Looking White People in the Eye: Gender, Race and Culture in the Courtrooms and Classrooms*. Toronto: University of Toronto Press.

Shapland, J., Atkinson, A., Atkinson, H., Chapman, B., Dignan, J., Howes, M., Johnstone, J., Robinson, G. and Sorsby, A. 2007. *Restorative Justice: The Views of Victims and Offenders*. Ministry of Justice Research Series 3/07. London: Ministry of Justice.

Sherman, L. and Strang, H. 2007. *Restorative Justice: The Evidence*. London: Smith Institute.

Smith, K. 2006. Dissolving the Divide: Cross-Racial Communication in the Restorative Justice Process. *Dalhousie Journal of Legal Studies*, 15, 168–203.

Stark, E. 2007. *Coercive Control: How Men Entrap Women in Personal Life*. New York: Oxford University Press.

Strang, H. 2002. *Repair or Revenge: Victims and Restorative Justice*. Oxford: Clarendon Press.

Strang, H. and Braithwaite, J. (eds). 2002. *Restorative Justice and Family Violence*. Melbourne: Cambridge University Press.

Straus, M. 2006. Future Research on Gender Symmetry in Physical Assaults on Partners. *Violence against Women*, 12, 1086–97.

Stubbs, J. 2007. Beyond Apology? Domestic Violence and Critical Questions for Restorative Justice. *Criminology and Criminal Justice: An International Journal*, 7(2), 169–87.

Theoretical Criminology. 2006. Special Issue on Restorative Justice. *Theoretical Criminology*, 10(1).

Walklate, S. 2006. Changing Boundaries of the 'Victim' in Restorative Justice: So Who Is the Victim Now?, in *Handbook of Restorative Justice: A Global Perspective*, edited by D. Sullivan and L. Tifft. New York: Routledge, 273–85.

Wemmers, J. 2002, Restorative Justice for Victims of Crime: A Victim Oriented Approach to Restorative Justice. *International Review of Victimology*, 9, 43–59.

Wemmers, J. and Cyr, K. 2006. What Fairness Means to Crime Victims: A Social Psychological Perspective on Victim-Offender Mediation. *Applied Psychology in Criminal Justice*, 2(2), 102–28.

Chapter 18

Reflections on Family Violence and Restorative Justice: Addressing the Critique

Anne Hayden

Introduction

There is more agreement in this debate about whether or not to use restorative justice for family violence than is generally acknowledged. For example, both critics and proponents concur that much family violence remains behind closed doors and is under-reported; and both stress the importance of ensuring victims' safety and using sound processes. This chapter explores further the agreements and disagreements between the two groups and, where disagreements remain, reflects on whether or not restorative justice could, in effect, address these concerns. This is a key issue because as long as the focus is on the points of difference, little attention is given to shared priorities and policy makers, researchers and many practitioners seem to prefer to maintain the status quo. The consequence of this for those directly involved – victims, perpetrators and families – is that they are likely to continue to experience or commit violent acts and their choices to deal with this violence will remain limited: call the police, seek refuge or do nothing. The consequences for society more broadly are that there are likely to be few opportunities for relevant empirical research to examine the relative advantages or disadvantages of both approaches – the criminal justice system and restorative justice processes – and the bulk of resources will continue to be allocated to the criminal justice system despite its acknowledged failings.

In this chapter, I try to address some of the criticisms made about the use of restorative justice for family violence. I primarily use intimate partner violence as an example, as there has been much more debate around it. However, the criticisms and my responses are of wider relevance and relate to family violence. I discuss research which provides new ways of thinking about family violence, restorative justice and power and explore the implications of gatekeeping which has been used to prevent restorative justice being available for family violence. I also draw attention to, as I alluded to above, some of the often ignored agreements which advocates for both sides of the debate share.

The Debate: The Example of Intimate Partner Violence

The battered women's movement worked hard in relatively recent years to bring intimate partner violence into the public arena and feminists have expressed many concerns about the limitations of the criminal justice system to stop violence against women (Busch 2002, Ptacek 2010). At around the same time, contemporary restorative justice was developing with the aim of empowering communities, in particular victims, with a voice about what should be done to address what had happened to them and about their needs (see, for example, Zehr 1990). Advocates from the battered women's movement, however, were concerned that restorative justice for intimate partner violence could re-victimize the victims.

A useful perspective on these two approaches was provided by Frederick and Lizdas (2010). They described a crossing of paths of the two reform movements, each of which was challenging the criminal justice system. These 'both ... [held] the promise of being truly effective responses to domestic violence' (Frederick and Lizdas 2010: 39). They observed that both movements shared four principles: restoring victims of crime; preventing individual perpetrators from re-offending; engaging the community in mending the harms caused by crime; and addressing the context of crime. This crossing of paths has yet to lead to mutual understanding, however, despite proponents and critics of restorative justice for gendered crimes agreeing that intimate partner violence and sexual assault warrant a significant response (Hudson 2002).

Evelyn Zellerer (2004) described the debate as an example of dichotomous thinking which considered the interests of victims versus the interests of perpetrators and intervention by the state versus intervention by the community. She saw the restorative justice paradigm as having the potential to overcome this dichotomous thinking and to resolve the dilemmas facing proponents and critics. Instead, what had happened, she wrote, was that 'dialogue between feminists and restorative justice advocates has been limited and oftentimes strained' (2003: 3). Also compounding this debate is the fact that there is no one feminist perspective: feminists do not take a uniform position on these matters (Merry 2009, Zellerer 2004). Furthermore, the dichotomy or either/or assumption in much of the literature fails to take account of the community service providers already working in conjunction with the criminal justice system, for example, in pre-sentence conferencing as discussed in Part III of this volume.

The Critique: The Example of Intimate Partner Violence

Julie Stubbs, in her valuable contribution to this volume, identified a series of concerns which are held by critics to the use of restorative justice for family violence. The main focus relates primarily to the experience of victims. These include limitations on victims being able to speak freely; the demands placed by restorative justice on victims; victims' unwillingness to be involved in restorative justice processes; the claim that restorative justice is incident-based; power imbalances between men and women, the abused and the abuser; and potential deficiencies in restorative justice practice. I will briefly comment on each of these.

Victims' Voices

Critics of using restorative justice for intimate partner violence often allude to the possibility of coercion of the victim at a restorative justice conference by the perpetrator's use of a subtle word or gesture, which can effectively silence and re-victimize the victim. On the other hand, advocates of restorative justice often highlight the importance of victims being able to tell their story which serves as both a catharsis and to empower (see, for example, Sherman and Strang 2007). However, Stubbs and other critics warn that restorative justice facilitators dealing with intimate partner violence need to be fully conversant with the dynamics and implications of this violence. This point is not in dispute. The important issue here is the contrast between what the criminal justice system and restorative justice offers victims. Restorative justice does provide an opportunity for victims to be heard and to express whatever they want to say; the criminal justice system rarely does. In New Zealand, as elsewhere, on the occasions when victims are allowed to read their victim impact statements in court they are constrained in what they are allowed to say. For example, they are not allowed to tell the court what they think the sentence should be and the use of any derogatory or rude language is also forbidden. Significantly, too, in a restorative justice process, a potentially wider audience hears what is said.

Also there is the belief among critics that victims want a criminal justice solution to the violence they have experienced. This is by no means the case. Morris and Gelsthorpe (2000: 414) noted that when women do call the police, there could be many reasons for this which 'may or may not include wanting their partner arrested … Whatever the reason – and whether we as outsiders agree with it or not – if a woman does not want her partner arrested, prosecuted or imprisoned, it is arguable that she should be listened to.' And so listening to victims must begin at an early stage in any process.

Restorative Justice's Demands of Victims

It has been argued that restorative justice demands and expects more from victims than the criminal justice system, thus putting victims' safety at issue. I agree with this in the sense that restorative justice does give victims greater responsibility. It offers them opportunities to share in the decision-making as well as to speak for themselves. In the criminal justice system, again, this is unusual. Instead, victims have to accept the decisions made 'for them' in the court and these can place heavy and unwelcome demands on them: for example, financial hardship, becoming a single parent and isolation.

Victims' Take-Up Rates

Research has shown that take-up rates by victims vary extensively in different schemes (see, for example, Dignan 2005, though it should be noted that his research related to victims in general and not to victims of intimate partner violence). This raises further key questions: whether or not victims have been advised of the possibility of using restorative justice processes and, if they have been, how this information is presented. For people to give informed consent to access a service, they need to be given information about not only its existence, but also its potential benefits (or drawbacks for that matter). If they have not been given full information, they have, in effect, been denied the opportunity to give informed consent to participate in the process. This is gatekeeping (for a fuller discussion of this point, see Hayden (2013).[1] Because accessing restorative justice depends largely on police gatekeeping in criminal matters and social services gatekeeping in care matters, there is a need for the police and social workers to have a greater understanding of the philosophy and practice of restorative justice.

Restorative Justice is Incident-Based

Critics point out that much of the literature on restorative justice refers to it being incident-based, which is inadequate for understanding intimate partner violence (and family violence more generally). I agree that this is often the case, but it is not necessarily so. Good restorative justice practice can give victims, perpetrators and their support people an opportunity to address their past histories. This is particularly relevant in intimate partner violence when possibly learning about intergenerational violence experienced by one or both parties can help them gain a more in-depth mutual understanding of the violence, its effects, and where it has come from. Again, too, it is important to contrast this with what the criminal justice system offers. Similar previous behaviour by a perpetrator is not usually revealed during a trial and there is often a public outcry when previous criminal behaviour is exposed after conviction on a single incident. Generally also, previous convictions cannot be taken into account in sentencing (though they can be when similar offending is repeated). The criminal justice lens is, therefore, much narrower than restorative justice processes.

Power Imbalances

Power imbalance is one of the most frequently made criticisms against using restorative justice for family violence. The rationale for this is that power

---

1 Despite the pivotal gatekeeping role of police officers, Stewart and Smith (2004) observed that there was limited research on police officers' understandings of, and attitudes towards, conferencing. Their research did, however, discuss the views of police officers involved *in* the conference and found that their responses were enthusiastic.

imbalances are believed to lie behind much family violence: young children are subordinate to their parents and the abused child is likely to be even more submissive to the dominant abusive parent; elderly parents are often reliant on and become submissive to their adult children and this is reflected in violence against the elderly by their adult children; some women feel subordinate to their (male) partners and abusive relationships between women and men are characterized by submission by the abused woman and dominance by the abusive man.

There is little research directly on this point with respect to child abuse (though there is some information in Daly and Wade's and Swift's chapters in this volume). But, citing New Zealand research into youth justice and family group conferences (Maxwell and Morris 1993), Morris (2002a) challenged the argument that restorative justice reproduces power imbalances in the family and in society. There, young perpetrators could be confronted by angry adult victims and parents, but the research found that nearly half of the young people felt involved in some way. Morris (2002a: 101) commented: 'They were able to say what they wanted to and to speak without pressure.' I made similar points in my earlier chapter on intimate violence, as has Kingi in her chapter on family violence more generally. Furthermore, Morris (2002b) points out that reducing power imbalances was not an objective that the criminal justice system either aspired to or achieved and so again there is no evidence that the criminal justice system offers more than restorative justice. Conversely, restorative justice processes often consciously attempt to address any imbalances by, for example, silencing the perpetrator or ensuring wider support for the victim.

Rethinking Power

I want to argue for a more complex analysis of power and suggest that an integral part of any relationship is power, whether or not it is equally distributed, and that this is especially significant in intimate relationships. In my view, power occurs in a particular situation or context and the use of that power leads to consequences which may be positive or negative. As mentioned earlier, usually in the literature about intimate partner violence, power is referred to as a form of abuse by men and its negative effects on victims and their families are stressed, including the disempowerment of women. However, research suggests that this is too simplistic.

Houry et al. (2008) concluded that their results validated the view of intimate partner violence as an abuse of power and control, but described it as affecting both sexes. In other words, power could be used by men and women over women and men. Similarly, Meyer, Wagner and Dutton's (2009) research found that some abused women were more willing and able than others to take steps to deal with their partner's violence – in other words, to empower themselves. However, it also showed that, despite accessing the network of power that exists within the criminal justice system, victims were not necessarily more empowered by it.

I contend that each individual has, and can exercise, personal power. This entails a person: becoming informed about matters directly related to their social, physical, psychological and emotional well-being; prioritizing those aspects of their life that are most important for them; making informed decisions about their priorities; taking responsibility for their decisions; and getting involved in outside/community activities.[2] Personal power can be used positively or negatively. Victims' reporting violence against them to the police or seeking help is an example of exercising positive personal power. So too is making the decision never to be in another abusive relationship, having raised self-belief and control of their lives and the adoption of new safety strategies. The negative use of personal power by victims include not seeking help, choosing to remain in the abusive situation, defending their partner's aggression and self-blame for the violence.

Relational power is power which is integral to relationships between individuals in a couple, family, friendship, work or social situation. Positive relational power is behaviour towards other people that is pleasant, constructive, conciliatory and/or likely to promote a healthy relationship. Negative relational power is the opposite. Examples of positive relational power include safety strategies to prevent intimate partner violence or to minimize its impact, planning a public venue for informing the abuser that the relationship is over, adapting behaviour while still in the relationship, and negotiation. Examples of negative relational power include stopping access to financial resources, the threat of physical violence, anger and verbal abuse.

Institutional or macro power is the power exercised by governmental or non-governmental organizations in response to a victim calling the police after an assault or involving social services or lawyers in an access or custody dispute. Reporting intimate partner violence to the criminal justice system can have positive or negative effects. Victims can clearly feel empowered by having the macro power of the police on their side, while perpetrators are most likely to experience the negative power of the state.

According to the participants in my research,[3] power was exercised positively and negatively at the micro and macro levels by both perpetrators and victims. Furthermore, micro and macro power were sometimes used simultaneously. For example, micro (relational) power and macro power were frequently used together in the area of child custody and access.

Power in Restorative Justice Practice

It is important for practitioners to understand that power is a multidimensional concept in intimate partner violence. Much of the literature on restorative justice refers to

2 This definition of personal power was derived from my observation of my friend, the late Maxine Burgham-Page, key informant in my PhD research and breast cancer sufferer, whose 24-year management of her disease epitomized 'personal power'.

3 The participants included 8 victims, 6 perpetrators and 15 key informants who worked in the fields of intimate partner violence and/or restorative justice.

the need for a balance of power at restorative justice conferences (Marshall 1999, Morris and Gelsthorpe 2000, Zehr 1990). However, the achievement of this balance is more complex than may be understood by many (Hayden 2012). To work top down, if a perpetrator is currently being prosecuted in the criminal justice system, it is probable that he/she is in a less powerful position than within his/her domestic environment. This has given the victim who reported the violence to the police more power. Giving a victim more power than the perpetrator in a conference (through, for example, greater speaking rights or more support people), in addition to the power already held through incorporating the assistance of the police, could create a more adversarial situation by increasing the defensiveness of the perpetrator and shaming him or her. This could reduce the possibility of a successful outcome.

On the other hand, in cases where the victim has not reported the violence because, for example, reporting occurred through the initiative of a neighbour, both the victim and the perpetrator are less empowered than in their domestic environment. At home, one or both partners make the decisions. In these circumstances, it could be helpful for the criminal justice process to be deferred for some months after a restorative justice conference and following a review of the situation, possibly by holding a second conference. This would enable a follow-up report to be sent to the court outlining the perpetrator's progress relating to his or her fulfilment of the outcomes from the conference before sentencing.

The presence of appropriate support people can help a couple gain equal power at a restorative justice conference (Hayden 2012) and this should be an integral part of thorough preparation. One participant in my research, a perpetrator and men's group leader, also emphasized that the support needs to be the 'right' support. The role of these support people is to equalise relational power, preferably in a restorative justice conference that is 'not anyone–centred', as suggested by a restorative justice practitioner. Moreover, as stated by Morris and Gelsthorpe (2000), these support people can continue to give support and oversight after the restorative justice conference as well.

The personal power of participants can be enhanced through restorative justice, for example, in ways suggested by Morris (2002a) and Morris and Gelsthorpe (2000). A well-managed restorative justice conference could be the catalyst for each party to develop their personal power and ways to use it positively. By this, I mean they could perhaps be guided towards prioritizing, becoming fully informed before making decisions, taking responsibility for those decisions, and establishing outside activities.

Conclusion

The criminal justice system 'has had its chance' as the dominant form of justice for a long time without proving to be effective for dealing with family violence (Hudson 2002). It is time, therefore, for recognition, resources and appropriate opportunities to be given to victims and perpetrators of family violence through alternative approaches such as restorative justice. Both proponents and critics of using restorative justice for family violence agree that there is a need for further empirical evidence to fill the research void in this field. Without it, the voices of critics will continue to persuade practitioners and policy makers not to use restorative justice for family violence. Continuing to rely solely on the criminal justice system has not served victims well (or perpetrators for that matter).

There is no disagreement between critics and proponents that the parties participating in a restorative justice conference should have appropriately informed facilitators and support people before, during and after a restorative justice process. Stubbs and others are justified in their comments that, although some restorative justice programmes state they are victim-focused, the reality is that they vary and are often perpetrator-oriented. The recent development of legislation supporting victim-initiated restorative justice programmes in the UK and USA may go a long way to counter this. The key concern, however, must be to maintain *a balance* between the needs and rights of both victims and perpetrators.

It may be, too, that opposition to the use of restorative justice for family violence is exaggerated or unfounded. This is suggested by an empirical study in Australia by Curtis-Fawley and Daly (2005) which showed that victim advocates were moving towards acceptance of restorative justice for these cases. They commented:

> The advocates interviewed for this study were in fact more receptive to restorative justice than policy makers and academic commentators may think, and even we had initially imagined ... The 'victim perspective' has been used (and some would say, abused) to provide ammunition for the competing claims that victims want increased punitive sanctions (thus supporting more vigorous criminal law interventions), or that they ultimately want acknowledgement and apology rather than punishment (Curtis-Fawley and Daly 2005: 11).

The same researchers found that all victim advocates 'spontaneously' made negative comments about the ability of the criminal justice system to effectively address gendered violence. Research has also shown that most abused women do not want their partners prosecuted (Frederick and Lizdas 2010, Morris and Gelsthorpe 2000) and that many abused elderly victims do not want their adult children or partners prosecuted (Beaulaurier et al., cited by Barnett et al. 2011). Similarly, it is unlikely that children favour the prosecution of their abusive parent or caregiver. They all want the abuse to stop but, paradoxically, their reluctance to involve the criminal justice system can have the effect of allowing that abuse to continue.

Participating in a restorative justice conference may pose risks (as does participation in the criminal justice system). This is especially so if victims and perpetrators wish to continue their future together (Hayden 2010). But it does not have to be *either* a criminal justice system *or* a restorative justice process. Processes involving both appropriately skilled and informed restorative justice practice and the criminal justice system can and do offer a moderate and more empowering experience for victims and perpetrators and a path forward after family violence.

It is sometimes suggested that not all victims or perpetrators are 'suitable' for participating in a restorative justice process. In the New Zealand Court-Referred Restorative Justice Pilot (Ministry of Justice 2005) coordinators and facilitators were asked for their main reasons for assessing perpetrators and victims as 'unsuitable' for referral to a restorative justice conference. Although this pilot excluded family violence cases, the research findings have some general relevance to this issue. The researchers found that a wide range of reasons were given for not referring victims or perpetrators for restorative justice processes, including a lack of remorse or responsibility by the perpetrator or a lack of commitment to the restorative justice process by both victims and perpetrators. However, the researchers observed: 'What this potentially ignores is that restorative justice processes can serve as a trigger for the acknowledgement of responsibility and for remorse and that it is often only after participating in a restorative justice process that participants fully appreciate them' (Ministry of Justice 2005: 100). What we need now is more good practice and careful evaluations. The 'embargo' which currently so often prevents the use of restorative justice for family violence means that those who want to use it are often denied this opportunity through gatekeeping based on misinformation, bias or prejudice.

Both critics and proponents of the use of restorative justice for family violence need to remember that the use of power is not straightforward. Collectively, the research (Hayden 2010, Houry et al. 2008, Meyer et al. 2009) has indicated that both victims and perpetrators use it positively and negatively at multiple levels, sometimes simultaneously. If this finding in the context of family violence is given greater credibility in future discussion and practice, it is possible that more headway will be gained in attempts to reduce the incidence of family violence. Furthermore, if the voices of those directly affected are listened to, restorative justice might become more available in certain cases, with the proviso that it is carried out by suitably specialized practitioners. Having choices is having power.

References

Barnett, O.W., Miller-Perrin, C.L. and Perrin, R.D. 2011. *Family Violence across the Lifespan: An Introduction.* Malibu, CA: Sage Publications.

Busch, R. 2002. Domestic Violence and Restorative Justice Initiatives: Who Pays if We Get it Wrong?, in *Restorative Justice and Family Violence*, edited by H. Strang and J. Braithwaite. Cambridge: Cambridge University Press, 223–48.

Curtis-Fawley, S. and Daly, K. 2005. Gendered Violence and Restorative Justice: The Views of Victim Advocates. *Violence against Women*, 11(5), 603–38.

Dignan, J. 2005. *Understanding Victims and Restorative Justice.* Maidenhead: Open University Press.

Frederick, L. and Lizdas, K. 2010. The Role of Restorative Justice in the Battered Women's Movement, in *Restorative Justice and Violence against Women*, edited by J. Ptacek. New York: Oxford University Press, 39–59.

Hayden, A. 2010. Why Rock the Boat? Non-Reporting of Intimate Partner Violence. PhD thesis, Auckland University of Technology.

Hayden, A. 2012. Safety Issues Associated with Using Restorative Justice for Intimate Partner Violence. *Women's Studies Journal*, 26(2), 4–16.

Hayden, A. 2013. Gatekeeping in Restorative Justice and Related Research, in *Reconstructing Restorative Justice Philosophy: Values, Norms, and Methods Reconsidered*, edited by T. Gavrielides and V. Artinopoulo. Farnham: Ashgate.

Houry, D., Rhodes, K.V., Kemball, R.S., Click, L., Cerulli, C. and McNutt, L.A. 2008. Differences in Female and Male Victims and Perpetrators of Partner Violence with Respect to WEB Scores. *Journal of Interpersonal Violence*, 23(8), 1041–55.

Hudson, B. 2002. Restorative Justice and Gendered Violence. *British Journal of Criminology*, 42, 616–34.

Marshall, T. 1999. *Restorative Justice: An Overview*. London: Home Office.

Maxwell, G. and Morris, A. 1993. *Families, Victims and Culture: Youth Justice in New Zealand*. Wellington: Social Policy Agency and Institute of Criminology.

Merry, S.E. 2009. *Gender Violence: A Cultural Perspective*. Chichester: Wiley-Blackwell.

Meyer, A., Wagner, B. and Dutton, M.A. 2009. The Relationship between Battered Women's Causal Attributions for Violence and Coping Efforts. *Journal of Interpersonal Violence*, 25(5), 900–98.

Ministry of Justice. 2005. *New Zealand Court-Referred Restorative Justice Pilot: Evaluation*. Wellington: Crime and Justice Research Centre, Victoria University of Wellington.

Morris, A. and Gelsthorpe, L. 2000. Re-Visioning Men's Violence against Female Partners. *The Howard Journal of Criminal Justice*, 39 (4), 412–28.

Morris, A. 2002a. Children and Family Violence: Restorative Messages from New Zealand, in *Restorative Justice and Family Violence*, edited by H. Strang and J. Braithwaite. Cambridge: Cambridge University Press, 89–107.

Morris, A. 2002b. Critiquing the Critics: A Brief Response to Critics of Restorative Justice. *British Journal of Criminology*, 42, 596–615.

Ptacek, J. 2010. Resisting Co-Optation, in *Restorative Justice and Violence against Women*, edited by J. Ptacek. New York: Oxford University Press, 5–36.

Sherman, L.W. and Strang, H. 2007. *Restorative Justice: The Evidence*. London: The Smith Institute.

Stewart, A.L. and Smith, F. 2004. Youth Justice Conferencing and Police Referrals: The Gatekeeping Role of Police in Queensland, Australia. *Journal of Criminal Justice*, 32(4), 345–57.

Zehr, H. 1990. *Changing Lenses: A New Focus for Crime and Justice*. Windsor, ON: Herald Press.

Zellerer, E. 2004. Dangerous Dichotomies: The Potential for Restorative Justice to Resolve Feminist Dilemmas. Conference Paper to the World Congress of Criminology, Rio de Janeiro, Brazil, 10–15 August 2003. Available at: http://www.restorativejustice.org/10fulltext/?b_start:int=240

Chapter 19
Concluding Thoughts

Heather Strang

It is not surprising that this volume is largely a product of New Zealand and New Zealanders. For all that restorative justice may be the oldest way of resolving disputes and conflicts throughout the world, it was New Zealand who took the world by surprise in the late 1980s by engineering and promoting its modern manifestation. The Children, Young Persons and Their Families Act 1989 courageously incorporated traditional *Māori* ways of dealing with crime and conflict with the introduction of family group conferences for addressing youth offending. This was the spark that ignited so much interest and enthusiasm around the world as a new way of 'doing justice' that recognized the limits of court-based justice in dealing with perpetrators.

Restorative justice as a concept continues to gain momentum around the world, even if not solid traction in many places outside the Antipodes. One of the most important and widely used versions of restorative justice – face-to-face conferencing – has been the subject of more research than almost any other justice innovation. We certainly know more about its effects than, say, the effects of imprisonment. This body of work clearly concludes that restorative justice of this kind can reduce re-offending and benefits victims willing to participate (Shapland et al 2007, 2008, Sherman and Strang 2007). But we know little about the effects or effectiveness of many of the other interventions that are said to be versions of restorative justice but which do not always conform to the widely accepted principles underpinning restorative justice. These have been codified in the United Kingdom by the Restorative Justice Council in its reports *Principles of Restorative Processes* (2004) and *Best Practice Guidance for Restorative Practice* (2011). The Canadian government has published its views in *Values and Principles of Restorative Justice in Criminal Matters* (Department of Justice, Canada 2010) and the New Zealand Ministry of Justice's *Statement of Restorative Justice Values and Processes* (2004) is a particularly useful publication. All of these statements coalesce around similar core principles about respect, accountability, voluntary and engaged participation, and direct, unmediated communication. They are operationalized in practice through impartial and competent facilitators managing inclusive, confidential and fair meetings between everyone willing to attend who has been affected by the crime. Although there is no fixed list of *sine qua non* fundamentals for restorative justice, the principles articulated are clear enough to recognize what is *not* restorative justice. Still, programmes such as youth referral panels or restorative resolutions in the United Kingdom and Community

Reparation Boards or school peer mediation in the United States sometimes stray far from these principles. New Zealand, too, has had its critics in terms of the practice of family group conferences, mainly around issues of confidentiality, follow-up to outcome agreements and the lack of rigorous evaluation (see for example, Huntsman 2006). In spite of these problems, however, restorative justice survives and flourishes, with much interest in a wider application as an addition or alternative to formal justice processing.

It may not be altogether surprising either that the rise of restorative justice over the past 25 years has coincided with a huge increase in interest and concern about violence perpetrated in the privacy of family homes against some of the most vulnerable in our society. The phenomenon of intimate partner violence and of family violence more generally has been with us for millennia. But perhaps some of the same forces were at work in the 1980s in bringing to the fore both the shortcomings of the formal criminal justice system for many of the crimes that affect communities and individuals the most and the impossibility of tolerating any longer violence behind closed doors.

At that time, the rightness of the cause and the strength of public opinion, led by a newly empowered women's movement, swiftly led to governments across the Western world changing their policies towards family violence. It was widely believed that family violence in all its manifestations could be addressed most effectively by exposing it to the cold light of day and treating it like any other crime. Instead of being hidden because of the shame felt by its victims, such violence needed to be sought out by police and perpetrators needed to be arrested, charged, prosecuted and sentenced just as they would be if the offence had occurred between strangers. The research on the effects of mandatory arrest carried out at that time (Sherman and Berk 1984) seemed initially to support the view that a punitive approach by the criminal justice system was indeed the best way to reduce the incidence of family violence. No one was particularly interested in follow-up studies published later (see Pate et al. 1991, Sherman et al. 1992) that showed all was not so simple – that arrest often backfired among poor unemployed men – increasing the likelihood of more victims and more victimization among the most vulnerable. Nonetheless, there seemed to be normative virtue in a full enforcement approach that swept all before it. Police across the English-speaking world adopted mandatory arrest policies, or at least a presumption of arrest, holus bolus: the New South Wales Police, for example, continues to work to a rule requiring arrest in at least 60 per cent of all domestic call-outs, a proportion with no empirical basis in terms of deterrence.

While research began to teach us a good deal about how restorative justice should be conducted, for whom it was likely to be most effective and, most clearly, the enormous benefits that could accrue to crime victims who agreed to meet their perpetrators, one iron rule presided: under no circumstances would governments agree to the use of restorative justice in cases of family violence or, except under the most particular and limited conditions in one or two locations, sexual assault. Those opposed to the use of restorative justice in general sometimes would try to stop further discussion by simply demanding 'But you wouldn't use it for rape, would you?', as if it was an intervention that could ever be imposed on victims of any crime or, indeed, on any perpetrator.

Nevertheless, dissatisfaction with a strictly formal approach in dealing with family violence, and violence against women in particular, has grown in recent times with the recognition that it continues to be a widespread problem, despite both a heightened awareness of its criminal nature and a much more proactive response by police and other agencies when it is disclosed. But its prevalence remains in large measure a matter of conjecture requiring the piecing together of various sources of information. Both Janet Fanslow and Loraine Gelsthorpe discuss this problem in this volume, with similar issues arising in both New Zealand and England and Wales. This is partly because of changing definitions of what constitutes family violence: for example, the Home Office in the UK now officially includes emotional abuse for counting purposes, a term which encompasses a wide range of behaviours.

It may also be a result of changing societal views on the acceptability of any kind of abusive behaviour, so that what appears to be a growing problem may in fact be an artefact of a greater willingness to disclose and to reach out for help. For example, a study by Starke et al. (1981) in New Haven, Connecticut, estimated that as few as one-fifth of women presenting at an Accident and Emergency Department who were 'probably' suffering injuries resulting from intimate partner abuse were accurately identified (almost none of the victims identified their own injuries as such). In contrast, a study currently underway in Hampshire, England (by Cornelius and Strang – as yet unpublished), is finding that very few women who called the police in the past year in relation to low-level abuse (with no physical violence) at the hands of their partners had experienced any abuse prior to the instant offence. Both of these studies are small and unreliable in terms of generalizability for all kinds of methodological reasons, but may at least indicate that women are not as reluctant as they used to be to disclose abuse by their partners. Studies of the kind Janet Fanslow has undertaken to try and assess prevalence are valuable parts of the jigsaw and make a helpful contribution to our understanding of the problem's dimensions and character.

But no matter the precision or otherwise of the numbers, there is no doubt that family violence remains an issue that our communities and our criminal justice systems struggle to address. Throughout these chapters we can discern a weariness about the shortcomings of a strict enforcement approach to intimate partner violence and family violence more broadly. And no wonder considering the difficulty of shoe-horning the law – of which we have no shortage, as Loraine Gelsthorpe comprehensively describes in relation to England – into complex human relationships described so well by David Mather and Chris McGuire in this volume and by Heeni Rongo in the opening chapter.

This problem becomes all the clearer when we consider what Loraine Gelsthorpe reports on what women want in response to violence from their partners. Once again the research is hampered by methodological and other problems but a picture emerges of the bluntness of a full enforcement punitive approach where reporting is likely to lead to arrest, an outcome that perhaps only a minority of victims want, and which may have the perverse effect of actually discouraging future reporting. This likelihood is supported by American research (Iyengar 2008) which found that intimate partner homicides increased by about 60 per cent in states with mandatory arrest laws. The research further investigated whether this was due to decreased reporting by victims of earlier offences or to increased reprisal by abusers after arrest, by examining the effect of mandatory arrest laws on family homicides, where the victim is less often responsible for reporting prior abuse. There appeared to be consistent evidence for the decreased reporting hypothesis, as mandatory arrest laws appeared to reduce the number of family homicides. This study concluded that 'these laws may have perverse effects on intimate partner violence; harming the very people they seek to help' (Iyengar 2008: 2).

Added to this, new findings about the long-term effects on both perpetrators and victims of arrest for low-level offences involving intimate partner violence give even more cause for concern. A 23-year follow-up study by Sherman and Harris (2013) investigated the effect of arrest in the Milwaukee intimate partner violence experiment (Sherman 1992). This study found that arrest had no effect for employed men but actually increased the prevalence of re-offending for the unemployed. Importantly, the harmful effect of arrest was only apparent after six years and continued growing for the next 17 years. Moreover, the long-term effects on victims was even more alarming: substantially more of those whose cases which had been disposed of by arrest were dead as a result of various non-violent causes after 23 years, possibly as a consequence of the stress of the arrest experience and its sequelae. If the reasons for arrest and processing through the courts is to protect victims and prevent future victimization, strong evidence is emerging that it serves neither of these purposes.

In spite of a growing sense of failure around mandatory arrest policies and court action, there is an understandable reluctance in many quarters to pursue a restorative justice alternative for family violence. This is partly because of a feeling that a restorative justice process without a court appearance is not a serious enough response to such a serious social problem and partly because of concerns about power imbalances between the parties and other legitimate concerns articulated by Julie Stubbs and responded to by Anne Hayden in this volume. Such is the level of concern that it has been almost impossible to conduct any research on the possible benefits (or harms) that might result from this approach. The study conducted by Joan Pennell and Gale Burford in the late 1990s remains one of the only successful attempts to set up a rigorous test to compare the use of restorative justice with the standard court response (Burford and Pennell 1998, Pennell and Burford 2000). Their contribution to this volume, which highlights the role of fathers and the imperative to engage them in resolving family violence, refers to findings from this landmark piece of research.

Almost everywhere that restorative justice has been introduced, whether for serious or not so serious crimes, governments have explicitly excluded intimate partner violence as an eligible offence category. This has been the case even in pilots or experiments, thus precluding the opportunity for a rigorous investigation of its effectiveness compared with what has become the conventional criminal justice response. The closest this author has come to such an opportunity occurred in 2003 when Cherie Blair, wife of the then British Prime Minister and a part-time judge in a London Crown Court with a deep interest in the potential of restorative justice, set up a meeting between our research group, then beginning a series of experiments to evaluate the effectiveness of restorative justice for serious crime, and leaders of various criminal justice agencies. The purpose was to discuss the possibility of including certain kinds of family violence in these experiments. This meeting was also attended by the then Solicitor General who listened briefly to what was proposed before stating that such a study would take place 'over my dead body' and immediately leaving the meeting.

But even if we seriously lack research on the effects of restorative justice in family violence, we know something about the views of those who have taken part in such meetings. Venezia Kingi reports here on her review of the delivery of restorative justice in family violence cases through interviews with both victims and perpetrators. Although we do not have any outcome measures on re-offending, we do know that, in this rare attempt to assess empirically this application of restorative justice, there was a relatively high level of satisfaction with the process, with almost all participants saying they would recommend it to others. There are some solid pointers here to the question of what kind of cases are best suited for restorative justice, namely for those where the parties want their relationship to continue or where both hope for a civil ending of the relationship, especially when children are involved. These findings echo Burford and Pennell's express caution about using restorative justice in family violence unless there are children with ties to both parties and their extended families: ties that provide real motivation for repairing relationships or ending them without rancour.

Exploring just the idea of restorative justice with victims and perpetrators in intimate partner violence can also provide useful indications of likely satisfaction, as Anne Hayden shows in the chapter reporting her research on this topic. Her respondents, some of whose cases had been dealt with through the criminal justice system, did not experience restorative justice themselves but were asked their opinion based on information provided about it. They reported support for the early involvement of the approach, especially because of the failures of the formal criminal justice system in reducing violence; few of them had chosen to involve the court in their cases and even fewer of them were satisfied with their experience.

But there is much to be learned from the experience of those who are already boldly exploring restorative justice in the family violence arena. Julia Hennessy and her colleagues draw on New Zealand examples of best practice, prioritizing attention to safety. Their contribution describes every aspect of preparation, including separate meetings with victims and acknowledged perpetrators and their supporters, the composition of the meeting itself, the atmosphere to be engendered and how to minimize risks.

We have many useful contributions in this volume that will encourage others to be bolder, none more so than those concerning the *Mana* Social Services Trust in Rotorua. This restorative justice programme, established in 1996 specifically to address intimate partner and family violence in *Māori* communities, is vividly described from the inside by Maxine Rennie, who articulates their style of practice in a most useful and practical way. She describes how the programme draws on important social and cultural aspects of *Māori* life that have synergy with the restorative justice process employed, in similar ways to that described by Marie Ropeti from a Samoan perspective. The challenge for us is to locate and draw on similar forces in non-Indigenous cultures (Strang 2002).

These contributors really tell us 'how to do it', setting up the possibility of a true test of restorative justice for family violence, including intimate partner violence, moderated to address the concerns of Julie Stubbs discussed in this volume. Their experience can teach a great deal and even open up the possibility for a change in approach around the world: 'changing tack' indeed.

Ken McMaster, too, draws on this programme in discussing the central question of the conditions under which restorative justice may be appropriate for family violence. He argues that strict use of formal court proceedings can be counterproductive for the families involved and suggests that a consensus may be emerging in which conventional criminal justice and restorative justice may be able to work together so that the seriousness of the crime can be recognized via a court sanction while the community input available via restorative justice can provide a mechanism for the perpetrator's reintegration.

Two New Zealand judges also contribute important perspectives in this volume on the role and use of the court in family violence. Chris McGuire draws on the experience in Rotorua and its use of restorative justice alongside the formal justice system. He observes that there is no controversy there about the use of restorative justice and uses a series of case studies to illustrate the complex relationships that come before the court and which the court alone is sadly deficient in resolving. Unfortunately, the case studies also show the difficulties arising from the lack of any systematic follow-up about the effectiveness of restorative justice in these cases, all of which have the potential for future serious harm. David Mather, likewise, discusses some complex and ambiguous cases coming before the court and describes the dilemmas accompanying a judge's responsibility for applying legal sanctions to messy human relationships with the benefit of only a partial glimpse of the dynamics of often unstable relationships – and, of course, no information about the consequences of any judicial decision.

Once again we see the need for hard empirical evidence about restorative justice where the violence is not necessarily perceived as a unitary phenomenon but rather as behaviour on a continuum of seriousness. It is after all conceivable that restorative justice in family violence, especially between partners, may be like restorative justice with non-domestic violence and prove to be more effective with more serious than less serious cases for reasons to do with the emotional power of the offence and of the bond between the parties. But such speculation is useless: we need information, not just stories.

The versatility of restorative justice is demonstrated in this volume with several chapters devoted to examples of practice in the most intractable kinds of family violence, beyond intimate partner violence. Kathleen Daly and Dannielle Wade vividly describe the complexity of sibling sexual abuse cases and the dilemmas that make them so difficult for formal judicial settings to deal with, especially when both perpetrators and victims are children. Likewise, the character of elder abuse and neglect often makes the criminal law inappropriate for addressing it, especially when it is family members themselves who are responsible for the harm. As Judith Davey suggests, restorative justice may have a real advantage in obliging perpetrators to face up to the impact of their actions on their victims by dealing with the crime in the context of the family. She reminds us though that, as with intimate partner violence, the very closeness and ongoing nature of the relationship that may alter the behaviour of the perpetrator may also entrench it, if there is insufficient attention to the risks arising from the victim's vulnerability.

The consequences of living with family violence are discussed in Donna Swift's investigation into the aetiology of violence among girls. She describes the violence in terms of coping behaviour that gives these girls a sense of personal power in a world where they believe feeling safe can only flow from being prepared to fight for it. She observes that any intervention to address their violence must recognize this reality and the need to involve all members of their family in resolving it. Paul Nixon echoes this in his discussion of restorative justice in the broader context of child protection. He believes that increasing family and community involvement in family group conferences for child welfare as well as youth justice is the best and most effective way forward.

All of the contributors to this volume share a recognition of the limits of formal criminal justice processes in addressing intimate partner and family violence. Some of them may feel the courts are simply inappropriate for these crimes and that a radical alternative is needed: that in the memorable phrase of Barbara Hudson, a feminist criminologist who had been one of the strongest advocates of a full enforcement approach, quoted in this volume by Anne Hayden: 'The court has had its chance'. Others believe that restorative justice can, and indeed does, have an important role as an addition to the court process: that the interaction between formal, court-based, justice and informal justice can have tensions but can also be positive and might allow for the expansion of restorative justice, even in very serious family violence. And there is a growing consensus, even among those who do not support restorative justice for family violence in the form that it is used for offences perpetrated by strangers, that, as Julie Stubbs says in this volume: 'a different approach is needed'.

The problem is that we are mostly speculating about the effectiveness of restorative justice with family violence because so little rigorous research has been conducted. So I end my commentary with a renewed plea for the opportunity to find out much, much more, through a programme of research that can finally answer questions that are posed again and again: what sort of restorative justice programme would be most appropriate? What do we need to know about safety? What sorts of cases are most likely to benefit from restorative justice? In what sorts of cases would restorative justice be contra-indicated? Would a cooperative arrangement with courts be desirable, especially family violence courts? Who should be included in such restorative justice conferences? What kind of outcomes should be sought? The questions flow thick and fast but we know almost nothing at present about the answers. Let us hope that this volume will be the start of a fresh view about the use of restorative justice in family violence so that the research can be done to allow the answers to flow too.

References

Burford, G. and Pennell, J. 1998. *Family Group Decision-Making: After the Conference – Progress in Resolving Violence and Promoting Well-being: Outcome Report* (vols 1 and 2). St John's, NF: Memorial University of Newfoundland, School of Social Work.

Department of Justice, Canada. 2010. *Values and Principles of Restorative Justice in Criminal Matters*. Ottawa, ON: Department of Justice. Available at: http://www.iirp.edu/pdf/RJValues-DOJCan.pdf.

Huntsman, L. 2006. *Family Group Conferencing in a Child Welfare Context*. Sydney: New South Wales Department of Community Services.

Iyengar, R. 2008. *Does the Certainty of Arrest Reduce Domestic Violence? Evidence from Mandatory and Recommended Arrest Laws*. Working Paper No. 13186. Cambridge, MA: National Bureau of Economic Research.

Ministry of Justice, New Zealand. 2004. *Restorative Justice in New Zealand: Best Practice*. Wellington: Ministry of Justice. Available at: http://www.justice.govt.nz/publications/global-publications/r/restorative-justice-in-new-zealand-best-practice.

Pate, A., Hamilton, E. and Annan, S. 1991. *Metro-Dade Spouse Abuse Replication Project Draft Final Report*. Washington, DC: Police Foundation.

Pennell, J. and Burford, G. 2000. Family Group Decision-Making: Protecting Children and Women. *Child Welfare*, 90(4), 9–16.

Restorative Justice Council. 2004. *Principles of Restorative Processes*. Available at: http://www.restorativejustice.org.uk/resource/rjc_principles_of_restorative_processes/#.UgD4XlOfI7A.

Restorative Justice Council. 2011. *Best Practice Guidance for Restorative Practice*. Available at: http://www.restorativejustice.org.uk/resource/best_practice_guidance_for_restorative_practice_2011/#.UgDsoFOfI7A.

Shapland, J., Atkinson, A., Atkinson, H., Chapman, B., Dignan, J., Howes, M., Johnstone, J., Robinson, G. and Sorsby, A. 2007. *Restorative Justice: The Views of Victims and Offenders. The Third Report from the Evaluation of*

Three Schemes. Ministry of Justice Research Series 3/07. London: Ministry of Justice.

Shapland, J., Atkinson, A., Atkinson, H., Dignan, J., Edwards, L., Hibbert, J., Howes, M., Johnstone, J., Robinson, G. and Sorsby, A. 2008. *Does Restorative Justice Affect Reconviction? The Fourth Report from the Evaluation of Three Schemes*. London: Ministry of Justice.

Sherman, L. and Berk, R. 1984. The Specific Deterrent Effects of Arrest for Domestic Assault. *American Sociological Review*, 49(2), 261–72.

Sherman, L. and Harris, H. 2013. Effects of Arrest over the Life-Course: A 24-Year Follow-Up of the Milwaukee Domestic Violence Experiment. Paper to the Stockholm Criminology Symposium, Stockholm, Sweden, 11 June 2013.

Sherman, L. and Strang, H. 2007. *Restorative Justice: The Evidence*. London: The Smith Institute.

Sherman, L. Schmidt, J. and Rogan, D. 1992. *Policing Domestic Violence: Experiments and Dilemmas*. New York: The Free Press.

Stark, E., Flitcraft, A., Zuckerman, D., Grey, A. and Robison, J. 1981. *Wife Abuse in the Medical Setting: An Introduction for Health Personnel*. Rockville, MD: National Clearinghouse on Domestic Violence.

Strang H., 2002. *Repair or Revenge: Victims and Restorative Justice*. Oxford: Oxford University Press.

Appendix 1
Glossary of *Māori* Terms

Aotearoa	New Zealand
Hapū	a subdivision of a tribe
Hui	a meeting
Iwi	a tribe, the largest political unit in *Māori* society – one *iwi* comprises many *hapū*
Kai	food, meal
Karakia	prayer or incantation
Kaumātua	respected male elder, keeper of tribal knowledge and traditions
Kaupapa	the policy or way of doing things
Kia Ora	hello
Koha	gift
Kōrero	speech, talk
Kupu	word(s)
Kuia	female elder
Māori	New Zealand's Indigenous people
Mana	status, prestige, authority, spiritual power
Manawhenua	*Māori* who are linked to the area/land by *whakapapa* (genealogy) whose ancestors have lived and died there
Marae	all buildings associated with a *Māori* community facility are collectively known as a *marae*; the *marae atea* is the open area of land in front of the meeting house
Ma matou mo tatou	one for all and all for one
Mokopuna	grandchild
Pākehā	a person of predominantly European descent
Puao-te-ata-tu	daybreak
Rangatahi	youth, adolescent
Rūnanga	governing council or administrative group of a *Māori Hapū* or *Iwi*
Tamariki	children
Tāne	man
Tangata whenua	people of the land, hosts, local people
Te Oritenga	equal balance
Te Reo	language
Te Rununga	council

Te Whanau Awhina	family assistance
Tikanga	customs and traditions
Tinana	physical body
Titiro	look
Tūhononga	standing together
Wairua	spirituality
Wāhine	*woman*
Whakamā	shame, embarrassment
Whakamua	forward
Whakamuri	back
Whakapapa	family networks, genealogy
Whānau	family/extended family
Whānau hui	family meeting
Whānau ora	programme to look after a family's well-being
Wharenui	meeting house

Appendix 2
Glossary of Samoan Terms

Aiga	extended family
Ali'i	leader of *fono*
Ava	ceremonial drink marking a special occasion
Fa'a Samoa	Samoan way
Fono	council
Ie toga	special fine hand-woven mat
Ifoga	submission ceremony seeking forgiveness
Matai	chief
Mu le foaga'	form of punishment involving the burning of an offender's property
Tulafale	talking chief
Va	the maintenance of relationships between people

Index

For Product Safety Concerns and Information please contact our EU
representative GPSR@taylorandfrancis.com
Taylor & Francis Verlag GmbH, Kaufingerstraße 24, 80331 München, Germany

www.ingramcontent.com/pod-product-compliance
Ingram Content Group UK Ltd.
Pitfield, Milton Keynes, MK11 3LW, UK
UKHW010958180926
475701UK00004B/445
9781138248236